T0339958

The Living Wage

As wealth inequality skyrockets and trade union power declines, the living wage movement has become ever more urgent for public policymakers, academics, and – most importantly – those workers whose wages hover close to the breadline. A real living wage in any part of the world is rarely its minimum wage: it is the minimum income needed to cover living costs and participate fully in society. Most governments' minimum wages are still falling short, meaning millions of workers struggle to cover their living costs.

This book brings new, vital insights to the conversation from a carefully selected group of contributors at the forefront of this field. By juxtaposing advances across sectors and countries, and encompassing many different approaches and indeed definitions of the living wage, Dobbins and Prowse offer a rich tapestry of approaches that may inform public policy.

By including the experiences and voices of those workers earning at, or near, the living wage alongside the opinions of leading experts in this field, this book is a pioneering contribution for public policymakers as well as students and academics of work and employment relations, public policy, organizational studies, social economics, and politics.

Tony Dobbins is Professor of Work and Employment Relations at the University of Birmingham, UK. He is Visiting Professor at the University of Limerick, Ireland; the Centre for Labour Studies at the University of Malta; and president of the British Universities Industrial Relations Association. His research interests include the living wage and decent work.

Peter Prowse is Professor in Human Resource Management and Employment Relations at Sheffield Hallam University, UK. His research interests include the living wage in care homes and football clubs, negotiating, work-life balance, and HR performance. He is a member of collaborative international research groups on the living wage.

The Living Wage

Advancing a Global Movement

Edited by
Tony Dobbins and Peter Prowse

LONDON AND NEW YORK

First published 2022
by Routledge
2 Park Square, Milton Park, Abingdon, Oxon OX14 4RN

and by Routledge
605 Third Avenue, New York, NY 10158

Routledge is an imprint of the Taylor & Francis Group, an informa business

British Library Cataloguing-in-Publication Data
A catalogue record for this book is available from the British Library

Library of Congress Cataloging-in-Publication Data
Names: Dobbins, Tony, editor. | Prowse, Peter, editor.
Title: The living wage : advancing a global movement /
edited by Tony Dobbins and Peter Prowse.
Description: New York : Routledge, 2022. |
Includes bibliographical references and index.
Identifiers: LCCN 2021014348 (print) | LCCN 2021014349 (ebook) |
ISBN 9780367514907 (hardback) | ISBN 9780367514877 (paperback) |
ISBN 9781003054078 (ebook)
Subjects: LCSH: Minimum wage. | Living wage movement. |
Cost and standard of living. | Working class.
Classification: LCC HD4917 .L578 2022 (print) |
LCC HD4917 (ebook) | DDC 331.2/3–dc23
LC record available at https://lccn.loc.gov/2021014348
LC ebook record available at https://lccn.loc.gov/2021014349

ISBN: 978-0-367-51490-7 (hbk)
ISBN: 978-0-367-51487-7 (pbk)
ISBN: 978-1-003-05407-8 (ebk)

DOI: 10.4324/9781003054078

Typeset in Bembo
by Newgen Publishing UK

Contents

Figures and tables

Contributors

Siautu Alefaio-Tugia (Samoan lineage of Matautu-Tai, Sasina, Manunu ma Fagamalo) is Associate Professor in the School of Psychology, Massey University, New Zealand. Her research specialty is Pacific-indigenous humanitarian psychology and she combines extensive practice and academic experience to reinform psychology from Pacific-indigenous knowledge frameworks. Siautu has been awarded major research grants from, and acted as adviser to, various New Zealand bodies including the Ministry of Social Development (MSD), the Ministry of Education, the Counties Manukau Police Pacific Advisory Board, and the Department of Corrections. She has published extensively on issues concerning Pacific well-being for over ten years.

Kristin Alsos is Research Director at Fafo Institute for Labour and Social Research in Oslo, Norway. Her research interests include employment relations and collective bargaining, labour law and collective agreements, as well as labour migration (https://fafo.no/en/staff/fafo-management/kristin-alsos). She is currently leading a Nordic comparative project on the future of work, financed by the Nordic Council of Ministries (https://fafo.no/en/project-home).

James Arrowsmith is Professor in the School of Management, Massey University, New Zealand. He has published over 50 articles in top-ranked journals and been awarded over $1m in grant funding in New Zealand and from the UK Economic and Social Research Council (ESRC). Jim has acted as a consultant for employers, government agencies, and trade unions, including a recent series of projects for the International Labour Organisation advising Pacific Island countries on labour reform. He is co-director of MPOWER – the Massey People, Organisations, Work and Employment Research group. Jim is on the editorial board of five leading HR and employment relations journals; is co-editor-in-chief of *Labour and Industry: A Journal of the Social and Economic Relations of Work*; and Associate Editor of the *International Journal of Human Resource Management*.

Stuart Carr is Professor of Psychology, Industrial and Organizational (I/O) Psychology Program, Massey University, New Zealand. Stuart co-facilitates the End Poverty and Inequality Cluster (EPIC), which includes a focus on transitions from precarious labour to decent work and living wages. Intersecting with EPIC is Project GLOW (Global Living Organizational Wage), a multi-country, multigenerational, interdisciplinary study of the links between decent wages (in purchasing power parity) and sustainable livelihoods for the eradication of poverty – the primary UN Sustainable Development Goal (SDG1).

Calum Carson is a labour market and policy researcher at the Employment Related Services Association (ERSA), with a particular research focus on the Decent Work agenda. In 2020 he completed his doctoral thesis on the UK Living Wage campaign, and was previously a researcher at the International Labour Organisation, Geneva.

Samantha Coronel obtained her Master's of Public Policy and Global Affairs degree from the University of British Columbia, specializing in Development and Social Change. She received her BA in International Development Studies from McGill University. Her research interests include corporate social responsibility, business ethics, and the intersection of business and public policy both nationally and globally.

Tony Dobbins is Professor of Work and Employment Relations in the Department of Management at Birmingham Business School, University of Birmingham, UK. Tony is Visiting Professor at the University of Limerick, Ireland, and the Centre for Labour Studies at University of Malta. He is president of the British Universities Industrial Relations Association (BUIRA). His research interests include employee voice/democratizing work, sociology of work, the future of work, and the living wage.

Reed Eaglesham is an MS/PhD student in the Industrial Labor Relations School at Cornell University studying Human Resources. He completed his BA in International Economics at the University of British Columbia. His research interests include compensation, scarcity, low-wage workers, and the effects of minimum wage policy.

Ray Fells is Professor and honorary senior research fellow in the Business School at the University of Western Australia (UWA). Building on his earlier practical experience, Ray's academic career has focused on the resolution of workplace issues, particularly through management–union negotiation and through mediation. His research into workplace relations and business negotiation has been published internationally; his book, *Effective Negotiation*, published by Cambridge University Press, is now in its fourth edition. In addition to his UWA teaching, he has taught on MBA and other programmes at a number of universities, including at Cambridge, Copenhagen Business School, and the Australian Graduate School of Management.

Michele Ford is Professor of Southeast Asian Studies and director of the Sydney Southeast Asia Centre at the University of Sydney, where she researches labour internationalism and Southeast Asian labour movements. Her books include *Labor and Politics in Indonesia* (Cambridge 2020, with Teri Caraway), *From Migrant to Worker* (Cornell 2019), and *Workers and Intellectuals* (NUS/Hawaii/KITLV 2009).

Michael Gillan is Associate Professor at the UWA Business School, University of Western Australia. His current research interests encompass global union federations; transnational labour regulation; and state governance and labour movements in Asia. He is currently engaged in a multiyear Australian Research Council Discovery Grant project on global production networks and worker representation in Myanmar.

Jarrod Haar (PhD), Ngati Maniapoto/Ngati Mahuta descent, is Professor of Human Resource Management at Auckland University of Technology, New Zealand. His research focuses on (1) work–family and work–life balance, (2) Māori employees and Mātauranga Māori, (3) leadership, (4) well-being, and (5) R&D, entrepreneurship, and innovation. Professor Haar is ranked world-class (PBRF research assessment exercise); won industry and best-paper awards; research grants (Marsden, FRST); and currently researches on a National Science Challenge (Science for Technological Innovation), a Marsden grant (Living Wage), and a Ngā Pae o te Māramatanga grant (Māori HRM). He has over 390 refereed outputs (including 100+ journal articles) and convenes the Economics and Human Behaviour Marsden panel.

Deborah Hann is a senior lecturer in Employment Relations at Cardiff Business School. She is currently working on a research projects in two main areas: the role of social actors in regulating the workplace and the management of conflict in the workplace. Her research has been in conjunction with the Living Wage Foundation, the Advisory, Conciliation and Arbitration Service, and the Labour Relations Commission.

Joshua Healy is senior lecturer in Employment Relations and Human Resource Management at the University of Newcastle, Australia. His research and teaching focus on aspects of the future of work, including the gig economy, workforce ageing, and earnings inequality. His recent published work appears in prestigious international journals, including *New Technology, Work and Employment*, and *Human Resource Management Journal*.

Edmund Heery is Professor Emeritus at Cardiff Business School and in recent years has been researching the involvement of 'new actors' in shaping the world of work. In a series of projects, he has examined the role of civil society organizations in developing voluntary regulation of the employment relationship, culminating in the research on the Living Wage Foundation reported in this book.

Darrin Hodgetts is Professor of Societal Psychology at Massey University, Auckland, New Zealand. His research interests lie in the interdependent domains of the social determinants of health, work, poverty, community, and human flourishing. Darrin's recent book-length publications include the *SAGE Handbook of Applied Social Psychology*, *Asia-Pacific Perspectives on Inter-cultural Psychology*, *Social Psychology and Everyday Life* (2nd ed), and *Urban Poverty and Health Inequalities*.

Daniel Howard is programme manager at the Living Wage Foundation, where he leads the Living Hours campaign and Living Wage strategy in the North West of England. He has previously held positions at the Joseph Rowntree Foundation and Department for Work and Pensions.

John Hurley is a senior research manager in the Employment unit at the European Foundation for the Improvement of Living and Working Conditions, an EU agency based in Dublin. He has authored or co-authored over 20 reports during his time at the Foundation including the *Concept and Practice of a Living Wage* (2018). His main research interests are comparative labour market analysis and the changing employment structure in Europe and other advanced economies.

Karen Jaehrling received her PhD in political science from the University of Hamburg (2003). Karen now works as a senior researcher at the Institute for Work, Skills and Training (IAQ), University of Duisburg-Essen. Prior to joining the IAQ, Karen worked at several projects within the Institute for Work and Technology (IAT), Gelsenkirchen, and had teaching assignments at the Universities of Bochum and Hamburg. Her research interests are in the area of labour sociology, the labour market, and social policy and industrial management, with a particular focus on low-wage/low-skill segments of the labour market. Karen gained expertise from various national as well as international comparative projects on industrial relations and some of her current research focuses on the role of public procurement in regulating low-wage labour markets.

Mathew Johnson is a lecturer in Employment Studies based in the Work and Equalities Institute at The Alliance Manchester Business School. After completing his PhD at Manchester, Mat worked as a postdoctoral researcher on a comparative study of precarious work funded by the European Commission (2015–16), and has been involved in a number of locally funded projects looking at the changing nature of work and employment in cities, and the role of public procurement in regulating labour standards. Mat recently secured a £1m grant from the United Kingdom Research and Innovation (UKRI) Future Leaders Fellowship to support a comparative qualitative study of work and employment in six cities around the world (2020–27). Mat has published articles in the *Industrial Relations Journal*; *Employee Relations*; *Work, Employment and Society*; *Economic and Industrial Democracy*; *Transfer*; and the *Journal of Common Market Studies*, and has co-authored several book chapters.

Stephanie Luce is Associate Professor of Labor Studies at the Murphy Institute, City University of New York. She is a leading expert on living wages. Professor Luce worked as an economist at the US Department of Labor and a Congressional Commission on Agricultural Workers before earning her PhD in Sociology at the University of Wisconsin-Madison in 1999. She has also worked as a researcher at the Center on Wisconsin Strategy and the Political Economy Research Institute.

David Nash is a senior lecturer in Employment Relations at Cardiff Business School. His research involves a number of international and UK projects with a focus on employment regulation and workplace conflict resolution. He has undertaken research projects for the Living Wage Foundation and the Advisory, Conciliation and Arbitration Service, and has published widely in leading industrial relations journals.

Kristine Nergaard is senior researcher at Fafo Institute for Labour and Social Research, Oslo, Norway. She has throughout the years done research on collective bargaining and the role of collective agreements, trade unions and employer organizations, atypical work, and labour market mobility both nationally and internationally, and has published widely on these issues (https://fafo.no/en/staff/kristine-nergaard).

Jane Parker is Professor of Employment Relations and Human Resource Management (HRM) at the School of Management, Massey University (New Zealand). She has authored multiple books, chapters, articles, and commissioned reports, including for the International Labour Organisation and the European Foundation for the improvement of Living and Working Conditions. Jane is the co-editor-in-chief of *Labour and Industry*, an editorial board member of *Human Relations*, editorial advisory board member of *Employee Relations*, and co-director of the Massey People, Organisations, Work and Employment Research group, public service, transdisciplinary research processes, and social movement unionism.

Andreas Pekarek is a lecturer in the Department of Management and Marketing at the University of Melbourne, Australia. He has published in such journals as *The British Journal of Industrial Relations*, *New Technology, Work and Employment*, *European Journal of Industrial Relations*, and *Industrial and Labor Relations Review*. His research focuses on unions and worker representation, the gig economy, the future of work, interdisciplinary approaches to work, human resource management, and industrial relations.

Julie Prowse is Associate Professor at the University of Bradford, School of Healthcare and Leadership. Her research interests include the work of social care workers and low pay, work–life balance, National Health Service reforms, and policy developments. Julie is on the Associate Board of *Work, Employment and Society* as a reviewer. Julie regularly reviews for *Economic and Industrial Democracy, New Technology Work and Employment,* and *Work, Employment and Society.*

Peter Prowse is Professor in Human Resource Management and Employment Relations at Sheffield Business School, Sheffield Hallam University. He has authored multiple book chapters, articles, and commissioned reports. He is an active member of collaborative international research groups for the living wage and has co-edited special issues of *Labour and Industry* and *Employee Relations* on the living wage. His research has been funded by Department of Employment, The British Academy/Leverhulme, and the UK Research and Innovation/Economic and Social Research Council. Peter is an associate board member of *Work, Employment and Society* and reviews articles for a range of international ranked journals.

Jeremé Snook is a senior lecturer in Human Resource Management at Sheffield Hallam University. His research interests focus upon employment issues, employment relations, and employment law. Specifically, Jeremé has been involved in projects exploring the UK living wage, obesity and disability discrimination, employee representation, and comparative and international employment relations. Jereme has published in the *Industrial Relations Journal, Economic and Industrial Democracy,* and *The International Journal of HRM.*

Danielle van Jaarsveld is a professor at the University of British Columbia Sauder School of Business. Professor van Jaarsveld's research explores the changing nature of work and its implications for unions, organizations, managers, and the workforce. She has engaged in comparative international studies of management and employment relations to understand the impact of globalization and restructuring on service workplaces, service workers, and the unions representing them. She has written extensively on human resource practices and their influence on firm performance. Professor van Jaarsveld received her undergraduate degree from Princeton University, and her PhD and MS from Cornell University's School of Industrial and Labor Relations.

Andrea Werner is a senior lecturer at Middlesex University Business School specializing in Business Ethics and Corporate Social Responsibility. Her main research interest is in ethics in small and medium-sized enterprises (SMEs), on which she has published widely in leading business ethics journals. Recent projects have focused on the implementation of the living wage in SMEs, and the motivations, strategies, and practices of sustainable fashion design entrepreneurs.

Amanda Young-Hauser has a PhD from Waikato University, Aotearoa/New Zealand, and a background in community psychology. She works in the School of Psychology at Massey University, Auckland, and contributes to the Ending Poverty and Inequality Research Cluster (EPIC) and Project GLOW (Global Organisational Living Wage) that bring together a global network of researchers with the aim to examine the dynamics of living wages and their consequences for organizations and people.

Acknowledgements

Thanks to our families for their loving support during the time in which this book was developed and edited: Paula, and Julie and James. Thanks also to Alexandra Atkinson, Terry Clague, Amy Laurens, and Emmie Shand at Routledge for their guiding contributions throughout. We would like to acknowledge the British Academy and the Leverhulme Trust for grant funding for our research on the living wage, which provided the impetus to plan this book. Finally, we sincerely thank all the contributors to the chapters, from around the world. We gratefully acknowledge their support and enthusiasm, enabling this book to be published.

To greater equality around the world for the many, not the few.

1 Introduction

Peter Prowse and Tony Dobbins

Against a backdrop of rising income inequalities and the decline in collective trade union wage bargaining in many countries, the living wage (LW) has become an increasingly important issue for public policy, practitioners, academics and, most importantly, workers who are paid it and those who are seeking to be paid it. Civil society organisations like Citizens UK/The Living Wage Foundation in the UK, and other actors like unions, have mobilised LW campaigns to tackle the symptoms of income inequality. A real living wage (RLW) is the minimum income deemed necessary for workers to be able to afford their basic needs. Such needs include food, housing, and other basic essentials like clothing. The goal of a LW is to enable workers to afford a basic but decent standard of living. A RWL is voluntary and is therefore distinct from compulsory legal national minimum wages set by the state and its agencies. Real living wages tend to be quite significantly higher than statutory minimum wages. The latter are viewed by many observers as not providing enough for many people to live on, factoring in rising living costs. Our book will provide important new comparative insights from academics and public policy experts and researchers into the operation and outcomes of LWs in a variety of sectors in the UK, Europe, and globally.

History of living wages

Although the LW is attracting substantial interest in modern times, the concept has a long history. Figart (2004) evaluated the historical development of LW activism and how movements developed the LW in the past. Historically, the LW rate can be traced to medieval times and classic philosophical thinkers including Plato, Thomas Aquinas, and even modern religious statements such as Pope Leo XIII's *Rerum Novarum* (1891); all are highlighted by Anker (2011). Classical economist Adam Smith (1776) stated:

> A man must live by his work, and his wages must at least be sufficient to maintain him. They must even upon most occasions be somewhat more; otherwise it would be impossible for him to bring up a family.
>
> (p.46)

Smith essentially argued for the provision of bare necessities to provide food, accommodation, and health for the family to sustain their labour, known as a sustainability approach (Stabile, 2008). Between the 1890s and the 1920s, there was a social movement that challenged the poverty and exploitation in England during the Industrial Revolution, which was highlighted by Friedrich Engels (1845) in *The Conditions of the Working Class*

DOI: 10.4324/9781003054078-1

in England. Karl Marx would later use Engels' work as an exposé of exploitation by capitalism in *Capital* (1885). As a response, social reformers considered how to establish acceptable standards of living to develop and secure acceptable living standards (and wages). Early philanthropic employers such as Robert Owen (1920), Joseph Rowntree, and Seebohm Rowntree conducted detailed studies of costs of food, clothing, and other necessities that shaped how much a head of the family should earn (Rowntree, 1901). In 1912, theologian John Augustus Ryan, a US Catholic thinker, argued that 'every member of a community has an abstract right to a decent livelihood' (Ryan, 1912, p.37). In the UK, social reformers such as Sidney and Beatrice Webb (Webb and Webb, 1920) called for selective application of a minimum wage floor for all employment, providing more than a basic subsistence, rather than wages and conditions sufficient to both survive upon and sufficient to prevent the need for dependence on charity. Essentially this higher wage enables freedoms and provides the capacity to allow the worker to spend more time with their family and wider community, and experience a more meaningful life (Searle and McWha-Hermann, 2020).

Winston Churchill, when president of the Board of Trade in Britain, argued against low pay and sweated trades. He developed trade boards for wages, setting minimum wages in each industry, negotiated by employers, unions, and independent members. Churchill argued that there should be protection of low-paid workers who do not have access to representation of unions and collective bargaining. This was the first discussion of state protection by a statutory wage floor:

> It is a serious national evil that any class of His Majesty's subjects should receive less than a living wage in return for their most utmost exertions [...] where you have a powerful organisation on both sides [...] there you have healthy bargaining [...] But where we have what you call sweated trades, you have no organisation, no parity of bargaining, the good employer is undercut by the bad, and the bad employer is undercut by the worst [...] where these conditions prevail you have not a condition of progress, but a condition of progressive degeneration.
>
> (Churchill, 1909)

In contrast, the first national minimum wages were developed in New Zealand (1894) and in Australia (1907) with the landmark *Harvester Decision* (Fair Work Australia, 2011). This case arose out of an application made by a combine harvester manufacturer to seek exemption from excise duty on the basis it paid a 'fair and reasonable wage'. The case ruled in favour of the employee, stating that pay should not just ensure wages for survival but cover 'the normal needs of an average employee, regarded as a human being in a civilised community'. It formed the basis of the Australian minimum wage system (Fair Work Australia, 2011, p.57).

In the 1930s, the United States instituted a minimum wage as part of Franklin D. Roosevelt's New Deal, stating 'no business which depends for existence on paying less than LWs to its workers has any right to continue in this country' (Roosevelt, 1933). The US Supreme Court rejected the original edict as they argued it exceeded state power, but it should be at subsistence level, whilst Roosevelt argued for the 'wages of decent living'. In recent years, this level for 'decent living' has been increased predominantly at state level, enabling individual states to set their own state levels of pay higher than the US national minima (Hirsch and Valadez-Martinez, 2017, p.11).

This develops and follows in the tradition of the original International Labour Organization (ILO) Constitution and convention for 'the provision of an adequate living wage' and the ILO Philadelphia Declaration in 1944 calling for 'a minimum living wage to all employed and in need of such protection' (ILO, 2020a). The UN Universal Declaration of Human Rights Article 23 (3) (1948) recognises the 'need for workers to earn a living wage' (United Nations, 1948). A key issue is that global institutions and initiatives such as the ILO (ILO, 2020a) and the Project GLOW (2016) have evaluated the potential for a sustainable LW, which will be reviewed in the present volume in Chapter 14. Institutional support for international LWs also includes the influence of civil society organisations and associated global networks, such as the UK-based Living Wage Foundation/ACCA (2017a), which have developed a global and regional network of partnerships based on principles and global perspectives of the LW (LWF/ACCA, 2017b).

Living wages versus minimum wages

So, what exactly is the difference between national minimum wage regulations that set and establish legal and regulatory wage floors and the real LW? This definition can be best summarised by Anker and Anker (2017) in their review of the Global Living Wage Coalition (2016):

> Remuneration received for a standard work week by a worker in a particular place sufficient to afford a decent living standard of living for the worker and his family. Elements of a decent standard of living include food, water, housing, education, health care, transport, clothing, and other essential needs, including provision for unexpected events.

> (p.8)

Anker and Anker (2017) outline a methodology calculation relating to developing countries, but other commentators have also provided methodology for specific countries including the UK and New Zealand (Hirsch, 2017; King, 2016). The UK Low Pay Commission (2021) (LPC) method states in its terms of reference:

> The aim of the LPC is to recommend levels for the minimum wage rates that will help as many low-paid workers as possible without any significant adverse impact on the economy.

Finally, Searle and McWha-Hermann (2020) review articles on the LW from 2000 to 2020 to examine how the context of LW research has developed since early sociological and economic analysis, to incorporate a broader range of disciplines since around 2014. Articles now introduce more management and employment relations insights, as well as insights from psychology, medicine/health, sociology, and social/public policy, along with rekindling interest from theology. Special issues of journals covering the LW from an employment relations perspective have included *Labour & Industry* (Parker et al., 2016), *Employee Relations* (Prowse et al., 2017), and a special issue of *Transfer: European Review of Labour and Research* (Müller and Schulten, 2019). It is within the tradition of employment relations that this book has mainly focused and developed its approach.

The structure of the book

The chapters in the book distinguish between statutory minimum wages and LWs, both in the UK and other countries internationally (ILO, 2020a). In so doing, it also assesses sectoral differences in the UK and other country contexts. The book has three primary aims. Firstly, to examine the development of how the LW as a concept has emerged and developed in the UK and internationally. Secondly, how LWs are designed not simply to reduce poverty, like statutory minimum wage regulations, but to provide a sufficient and sustainable standard of living. Thirdly, it examines international growth in 'Voluntary' Living wage (VLW) initiatives and campaigns by civil society organisations like the UK Living Wage Foundation, and the 'Fight for $15' campaign in the USA by trade unions and other actors.

Part 1 The living wage in the UK – Sector studies

Part 1 examines the United Kingdom specifically and the emergence and development of the 'Voluntary' Living Wage (VLW) through campaigns by institutions such as Citizens UK/the Living Wage Foundation, community groups, and trade unions. Campaigners have campaigned for employers to pay wage rates above the national minimum wage to address widespread in-work poverty.

Estimates for the evidence on methodology to establish a minimum wage and address low pay in Britain have been developed using evidence-based research. A real challenge to address low pay are the methods that calculate exactly what level of pay and how many hours are required to earn a sustainable level of earnings (full-time) for a family or individual according to their needs. This method examines relative measures of low pay and how someone is classified as low paid if they earn less than a specified percentage of pay compared to an absolute measure and a specific amount (Cominetti and Slaughter, 2020).

Firstly, the relative measures include a 'core' full-time rate of the UK national median pay across all employees using the Organization of Economic Co-operation and Development (OECD) measure. This measure indicates that earning less than two-thirds of the national median across all employees is an insufficient sustainable level of earnings, even working full-time. This means calculating an average between full- and part-time workers per cent of the median and obviously a measure of the full-time median would be higher. This is calculated at a full-time pay rate of £8.81 pence per hour for a 38-hour week (OECD, 2020). This calculation is rarely used in the UK.

The second approach involves absolute measures, and a needs-based low pay definition set by the Living Wage Foundation (LWF) for a full-time worker at £9.50 per hour and a London rate of £10.85 per hour at 38 hours, as of 2020/2021 (Cominetti, 2020).

Finally, a statutory minimum wage for employees' earnings was established by the National Minimum Wage (NMW), which sets an adult rate for those over 23 years of age of £8.91 per hour (38 hours) with effect from April 2021. It must be noted that the Low Pay Commission adult rate establishes a rate an employer can afford to pay considering the effect on setting the minima rate and its consequent effect on employment. The adult rate was increased to 25 years of age in 2016 from a previous calculation of the full adult paid for employees aged over 21 years. Recently, the LPC decided to return the calculation and payment of the adult category to 21+ years of age by 2024 (LPC, 2020). It must also be noted that the National Minimum Wage was retitled the

'National Living Wage' in 2016. Nonetheless, this still remains a calculation for a statutory wage floor rather than the OECD and Living Wage Foundation calculated rates based on cost of living.

Chapter 2 explains the Living Wage Foundation's 'Real Living Wage' campaign. The Living Wage Foundation is an important new civil society 'actor' in the determination of pay in Britain, striving to improve wages for the lowest paid. Daniel Howard outlines the history and development of the Living Wage Foundation. The Living Wage campaign is based on the belief that a hard day's work deserves a fair day's pay. In the 20 years since the campaign started, over 250,000 people have had their wages uplifted as a direct result of the Living Wage movement. For each of these people, the increase to the RLW means the difference between struggling to pay for heating and being able to afford to put food on the table. The chapter also provides an overview of the Living Wage Foundation's work to increase the number of accredited employers and, therefore, the number of workers who are paid a wage that meets the cost of living. It outlines the work of the Foundation in different sectors and industries. The chapter continues by explaining how the Foundation is building on progress to promote the LW globally as well as deepening its impact with employers in the UK to tackle insecure work and underemployment, and provide living hours.

Chapter 3 discusses the theme and effect of the LW policy of a Living Wage Foundation-accredited employer in the sports sector in the UK. Peter Prowse and Tony Dobbins explore how Living Wage Foundation accreditation has transformed a football league club. In doing so, this chapter presents a qualitative case study of the RLW policy at Luton Town Football Club (LTFC) in the UK. The research enhances knowledge about the impact of LW policy and practice on lower-paid staff in a labour market sector that relatively little is known about: professional football. Only a few professional football clubs pay their low-paid staff and contractors a RLW, despite Premier League clubs, in particular, making vast revenues. It is significant that Luton Town was the first football league club to commit to pay a RLW and become accredited by the Living Wage Foundation in 2014; thus setting an all too rare 'good employer' benchmark in the sector context of UK professional football clubs. The research also outlines the effects of a pay uplift for events workers, hospitality staff, and agency staff used on match days. This provides a rare insight into the ripple effect of the RLW on non-footballing staff in the club and wider influences on the community.

Chapter 4 examines and evaluates the influence of the LW on improving the pay of outsourced (and low-paid) services. Edmund Heery, Deborah Hahn, and David Nash present evidence on the relationship between outsourcing and the LW. Many LW campaigners have called for the reversal of outsourcing and the transfer of contract workers back into direct employment. The main thrust of LW campaigns, however, has been to regulate, not reverse outsourcing, primarily by requiring employers that adopt the LW to extend it to their contract workers. These provisions have benefited tens of thousands of contract workers. Cleaners, receptionists, security guards, administrators, and catering assistants providing outsourced services to large corporations and public service organisations have been some of the main beneficiaries of the LW.

Attention extends to the effect of the RLW in the higher education, hospitality, and construction sectors in Chapter 5. In this chapter Calum Carson investigates the experiences of three separate case study employers across the UK regarding both their initial decision to adopt the RLW, and the consequences of doing so for their organisations and workforce. A key focus is placed on the decision-making processes within each organisation which led them to become accredited LW employers, and the organisational ripple effects that this decision created through a series of internal and external impacts. It examines both the benefits and the challenges of implementing the LW for each employer, determined in part by the geographical and industry-related circumstances that each operates within, and the wider implications of the implementation process for both individual workers and fellow organisations within each accrediting employer's sphere of influence. The chapter concludes with a discussion about the ways and means through which ethically led organisational change occurs and progresses across the British employment landscape in the twenty-first century.

Chapter 6 by Julie Prowse, Peter Prowse, and Jeremé Snook examines pay in the adult residential care sector (care homes) in Yorkshire in the UK, and the continued incidence of paying rates just above the 'bite' or bare minima rate set by the Low Pay Commission. This regional study examines the history of the UK adult care sector (ACS) and the changes in delivery by private companies whose workforce is projected to increase. The workers in the adult care sector are amongst the lowest-paid occupational workers in the UK. The chapter presents findings examining the care home workers's perspective of pay and working conditions in adult residential care, and more importantly, the lived experience of care workers. The study highlights the rise of in-work poverty for care home workers. Women still predominate in this sector's employment, and the chapter examines the increasing challenges for people working in care homes on low pay and the effects of increasing work intensification for staff on low pay. Given the tragedy of Covid-19 and challenges for the 1.49 million predominantly female staff working on the front line with their clients during the virus, they were constantly applauded as 'heroes', yet most remain under-rewarded.

Chapter 7 by Andrea Werner provides insights into a sector significantly challenged by Covid-19, the UK hospitality sector. The focus is on case studies of Living Wage Foundation-accredited small to medium-sized enterprises (SMEs) from the hospitality sector, a sector with low wages and poor working conditions. This evidence examines how SMEs adopt and implement a RLW. Analysis of case studies will draw out the range of SMEs' motivations for signing up to the RLW, encompassing moral, strategic, and political reasons. It will set out the multitude of benefits of Living Wage Foundation accreditation for these SMEs and challenges regarding implementation of the RLW, as well as some industry-related issues. The chapter will close with some reflections about the implications of RLW adoption in SMEs for individuals, businesses, and the economy, and about the prospects and conditions for future growth of RLW accreditations among SMEs, especially in low-wage sectors.

Part 2 The living wage in international comparative contexts

Part 2 examines how some selected countries and international regions including the European Union (EU), the Nordic countries, the USA, Canada, Australia, New Zealand, and South-East Asia have all developed RLW policies. Although Anker and Anker (2017) outlined a measure for an international LW, which is examined within national comparators, international comparisons are complex and include nutrition, housing, food prices, healthcare, and family size. These measures can be developed within different countries based on levels of subsistence and need. The UK Living Wage Foundation has links with some countries, which we have outlined earlier, but this second part of the book examines developments in LW policies internationally.

In Chapter 8, John Hurley outlines LW initiatives that have emerged in a small number of mainly English-speaking countries, including the UK and Ireland. The main concern of such campaigns – income adequacy for workers on low pay – are however increasingly visible in national and EU policymaking across Europe. Key recent developments have included the introduction of a statutory minimum wage in Germany (2015), fair wage commitments in the European Pillar of Social Rights (European Commission, 2017), and the European Commission's subsequent proposal of an EU framework for adequate minimum wages (2020). Living wage campaigns exist in large part to cast light on the shortcomings of legal wage minima based on the empirical approach of consensual budget standards research. They have in this way been instrumental in supporting the case for a more progressive uprating of national wage minima to reflect the needs of workers and their dependants. This chapter describes how LW initiatives and related policy discourse have impacted on public policy, notably minimum wage policy, across EU member states in recent years.

Chapter 9 by Mathew Johnson and Karen Jaehrling continues the European focus and examines and compares organisational outsourcing in three European countries: Germany, Spain, and the UK. Outsourcing is widely recognised as having a detrimental effect on pay and working conditions in low-paid industries, particularly where collective bargaining is weak and fragmented. This chapter presents a contextualised comparison of outsourcing examples from the metal sector in Germany, the catering sector in Spain, and the care sector in the UK, where social partners have sought to better protect pay, living standards, and working conditions for outsourced and subcontracted workers through different channels. These collective interventions included extending collective agreements, inserting labour clauses into public contracts, and implementing voluntary agreements over pay and conditions with client firms at the top of supply chains. Although not explicitly categorised as LWs initiatives, each of these examples was partly successful in tackling poor pay and conditions among precarious workers. However, this chapter argues that a combination of strategies is needed to reduce segmentation and temper the pressures that sustain cost-driven outsourcing.

In Chapter 10 Kristin Alsos and Kristine Nergaard examine the institutional alternative to secure the LW through strong trade unions and collective bargaining in Nordic countries. Experiences from low-wage industries reveal that definitions of a 'living wage' have not been a widely applied concept in the Nordic countries, and civil society campaigns like those seen in English-speaking countries to introduce a LW have been absent. This examination of selected Nordic states such as Denmark, Norway, and Sweden are important as they have not introduced statutory minimum wages that ensure a minimum wage level for all workers. Wage formation is still the voluntarist domain of employer organisations and trade unions through coordinated collective bargaining. There is widespread support among employers and workers for the idea that small wage differences serve the Nordic welfare states well, and that the lowest-paid workers must be guaranteed a decent standard of living. In this chapter, the authors take a closer examination of the trade unions' strategies for ensuring a minimum wage that means employees can earn sufficient pay in the food and beverage, retail, cleaning, and hospitality sectors. The study also examines the higher-paying construction sector, which continues to employ agency and subcontracted migrant workers, and explores challenges for the effectiveness of collective bargaining in this area.

Chapter 11 moves our studies across to North America and the establishment of the modern LW movement in the United States. Stephanie Luce provides a study of US LW trends, highlighting the 'Fight for $15' pay campaign and other low-wage worker campaigns in the US. This chapter provides a commentary on current efforts to raise wages in the US, focusing on the history and trajectory of the LW and minimum wage movements. This chapter examines the statutory and voluntary LW approaches. The author reviews debates about economic impacts of wage laws, discusses some of the tensions in the movement around goals and strategy, and offers suggested directions for the future of low-wage worker organising. Some themes addressed include the challenges of using wage regulations to improve the living standards of precarious and workers employed on irregular hours. The study also examines how to set wage levels, and how the LW movement intersects with demands for a federal jobs programme or universal basic income.

Chapter 12 continues this North American coverage and moves to examine the Canadian LW movement. In this chapter, Danielle van Jaarsveld, Samantha Coronel, and Reed Eaglesham explore heterogeneity in the development of LW campaigns across Canada. First, they describe the demographics and characteristics of the Canadian low-wage workforce. Secondly, they explore key themes and features of the LW movement across Canada, with a particular focus on British Columbia. Finally, through an analysis of qualitative data from interviews with key actors in the Canadian LW movement, they use focus groups with the low-wage workforce and case studies of LW Employers in British Columbia. They examine the benefits and challenges of implementing a LW policy across provinces and territories. Finally, the authors highlight distinct features of the Canadian LW movement to provide a broader context on policy discussions about how to respond to the Covid-19 pandemic.

In Chapter 13, Joshua Healy, Andreas Pekarek, and Ray Fells provide an interesting contrast on developments of LW initiatives in Australia. In this review they revisit the development of the Australian LW and consider the contemporary 'A Fair Go' for the 21st Century initiative. For much of the twentieth century, a distinctive system of compulsory arbitration sought to balance the competing criteria of workers' needs and employers' capacity to pay. This system, they argue, served Australia well, delivering equitable real-wage growth and coordinated responses to economic downturns. Starting in the 1980s, however, public policy shifted to emphasise workplace-level wage determination. The authors then examine how this agenda to 'free up' the labour market has affected Australia's ability to maintain, and enforce, its wage safety net. Comparisons with other OECD countries identify that Australia's real minimum wage remains high but has declined in recent years, relative to several other benchmarks. Incidences of employment at low pay, and below the minimum wage, are also explored for different industry sectors in Australia. The authors conclude with an assessment of the trade union movement's recent attempts to reinvigorate a LW campaign in the face of an increasingly fragmented workforce and a diminished arbitration system.

Chapter 14 examines Australia's close (sometimes referred to as 'Kiwi') neighbour – New Zealand. James Arrowsmith, Jane Parker, Amanda Young-Hauser, Darrin Hodgetts, Jarrod Haar, Stuart Carr, and Siautu Alefaio-Tugia outline that New Zealand has a long history of relatively generous minimum wage (MW) regulation, dating back to 1894. It is noted that the statutory MW has closed the 'gap' on the LW rate since the election of Labour governments in 2017 and 2020. This chapter explores employer attitudes and responses to this development, focusing on low-paying sectors. The study uses a series of interviews with sector employer associations and complements them with in-depth case studies to further examine the motivation and effects of becoming a LW Employer. The evidence recognises employer sympathy for the LW, informed by a labour market context of low unemployment, including in small firms where employee financial struggles are often evident. However, commitment to the LW is inhibited for many firms by a dual temporal uncertainty – they do not know what future rates will be, nor whether possible productivity or recruitment and retention returns will outweigh any immediate cost implications. In these circumstances, ethical considerations are likely to motivate firms to formally become LW Employers, unless the workforce is already generally paid well above MW rates. The case studies demonstrate a likely win–win from adopting the LW, although there may be complications around pay differentials in larger organisations.

Chapter 15 by Michele Ford and Michael Gillan examines the region of Southeast Asia, and the challenge of addressing low pay for garment workers in the global supply chain. Southeast Asia's pivotal role within various manufacturing global production networks (GPNs) has drawn international attention to its labour standards and employment conditions. Using the region's garment sector as a case study, the authors examine various global and regional LW initiatives driven by non-governmental organisations (NGOs), trade unions, employers/brands, and a combination of all these organisations. In doing so, it distinguishes between three different logics of LW interventions in Southeast Asia. The first of these is the 'technical fix', where an actor, or actors, propose a formula that can be used to calculate LW levels. The second is collaboration, whereby unions or NGOs work with lead firms and other actors to improve compliance and reconfigure network governance. The third is contestation, whereby workers, their unions, or their other allies engage in public campaigning and mobilisation to try to rectify the absence of a LW. As the chapter demonstrates, different wage initiatives each have limitations in scope and effectiveness, which have affected their capacity to translate their goals and aspirations into concrete outcomes for workers.

Finally, in Chapter 16 Tony Dobbins and Peter Prowse identify a number of important themes that emerge from the book, relating to the LW and the bigger picture of inequality and imbalances in wage bargaining power. These themes include: why minimum wages are not RLWs; why RLWs have (re-)emerged in the contemporary era of neoliberalism, rising inequality, and declining union bargaining power, especially in countries labelled as liberal market economies (LMEs); why the LW is not a prominent concept in some European countries, including the 'Nordic' countries, which retain strong trade unions and collectivism; why LWs are insufficient as a stand-alone policy measure to address low pay and inequality, and focus on a broader decent work agenda and a 'new social contract' are required; and an increasing interest in a global LW.

References

Anker, R. (2011) *Estimating A Living Wage: A Methodological Review*. Conditions of Work and Employment Series. ILO: Geneva.

Anker, R., and Anker, M. (2017) *Living Wages Around the World – Manual for Measurement*. Edward Elgar: Cheltenham.

Churchill, W. (1909) Speech Introducing the Trades Board Bill. 28 April. *Hansard Series* 5, vol. 4, col.38.

Cominetti, N. (2020) *Calculating the Real Living Wage for London and the Rest of the UK 2020-2021*. The Resolution Foundation Briefing. Resolution Foundation: London.

Cominetti, N., and Slaughter, H. (2020) *Low Pay Britain 2020*. Resolution Foundation: London.

Engels, F. (1845) *The Condition of the Working Class in England*. Panther: London.

European Commission (2017) *The European Pillar of Social Rights*. Publication Office of the European Commission, Luxemburg.

Fair Work Australia (2011) *Waltzing Matilda and the Sunshine Harvester Factory: The Early History of the Arbitration Court, the Australian Minimum Wage, Working Hours and Paid Leave*. Fair Work Australia: Melbourne.

Figart, D.M. (2004) *Living Wage Movements: Global Perspectives*. Routledge: London.

Hirsch, D. (2017) 'Contemporary UK Wage Floors and the Calculation of a Living Wage', *Employee Relations*, 39(8): 815–824.

Hirsch, D., and Valadez-Martinez, L. (2017) *The Living Wage*. Agenda Publishing: Newcastle-Upon-Tyne.

International Labour Organization (ILO) (2020a) Conventions of the International Labour Organization. ILO: Geneva. www.ilo.org/global/topics/wages/minimum-wages/definition/WCMS_439070/lang--en/index.htm. (accessed 17/2/2021)

International Labour Organization (ILO) (2020b) *Global Wage Report 2020-2021: Wages and Minimum Wages at the Time of Covid-19*. ILO Flagship Report, ILO: Geneva.

King, P. (2016) Setting the New Zealand Living Wage: Complexities and Practicalities, *Labour & Industry: A Journal of the Social and Economic Relations of Work*, 26(1): 8–23.

Living Wage Foundation/ACCA (2017a) *The Living Wage: Core Principles and Global Perspectives*. ACCA: London.

Living Wage Foundation/ACCA (2017b) *The Living Wage: A Global Overview on Initiatives and Regulation*. ACCA: London.

Low Pay Commission (2020) *National Minimum Wage: Low Pay Commission Report 2020*. Crown Copyright: London.

Low Pay Commission (2021) "Terms of Reference" available at www.gov.uk/government/organisations/low-pay-commission/about/terms-of-reference#the-aim-of-the-lpc

Marx, K. (1885) *Capital* (volume 2) International Publishers: New York.

Müller, T., and Schulten, T. (2019) 'From Minimum to Living Wages: Lessons from Different European Practices – Editorial'. *Transfer: European Review of Labour and Research*, 25(3): 262–265.

OECD (2020) *Minimum wages at current prices in NCU*. OECD Statistics.

Owen, R. (1970) *A Report to the County of Lanark – A New View of Society*. (Edited by V.A. Gatrell). Pelican Books: London.

Parker, J., Arrowsmith, J., Fells, R., and Prowse, P. (2016). 'The Living Wage: Contexts, Concepts, and Future Concerns', Editorial, *Labour & Industry*. Special Issue: *Low Pay and the Living Wage – Comparing Concepts, Practice and Evidence*, 26(1): 1–7.

Project Glow (2016) *The Sustainable Development Goals Need to Build a Social and Business Living Wage*. Society for Industrial and Organizational Psychology and Economic Council of the United Nations: New York.

Prowse, P., Fells, R., Arrowsmith J., Parker, J., and Lopes, A. (2017). 'Editorial: Low Pay and the Living Wage: An International Perspective', *Employee Relations*, 39(6): 778–784.

Rerum Novarum (1891) *On Capital and Labour – Encyclical of Pope Leo XIII On Capital and Labour*. St. Athanasius Press: London.

Roosevelt, F.D. (1933) Franklin Roosevelt's statement. http://docs.fdrlibrary.marist.edu/odnirast.htmlt on the National Industrial Recovery Act. 16th June. Franklin D. Roosevelt Library. (accessed 17/2/2021)

Rowntree, B.S. (1901) *Poverty: A Study in Town Life*. Macmillan: London.

Ryan, J. (1912) *A Living Wage: Its Ethical and Economic Aspects*. Macmillan: London.

Searle, R.H., and McWha-Hermann, I. (2020). '"Money's too tight (to mention)": A Review and Psychological Synthesis of Living Wage Research', *European Journal of Work and Organizational Psychology*, (forthcoming) doi: 10.1080/1359432X.2020.1838604.

Smith, A. (1776) *An Enquiry into the Causes and the Wealth of Nations*. W. Strahan and T. Cadell: London.

Stabile, D. (2008) *The Living Wage: Lessons from the History of Economic Thought*. Edward Elgar Publishing: Cheltenham.

United Nations (1948) *United Nations Declaration of Human Rights*. United Nations.

Webb, S., and Webb, B. (1920) *Industrial Democracy*. Longman: London.

Part 1

The living wage in the UK

Sector studies

2 The Living Wage Foundation's 'Real Living Wage' campaign

Daniel Howard

Introduction

The Living Wage campaign is based on the belief that a hard day's work deserves a fair day's pay. In the 20 years since the campaign started, over 250,000 people have had their wages uplifted as a direct result of the Living Wage movement. For each of these people, the increase to the real Living Wage means the difference between struggling to keep the heating on and being able to afford to put food on the table. There are now over 6,500 accredited Living Wage Employers, all making a voluntary commitment to protecting their workers from in-work poverty. These range from large, well-known organizations such as Google, Liverpool Football Club and IKEA, to thousands of small and medium-size enterprises, each implementing the new real Living Wage rates every November. Collectively, these employers have put more than £1 billion of extra money into the pockets of low-paid workers.

This chapter provides a brief history of the campaign for the real Living Wage before going on to give an overview of the Living Wage Foundation's work to increase the number of workers who are paid a wage that meets the cost of living. It outlines the work of the Foundation in different sectors and industries, highlighting the impact employers in the Living Wage network are making and the specific approaches of the Foundation to tackle low pay. It finishes by explaining how the Foundation is building on progress to share learning and promote the Living Wage globally as well as deepening impact with employers in the UK to tackle insecure work and underemployment.

Working in the same offices, living in different worlds: a brief history of the Living Wage campaign in the UK

In 2001, a group of people from churches, mosques, schools and synagogues across East London met in a community hall to talk about the issues affecting their lives. Brought together by Citizens UK, the home of community organizing in the UK, over 1,000 people were packed into the wood-floored room of York Hall in Bethnal Green, usually used as a boxing venue, to talk about the issues affecting their lives. The hall is a short ride away from Canary Wharf, an area that has seen huge change over the past few decades. When the docks closed in the 1980s, many skilled jobs were lost. Regeneration brought significant new investment from the financial and property sectors. But many of the people in that hall felt that their communities had not benefited, as house prices soared and the jobs available to them in the new steel and glass buildings were too often minimum wage positions as cleaners or security guards.

DOI: 10.4324/9781003054078-2

The minimum wage at the time was just £3.70 an hour. Many of these people were working full-time, sometimes in two or three minimum wage jobs, but still not earning enough to live on. The campaign for employers to pay a real Living Wage came out of that room, based on the idea that a hard day's work deserves a fair day's pay.

But it was years before campaigners saw any success. Their first action was to occupy a branch of HSBC on Oxford Street. The following year they attended the bank's annual general meeting, where a night cleaner called Abdul Durrant famously stood up to tell the chairman, Sir John Bond, and other board members that although they worked in the same offices, they lived in different worlds. He and his colleagues weren't earning enough to provide books, a decent lunch or school outings for their children. The campaigners picketed other big firms in the City, turned up at the board meetings of local hospitals and universities, marched down the Mile End Road to call on these and other major public and private sector employers in East London to ensure not only their employees but also their subcontracted staff earned a wage they could live on.

Finally, in 2004, Barclays and HSBC agreed to increase pay for their third-party contracted cleaning staff, followed over the next few years by Living Wage commitments from Deutsche Bank, Morgan Stanley, Lehman Brothers, Citigroup, KPMG, PWC and RBS. These early vanguard employers were crucial in building the legitimacy and evidence base for the campaign. They showed that paying a real Living Wage could have business benefits as well as being the right thing to do.

The Living Wage Foundation

In 2011, the Living Wage Foundation was founded to recognize and celebrate the leadership shown by Living Wage Employers in the UK. The Foundation has three core functions in growing the number of workers who are paid a wage that meets the cost of living:

1. Accreditation: offering accreditation to employers that pay the Living Wage, or those committed to an agreed timetable of implementation, by awarding the Living Wage Employer Mark. There is also a Service Provider Recognition Scheme for suppliers of outsourced services, such as cleaning, catering and security. The recognition is awarded to providers who pay their own staff the Living Wage and always offer a Living Wage option when submitting tenders.
2. Intelligence: giving advice and support to employers and service providers implementing the Living Wage including best practice guides; case studies from leading employers; model procurement frameworks; and access to specialist legal and HR advice. The Foundation also coordinate the announcement of the new Living Wage rates each November.
3. Influence: providing a forum for leading employers and service providers to publicly back the Living Wage. We work with Principal Partners who bring financial and strategic support to our work. We coordinate Living Wage Week each November, a UK-wide celebration of the Living Wage.

Becoming an accredited Living Wage Employer, as opposed to just paying the Living Wage, signals an organization's long-term commitment to protecting its workers from in-work poverty. It gives employees certainty that they will always earn a wage that reflects changes in the cost of living from year to year. Accredited employers are encouraged to display the Living Wage Employer logo and promote their commitment through recruitment. All accredited Living Wage Employers pay an annual accreditation fee, based on the size of their organization – these fees enable the Foundation to grow the Living Wage Employer network and, in turn, the number of workers who are paid at least the real Living Wage. Vitally, the public commitment of accreditation helps increase the public profile of the campaign, providing a benchmark of good employment practice for others to follow.

Rate calculation

The Living Wage is calculated by the Resolution Foundation and is overseen by the independent Living Wage Commission, which was established by the Living Wage Foundation in January 2016 to provide clear governance of the Living Wage rates. The Commission is drawn from high-profile representatives from civil society, accredited employers and expert stakeholders. It provides a transparent decision-making forum, free from political control, to resolve specific judgements about how to incorporate policy changes and new sources of data into the calculation, advises on how to manage extreme year-to-year variations from general rises in living costs, and ultimately recommends the UK and London Living Wage rates for the Living Wage Foundation to announce in November each year.

The calculation of the Living Wage rates is built on a basket of goods that represents a decent standard of living, using the Minimum Income Standard research determined through consultation with the public, and undertaken by the Centre for Research in Social Policy. The hourly Living Wage rates are then calculated by taking a weighted average of the earnings for a range of family types working full-time to reach a level of income that provides that decent standard of living. Regional variances in living costs for London and the rest of the UK are taken into account. The difference between the two rates is due to the much higher cost of housing and childcare in London, although in 2020 they rose less quickly compared to the rest of the UK.

Political support

The campaign has garnered cross-party political support, notably from successive London mayors, English Metro mayors and devolved governments in Scotland and Wales. In 2015, David Cameron declared the Living Wage a campaign 'whose time had come', and in 2016 his government announced a higher minimum wage for workers over the age of 25. The National Living Wage, inspired by the Living Wage campaign, has increased the hourly rate of pay for those on the lowest wages. However, the National Living Wage is not based on the cost of living in the UK. In April 2020, the UK Government set a new target for the National Living Wage to reach two-thirds of median earnings by 2024 (Low Pay Commission, 2020).

Business benefits

As well as being the right thing to do, paying the real Living Wage makes good business sense too. There is increasing evidence that Living Wage Employers experience improved recruitment, retention, motivation and quality of work – ultimately contributing to higher productivity – and that people are happier and more committed to an organization that invests in them and treats them with dignity and respect.

In a 2017 survey of accredited Living Wage Employers by Cardiff Business School (2017):

- **93 per cent** of employers reported they had gained as an organization after becoming a real Living Wage Employer
- **76 per cent** of large Living Wage Employers reported improved retention
- **64 per cent** of accredited organizations felt that accreditation differentiated them from others in the same industry
- **80 per cent** of employers felt that the Living Wage had increased consumer awareness of their commitment to be an ethical employer with **7 out of 10** consumers saying they would consciously shop in favour of a Living Wage-accredited retail chain

Tackling low pay in high-revenue industries

Many of the earlier adopters of the real Living Wage were in typically high-revenue industries, such as banking, finance and professional services. These organizations were often the target of early Living Wage campaigns as prominent employers in the economy. But, as the story of Abdul Durrant shows, the direct impact these employers can have on tackling low pay should not be underestimated. The commitment of employers in these industries not only has an impact on staff they directly employ, but also increases the pay of their regular third-party contracted staff. As part of becoming an accredited Living Wage Employer, organizations must commit to paying the real Living Wage to all workers who regularly provide labour to them through a third party. This often means increases to the rates of pay for cleaners, catering and security staff for the time they work on a Living Wage Employer's contract, broadening the impact of their accreditation and safeguarding more workers from in-work poverty. Importantly, this commitment to third-party contracted staff recognizes the integral role these workers play in the operation of these organizations.

Beyond the direct impact on their workers, employers in these industries have considerable influence in growing the profile of the Living Wage campaign through their networks and public presence. Many of these employers are household names and their public commitment demonstrates leadership, encourages others to follow and provides legitimacy to the campaign.

In addition to working directly with employers, the Living Wage Foundation works with responsible investors and campaign partners, such as ShareAction, to promote the Living Wage in publicly listed businesses. Investors have been instrumental in over 40 of the FTSE 100 becoming Living Wage Employers. These accreditations have resulted in the uplift of over 20,000 workers from the minimum wage to the real Living Wage, showing the impact that these organizations can have for low-paid workers. The Foundation is continuing to work with the UK's wide network of responsible investors to redouble their efforts to engage their portfolio companies on fair pay and encourage them to become accredited Living Wage Employers.

Accredited Living Wage Employers in high-revenue industries continue to champion the Living Wage in their own organizations and beyond. They show why paying the real Living Wage is not only the right thing to do but is good for business too.

One contract at a time – the role of service providers

Outsourcing and facilities management are two of the UK's most important industries, employing one in ten of all workers, and accounting for around 7 per cent of the UK's

GDP. However, despite the size and significant reach of these sectors, they, like many others, face real challenges, a major one being how to deliver a real Living Wage to their workers that covers their cost of living, while maintaining business competitiveness and commercial viability. It is for this reason that the Living Wage Foundation set up the Recognised Service Provider scheme. This scheme works by encouraging greater uptake of the real Living Wage in facilities management and the outsourcing sector, particularly in notoriously low-paid sectors such as cleaning, security and hospitality. Recognised Service Providers not only help advocate for the real Living Wage to their clients and suppliers but are also changing the public perception of the service industry, and the prevailing perception that certain sectors will always be blighted by low pay. In light of the current crisis, Service Providers are uniquely well placed to demonstrate to the public that they are responsible employers, and that the sector as a whole is moving towards fairer pay.

Since 2013, the Living Wage Foundation has worked with a number of trail-blazing service providers that want to take an active stance on the real Living Wage. There are currently over 140 Recognised Service Providers, including household names such as Mitie, ISS and Compass Group, who collectively operate some 10,000 contracts and employ over 90,000 workers on the real Living Wage. Collectively, the work of the Recognised Service Providers delivers pay rises annually to all of these workers, making a real difference to the lives of low-paid workers and their families.

Recognised Service Providers guarantee the real Living Wage to their directly employed staff and to regular third-party contracted staff who are not tied to client contracts. Where Recognised Service Providers differ from Living Wage Employers is in relation to staff and third-party contracted staff who are tied to client contracts. Recognised Service Providers pledge to always offer a real Living Wage option to prospective and current clients alongside every market rate tender bid, giving the client an opportunity to implement the real Living Wage through their contracts. These service providers are required to initiate a framework to promote and measure the impact of the real Living Wage internally and to actively promote the real Living Wage to their clients and supply chains. Recognised Service Providers are tackling low pay one contract at a time through the real Living Wage.

Holistic approaches to pay in retail and hospitality

Another area where low pay is concentrated in the UK economy is in the service industries. It is often assumed that higher wages in these labour-intensive industries, such as retail and hospitality, are 'bad for business'. But the decision by leading retail and hospitality employers to go beyond statutory requirements to pay their staff the Living Wage has confounded the traditional view of how to succeed in these sectors. From fast-growing UK-born companies such as the brewery and bar chain BrewDog, to the global low-cost furniture giant IKEA, accredited Living Wage Employers are demonstrating that the companies best placed to succeed in the twenty-first century will be those that put the customer–staff relationship at the heart of their business model. In an era where customer service is increasingly important, many retailers are looking at how to best invest in and engage their employees.

In a sector that operates with tight profit margins, this highly competitive context has led to an ongoing drive to control costs. Labour is the biggest and most tangible cost to employers in retail and hospitality. Efforts to improve competitiveness therefore often focus on reducing staff costs – with measures to limit the cost of employee pay and benefits, minimize investment in training and match staffing levels and contracts to patterns of customer traffic as closely as possible. As a result, low wages, chaotic schedules and a lack of training and progression opportunities are often seen as an inevitable feature of jobs in the sector.

This is not just bad for employees. Many employers are also concerned about the sustainability of this strategy, which is associated with high levels of staff turnover and absenteeism. The negative image of the industry and the lack of progression opportunities mean that retailers often struggle to attract or retain recruits with the right skills and attitude. These problems have indirect and direct costs to employers. Operational complexity has grown at the same time as many retailers have reduced investment in staff, driven by bigger product ranges, more complex service offers and frequent promotions.

The decision by leading retail and hospitality employers to go beyond basic legal compliance and pay their staff the real Living Wage rates demonstrates that low pay is not an inevitable feature of these sectors. Accredited Living Wage Employers in retail and hospitality see the wage increase as an investment, not a cost. For these companies, a modern workforce – well paid and motivated to perform to the best of its ability – is the key to good service. This drives customer loyalty, which, in turn, drives sales and profits.

Organizations that maximize the benefits of paying a Living Wage often take a holistic approach, combining the investment in staff pay with wider changes that result in permanent improvements in staff performance, productivity and customer service. This is sometimes underpinned by a move over time to flatter, more collaborative team structures that support both a higher entry rate of pay and longer and more stable contracts. Investments in training enable them to build a more skilled workforce that requires less supervision and can be deployed more flexibly across different job roles. In this way, the Living Wage can act as a catalyst for meaningful changes across the business. When the brewery and bar operator BrewDog became a Living Wage Employer in October 2014, they also abolished zero-hours contracts and introduced more stable hours, with the most common new contract set at 32 hours a week. The company simplified its pay structures, introduced greater pay transparency and increased managerial pay, so that more than 180 staff got a pay rise overall. BrewDog also improved its training and development programme, capitalizing on the expectation that its staff would want to stay longer with the business. In just a year these interventions had led to a 50 per cent increase in staff satisfaction with their pay, a 40 per cent reduction in staff turnover on the company's retail sites and an increase in the proportion of management roles filled by internal promotions from less than 50 per cent to 80 per cent.

As well as the commitments from employers, we've also recently seen an increased awareness on the part of consumers on where they spend their money. There has been acceleration towards new ways of shopping and consuming; people are embracing buying consciously and locally and taking advantage of innovations in digital commerce. The Foundation has been working to increase consumer awareness of the Living Wage as an ethical consideration. It seems as though many of these changes are here to stay, and the Living Wage can play a role in helping consumers choose which businesses they support.

Charities and grant makers

Employers in the third sector make up almost a third of the Living Wage Employer network. Whilst these organizations are often faced with limited budgets and financial constraints, for these employers paying the Living Wage and demonstrating public support for the campaign is about doing the right thing. Many charities are at the front line, seeing the day-to-day impact of low pay on people's lives. For accredited employers in the third sector, commitment to the Living Wage is often part of their ethos and purpose in improving lives and the health of society.

As well as working with charities to pay all of their directly employed and third-party staff the real Living Wage, the Living Wage Foundation runs a Living Wage Funders scheme to support charities to pay the Living Wage through their grant-making. Where charities are reliant on grants, their ability to pay their workers the Living Wage is dependent on how money is allocated to staff costs within these grants. For this reason, Living Wage Funders commit to budget so that all workers employed through their grants are paid at least the real Living Wage.

The purpose of this collaborative work is to end low pay in the voluntary and community sector. Hundreds of charities and funders have already embraced the Living Wage, but low pay remains a real challenge in this area. There are now over 50 Living Wage Funders in the UK, all committed to ensuring that all workers employed through their grant-making are paid at least the real Living Wage and tackling low pay in the third sector. The Foundation works with these funders to support grantees in paying the Living Wage and set targets for how many grantees they will impact and support to become accredited Living Wage Employers themselves.

Harnessing the power of local authorities

Local and combined authorities employ large numbers of people in the UK, both directly and through third-party contracts, and collectively procure over £40 billion worth of goods and services each year. By becoming an accredited Living Wage Employer, local authorities are ensuring that all of their directly employed and third-party contracted staff are earning a wage that meets the cost of living, safeguarding them from in-work poverty.

Research in 2018 found that the extra wages paid by local authorities accredited as Living Wage Employers are invested back into the local economy (The Smith Institute, 2018). The report found that if just a quarter of those on low incomes saw their pay rise to the real Living Wage in ten of the UK's major city regions, a subsequent increase in wages, productivity and spending could deliver a £1.1 billion economic boost to major UK cities. This highlights the cumulative impact of local authorities paying the real Living Wage. When workers earn enough to live, they have more income to spend in the local economy. By accrediting companies as Living Wage Employers, local authorities are not only improving the lives of their employees but also making an investment in the community and local economy. Providing workers with more disposable income means more money will be spent with local businesses, generating wealth in the area.

Local authorities have a key role to play in their communities by helping promote and grow the Living Wage movement. As prominent institutions in their communities, they can lead by example and catalyse change by demonstrating a public commitment to the real Living Wage. The Living Wage Foundation works with accredited local authorities to take steps to promote the Living Wage in their local employer communities by offering business incentive schemes, business engagement events and proactive publicity. Where accredited local authorities utilize their status as prominent employers, embed the Living Wage through their procurement processes and encourage other organizations to pay the real Living Wage, they can create a ripple effect, improving the lives of people who live and work in the local area. Through our experience of working with local authorities, we have seen that strong and visible leadership is important to the growth of the Living Wage, and there is a huge opportunity for local authorities to play an even greater role, beyond their own workers, in tackling in-work poverty in their communities.

Through accreditation, local authorities are making a commitment to tackle in-work poverty in their communities. They are ensuring that all staff are paid at least the real Living Wage and that the independently calculated rates are implemented each year to keep up with the cost of living.

One of the most challenging areas for local authorities when accrediting as Living Wage Employers is implementing and embedding the Living Wage in their third-party contracts. It is not uncommon for local authorities to have thousands of contracts in place, and it is often in contracted areas of business where most low-paid jobs are concentrated. So, whilst it can be challenging to implement the real Living Wage as a criterion in procurement, it is here that the decision to pay the real Living Wage has the greatest impact on low-paid workers. The Living Wage Foundation works with local authorities to do this effectively.

Through our experience of working with over 60 district councils, county councils, unitary authorities, metropolitan boroughs, London boroughs and combined authorities to become accredited Living Wage Employers, we are able to guide these employers through the process of implementation. We provide assistance and best practice in helping a local authority navigate these obstacles. It is also important to note that Living Wage-accredited local authorities have not found that they have become uncompetitive as a result of implementing the real Living Wage in their procurement processes. In most cases, contractors still compete and bid for their work as they did before. Within the complexities of implementing the Living Wage on third-party contracts, the most challenging area for local authorities is adult social care. In particular, residential adult social care is the toughest area to secure the real Living Wage for their contractors. The business model for most care homes in the country is usually predicated on workers being low paid, and the vast majority of costs are staff costs.

Despite these challenges, we know that where local authorities make a commitment to the Living Wage, this has an impact in their communities far beyond the workers they employ. Where these organizations lead the way, we have seen that local businesses follow by adopting the Living Wage, driving up pay and employment standards in the local area.

Place-based approaches to the Living Wage

Local authorities can redouble the impact they have on the Living Wage in their local communities by building coalitions with supportive employers in their area. There is a growing consensus that collective efforts within defined geographic places can help redesign the way our local economies work. Place-based large institutions – hospitals, councils, universities and big employers – are working together with small and medium-sized enterprises, local grass-roots groups and the third sector to focus on addressing the rise of in-work poverty and rebuild identity and prosperity within local communities.

Over recent years, the Living Wage Foundation, along with partners in Scotland and Wales, have been developing Living Wage Places. This project puts the real Living Wage at the heart of local debates around more inclusive economies, using place as a driver to increase the number of employers signing up to the Living Wage. The recognition scheme includes 'places' of all sizes, from buildings and zones to cities and towns. The aim of Living Wage Places is to use a place-based approach to uplift low-paid workers to the real

Living Wage. It provides an opportunity for employers to play a role in addressing low pay in the places they operate and to work in partnership to tackle low pay.

There are two elements to the Living Wage Places model. Smaller geographies such as zones and buildings can achieve recognition when 100 per cent of businesses working within them pay at least the real Living Wage to their staff and regular third-party staff. The model celebrates building management companies or leaseholders for achieving recognition as a Living Wage Place. For larger places like neighbourhoods, boroughs, towns and cities, the model begins a journey towards making the real Living Wage the expected norm in a place. The model recognizes that places of this scale will experience varying challenges and opportunities in encouraging all employers to sign up to the real Living Wage. For larger place-based approaches, the model celebrates local employer action groups for achieving recognition for a commitment to Making a Living Wage Place.

We have seen that all place-based efforts to increase take-up of the real Living Wage require effective partnership working. Neighbourhoods, boroughs, towns and cities interested in starting the journey towards Making a Living Wage Place must have a group of Living Wage-accredited organizations based in their locality. This group, otherwise known as a Living Wage Action Group, should be prepared to work in partnership on a Living Wage Action Plan over a period of three years.

Through the Action Group and the Action Plan, they need to demonstrate the ambition and commitment to 'Making a Living Wage Place' in their locality by encouraging other local employers to pay the Living Wage and increase the number of people in their area who are paid the real Living Wage. Importantly, the model appreciates that every place is unique and allows for flexibility and for different starting points. It is not a model that requires a set of predetermined standards to be met before celebrating local action. Instead, any place can aspire to make the real Living Wage the norm, and the Living Wage Places model is a way to help places begin a meaningful journey towards achieving that aspiration. Making Living Wage Places celebrates the fact that the neighbourhood, borough, town or city is on a journey to help tackle low pay through a partnership of local employers and the community working together. The unique element of Living Wage Places is recognition that place identity and local pride can be a powerful motivator to encourage employers to pay the real Living Wage.

Living Wage Places is harnessing the potential of employers to improve the lives of their communities when they coalesce around their common values. Not only do these employers share a commitment to paying the real Living Wage, but they also share an affinity with the local area in which they operate. Living Wage Places offers employers an opportunity to drive change and deliver a tangible increase in the number of workers earning enough to make ends meet.

Beyond the UK – Global Living Wage

In the UK, the Living Wage Foundation has set a model for how Living Wage campaigns can be operationalized and organized to win pay rises for low-paid workers. The success of the campaign has been based on bringing together a coalition of committed stakeholders to win change on the issue of low pay. However, the Living Wage is also a growing global concept that is crucial to achievement of many of the UN's 17 Sustainable Development Goals (SDGs) (Living Wage Foundation, 2019). Our work on the Global Living Wage is an attempt to share the learning and expertise we have developed to support Living Wage campaigns across the world.

The Living Wage Foundation is now contributing to the search for practical global solutions to help employers and civil society groups across the world tackle in-work poverty through living wages. Following extensive international multi-stakeholder engagement in 2015, the Living Wage Foundation developed a set of core Living Wage Principles (Living Wage Foundation, 2015) to inform a more unified approach to building a global Living Wage movement.

The Foundation is now using these principles to support national multi-stakeholder Living Wage coalitions at various stages of development in several countries, including Canada, Hong Kong, New Zealand, South Africa, and the USA, with the aim of creating a Global Affiliate Network of accreditation bodies similar to the Living Wage Foundation. The World Benchmarking Alliance is currently developing free, publicly available benchmarks that measure and rank the world's 2,000 most influential companies on how they contribute to the SDGs across seven critical systems transformations, including consideration of living wages. Through this work, the Foundation hopes to share learning on the development of a successful Living Wage campaign in the UK context, providing support and guidance to Living Wage campaigns across the globe.

Living Hours – tackling insecurity and underemployment

The campaign for a real Living Wage has always focused on asking employers to make sure full-time workers earn enough to make ends meet. However, whether low-paid workers can make ends meet is also dependent on the number and security of hours they can rely on week-to-week, month-to-month and year-to-year. While many people choose to work part-time, the UK has seen a rise in 'one-sided flexibility' – including the exploitative use of zero-hour or 'tiny hour' contracts as permanent workforce management tools, and false self-employment. This has created financial insecurity and exacerbates in-work poverty. While we have record employment levels in the UK, in-work poverty has not fallen.

Analysis conducted by the New Economics Foundation offers insights into the scale of vulnerable and insecure work among the lowest-paid workers (Living Wage Foundation, 2020). The research shows that 5.1 million UK workers experience insecurity and earn less than the real Living Wage. Two million of these workers have children to look after, but are trapped in low-paid, insecure work long term. Insecure and low-paid work is concentrated in industries such as wholesale, retail, and health and social care, and disproportionately affects Black, Asian and minority ethnic (BAME) workers and women.

Living Hours offers a practical solution that employers can adopt to help provide the security and stability that low-paid workers need to make ends meet. The Living Hours campaign was launched in June 2019, with the first accredited employers announced in October 2020. The campaign was developed over an 18-month period of consultation with workers, Living Wage Employers, trade unions and experts. This culminated in a set of measures to tackle the problems of underemployment and insecurity about working hours.

Living Hours sets out three core measures that constitute good practice on working hours and notice periods:

1   Decent notice periods of shifts of at least four weeks
    For many families, rent and other large outgoings are due monthly. Household bills such as utilities are also often cheaper when paid on a monthly rather than a

pay-as-you-go basis. Sharing rotas four weeks in advance means workers will know the amount of work they will be doing and what they can expect to take home in pay, helping them budget for the month ahead. Last-minute shift changes also impact on healthy family life and make it difficult to plan childcare arrangements. Under our proposals, workers would receive guaranteed full payment if a shift is cancelled within this four-week period. This creates an incentive for employers to plan effectively and share the risk of any fluctuations with workers, rather than expecting workers to shoulder the full cost of uncertainty.

2   A contract that reflects the hours you regularly work

Low-paid workers can't risk uncertainty and large fluctuations in pay from week to week and month to month. So, we are asking employers to give workers the right for their contracts to be reviewed and adjusted if they are regularly working more than the hours they are contracted to do. This would also reduce how vulnerable workers on variable-hours contracts are to arbitrary unfairness, such as cutting of hours to prevent staff from raising concerns or as an alternative to good performance management.

3   A guaranteed minimum of 16 hours a week (unless workers request fewer)

Through our consultation, we wanted to find out what people thought a good minimum number of weekly hours should be. In our consultation with workers and community leaders all groups said that between 12 and 20 hours was a decent minimum. We also wanted to make sure whatever we called for also aligned with requirements on workers in the benefits system. Under our proposals, workers who want to work fewer than 16 hours – for example, because they want to spend more time with their family or have a health condition that means they'd prefer to work fewer hours – would be able to opt out.

When working with employers, contractors and employees on the pilots to test Living Hours, we have seen the positive impact Living Hours could have long-term for both employees and employers. Employees we spoke to felt that Living Hours would enable them to plan better financially and spend more time with their families. It would make them feel valued, recognized and listened to – giving them more pride in their work and their employer. As they would be able to better balance work and care commitments, they would feel a greater sense of well-being and experience health (mental and physical) improvements

Employers we spoke to felt that Living Hours would result in happier and more motivated staff. They felt that this would lead to improved retention and internal progression rates because of higher staff morale and engagement. These factors would contribute to higher performing teams and more satisfied clients. Implementing systems to ensure better planning would also help businesses develop a more robust approach to peaks and troughs, which would lead to a reduction in the costs associated with last-minute demands, such as agency fees. Both employees and employers felt that better planning for everyone would contribute to more productive and decisive organizations.

Through Living Hours, the Foundation will work with employers who can and want to go further to protect their workers from in-work poverty by providing workers with secure hours and predictable shifts. This means continuing to build relationships with employees based on dignity and respect, as well as shaping employment cultures with shared responsibility and reciprocity at their heart.

Conclusion

The network of accredited Living Wage Employers has made a huge impact on tackling low pay and driving up living standards in the UK. The strength of the campaign is demonstrated not only through the number of workers who have been directly uplifted to the real Living Wage, but also by how the rate is now widely seen as a benchmark of responsible pay and has influenced the commitments made by the UK Government.

But there is still work to be done. Research in 2019 showed that 19 per cent of all jobs in the UK pay less than the real Living Wage, equating to 5.2 million jobs (IHS Markit, 2019). As we enter into a period of economic uncertainty following the coronavirus crisis, the Living Wage Foundation will continue to work with the network of Living Wage Employers and campaign partners who believe that a hard day's work deserves a fair day's pay. Paying the Living Wage has always been about doing the right thing, even when times are tough. The pandemic has shown just how much we need each other to get by and shone a light on the crucial role of cleaners, delivery drivers and millions of others in low-paid, insecure work. Now, more than ever, we need to recognize and celebrate employers who do the right thing by workers and their families and pay the real Living Wage. It is vital that we keep good work on the agenda to ensure that workers earn a wage that meets the cost of living to protect their living standards.

References

Cardiff Business School (2017), 'The Living Wage Employer Experience'.

IHS Markit (2019), Living Wage Research for KPMG.

Living Wage Foundation (2015), 'The Living Wage: Core Principles and Global Perspectives'. www.livingwage.org.uk/sites/default/files/pi-living-wage-core-principles%20final%20draft_0_0.pdf

Living Wage Foundation (2019), 'The Sustainable Development Goals and the Living Wage'. www.livingwage.org.uk/sites/default/files/LW_SDG_Report.pdf

Living Wage Foundation (2020), 'Over 5 Million Workers in Insecure, Low Paid Work'. 15 June. www.livingwage.org.uk/news/news-over-5-million-workers-insecure-low-paid-work.

Low Pay Commission (2020), 'The National Minimum Wage in 2020: Uprating Report April 2020'.

The Smith Institute (2018), 'The Local Living Wage Dividend: An Analysis of the Impact of the Living Wage on Ten City Regions'.

Additional resources

- For more information on the work of the Living Wage Foundation, see our website www.livingwage.org.uk/.
- Investing in the Living Wage: www.livingwage.org.uk/sites/default/files/Investing%20in%20the%20Living%20Wage%20toolkit_1.pdf.
- Good jobs in retail: A toolkit: www.livingwage.org.uk/sites/default/files/Living%20Wage%20Foundation%20-%20Good%20Jobs%20ToolKit_1_0.pdf
- Living Hours Final Report: www.livingwage.org.uk/sites/default/files/Living%20Hours%20Final%20Report%20110619_1.pdf.
- Becoming an accredited Living Wage Employer: An implementation toolkit for local authorities: www.livingwage.org.uk/sites/default/files/Living%20Wage%20Local%20Authority%20Toolkit.pdf.
- Living Wage Places: A toolkit on tackling low pay by celebrating local action: www.livingwage.org.uk/sites/default/files/LWP%20Low%20Pay%20Local%20Actions%20Report.pdf.

3 The real living wage and 'the good employer' in UK football clubs

Peter Prowse and Tony Dobbins

Introduction

There is an existing body of academic knowledge about living wage policy and practice in the UK (Heery et al. 2017, 2018; Hirsch, 2017; Johnson et al. 2019; Linneker and Wills, 2016; Prowse and Fells, 2016a and b; Prowse et al. 2017a and b). But there is no research on living wage policy, practice and outcomes in the context of football. This chapter explores the ethical management of 'real living wages' (RLW) for lower-paid staff in British Football League clubs.

A case study of the RLW policy at Luton Town Football Club (LTFC) was undertaken, involving semi-structured interviews with a range of internal participants at LTFC, as well as selected external participants from The Living Wage Foundation, trade unions and community/supporter representatives. The research enhances knowledge about the impact of living wage policy and practice on lower-paid staff in a labour market sector that relatively little is known about. It is significant that Luton Town was the first Football League club to commit to pay a RLW and become accredited by the Living Wage Foundation in 2014, thus setting a 'good employer' benchmark in football. Civil society organizations like Citizens UK/Living Wage Foundation play an important role in improving labour governance standards (Williams et al. 2017). As of 2021, there were approximately 8000 accredited Living Wage Employers (Living Wage Foundation, 2021). The next section considers the real living wage in the sector context of UK football clubs.

The living wage in the context of UK football clubs

Premier League football clubs are accumulating extensive wealth, especially elite clubs in the Deloitte Football Money League (2020). Deloitte estimated an overall income of £5.25 billion for Premier League clubs in 2019/20, before the Covid-19 crisis hit the UK. But, evidently, this wealth bonanza has not been distributed fairly between and within clubs. In particularly, while Premier League club executives and players receive lucrative financial rewards, wages are dramatically lower for staff at the lower echelons of the football labour market, with many encountering in-work poverty. Indeed, of 92 clubs in the English Football League and Scotland, only Chelsea, Everton, Liverpool, West Ham United, Crystal Palace, Luton Town, Derby County, Fulham, and Celtic and Hearts in the Scottish League, are fully accredited by the LWF, ensuring that all directly employed staff, and external contractors and agency workers earn at least the RLW rate of £10.75 an hour in London and £9.30 elsewhere (as of 2020). Staff in many other clubs – cleaners,

DOI: 10.4324/9781003054078-3

caterers, stewards and other match-day roles – are employed indirectly by agencies or contractors and not paid the RLW. Occupations such as catering, cleaning, security and hospitality in football clubs are casual and part-time due to the nature of the sports events sector, and are amongst the lowest-paid roles.

Despite various grass-roots campaigns by trade unions (notably the GMB Foul Pay campaign, GMB, 2016), supporters groups and civil society organizations like Citizens UK/Living Wage Foundation, and political exhortations, few football clubs are taking concrete measures to improve the wages and working conditions of lower-paid staff (Dobbins and Prowse, 2017). Football remains one of the lowest payers of the RLW (only a 3 per cent take-up), within the broader arts and entertainment category. Many British football clubs are embedded in urban communities, some classified as among the most impoverished places in Western Europe. It does not reflect well, ethically and morally, on wealthier Premier League clubs especially, when many match-day staff only receive the lower legal national living wage (NLW) or national minimum wage (NMW) (depending on age). The NLW/NMW are widely seen by labour market and social policy experts as not providing enough to live on in a context of widespread in-work poverty in the UK (Cominetti and Slaughter, 2020; Dobbins, 2019).

Case context and methods

Luton Town Football Club (LTFC) is a professional association football club based at Kenilworth Road in the town of Luton, Bedfordshire, England. The club currently competes in the Championship, the second tier of the English football league. Founded in 1885, it is nicknamed 'the Hatters'. The club's colourful history includes major trophy wins, several financial crises, numerous promotions and relegations. Luton employs approximately 500 staff, as follows: 350 match-day staff, 100 full-time non-match day staff and 50 professional footballers. Table 3.1 outlines current direct and indirect employment related to club activities.

The Head of Catering Operations (HCO) manages the day-to-day operations of the football stadium/games, including hospitality, match-day operations of food and drink, the training ground and oversees two stadium catering managers and a full-time head chef on a day-to-day basis, and the 350 events staff on match days. Management of match days is complex. The 350 match-day staff comprise stewards, hospitality (food and bar staff), including executive boxes, a directors' suite, a trophy room suite and a millennium suite mainly for drinks and buffet, a lounge and a range of stadium kiosks serving food and drinks.

There is quite a high degree of economic deprivation in Luton, and the club is cognizant of its important role in the local community as a good employer. Therefore, the club officially announced in December 2014 that it would be the first Living Wage Foundation-accredited employer in the football league paying a RLW. It significantly increased wages for staff, contractors and casual, match-day staff. This is likely to have had a subsequent multiplier effect by encouraging other employers in the town to pay RLW, including the local council. Office for National Statistics (ONS) Annual Survey of Hours and Earnings data identified a fall in workers in Luton paid less than the RLW, from 17,000 (21.4 per cent) to 14,000 (15.8 per cent) workers between 2017 and 2018 (ASHE, 2017/18).

We were keen to research the RLW initiative at Luton, especially as it was the first football league club to be accredited by the LWF and, therefore, to establish a 'good

Table 3.1 Direct and indirect employment related to club activities

Roles	Title	Tasks Include	Gender Male	Female
Board	10 Full Time	CEO	Male	
		Club Secretary	Male	
		Commercial and Hospitality Manager	Male Male	
		Financial Director	Male	
		Chief Operational Manager	Male	
Manager	Full Time	Catering Operations and Hospitality Manager	Male	
Football Professionals	Full Time Professionals	25	Male	
First Team Support Staff	Full time	8	Male	
Non Matchday Staff	Full-Time	50	25 Male	25 Female
Academy Staff	Full Time	12	11 Male	1 Female
Matchday Staff (Events)	Full-time 5% Part time- events 75% Agency staff 20%	150 catering and hospitality 100 stewards and events	50% Male 80% male	50% Female 20% Female
Luton Town Community Trust (Charity Link]	Charity not LTFC Employees	18 Full time 26 part-time 8 unpaid volunteers	15 Males Not available	3 Females Not available

employer' benchmark in British professional football. Moreover, we wanted to collect qualitative evidence on the experiences and voices of the people who receive the RLW and their perceptions of how it changed their lives. We gained access to the club with the assistance of the Living Wage Foundation.

The overarching research objective was to conduct exploratory research analysing the implications of a living wage policy for low-paid staff at LTFC. It was also important to explore corporate social responsibility (CSR) (Breitbarth and Harris, 2008; Fifka and Jaeger, 2020; Jenkins and James, 2013; Walters and Panton, 2014) of football clubs towards employees and the local community. From the research objective, we identified four research themes/questions. Firstly, why have some football clubs like LTFC decided to become fully accredited employers with the Living Wage Foundation, and pay all staff at least the RLW? Secondly, how has LTFC implemented the RLW? Thirdly, what, (if any), are the implications of a RLW for other related (internal) employment and Human Resource Management (HRM) policies and (external) community (CSR) policies in football clubs? Fourthly, what outcomes can be identified, notably the experiences of workers?

We visited LTFC a number of times during 2019 to conduct face-to-face semi-structured interviews with management and employees. Designing an interview population sample required identifying key actors in the club involved with/knowledgeable about living wage accreditation. To address this, seven senior managerial and football board members were interviewed, and all self-referred colleagues involved in the

Table 3.2 Respondents of the Luton Town FC study

Management Board
Chief Executive-[CEO] [Male, FT, 12 years at Club]
Finance Director-[FDO] [Male, FT, 5 years at Club]
Club Secretary-[ClubSec] [Male, FT, 15 years at Club]
Commercial Hospitality Manager-[CHM] [Male, FT, 11 Years at Club]
Head Catering Operations [HCO] [Male, FT Worked 2 Years at Club]

Staff Paid RLW
Commercial Sales [Ellen][Female, FT, 8 years at Club]
Worker -Kitchen Worker [Jaqi] [Female, FT, 5 years at Club]
Assistant chef [Billy] [Male, FT, 3 years at Club]
Security and Parking [Will] [Male, FT, Worked 20 years at Club]
Cleaner Jenny [Female, FT, Worked 13 years at Club]
Cleaner [Alison] [Female, FT, Worked 5 years at Club]
Kit Cleaner [Mary] [Female, FT, Worked 14 years at Club]
Maintenance [Joe] [Male, FT, Worked 3 years at Club]
Apprentice Chef [Jens] [Male, FT, age 17, Worked 2 years]

Part-Time Match Staff
Observation of 20 Inductees then follow up
Agency Food Catering Sales [Yolanda] [Female, aged 19, Works 12-14 hours PT, Worked
    3 months at Club]
Agency Food Catering Sales [Jay] [Male, aged 17, Works 2-14 hours PT, Worked 3 months
    at Club]

Head Luton Town Community Trust (Charity)
Community Trust Worker [KTCommTRust]- [Male, FT, Worked 20 years at Trust]

External interviews
Living Wage Foundation
GMB union

---

decision-making and implementation process, using a snowball technique (Noy, 2008). Exploring implications required interviewing senior managers, but we also needed to select a sample of employees whose wages were influenced by the RLW rise. Consequently, nine full-time staff, all personally affected by the RLW, were interviewed. In addition, the Head of Catering Operations and Hospitality facilitated access to chat to part-time agency events staff, through a new staff induction event, and we subsequently conducted follow-up telephone interviews with some of them. Significantly, visiting the club also provided opportunities to engage in ethnographic non-participant observation (Plows, 2018). Selected external participants (from the Living Wage Foundation, GMB trade union) were also interviewed by telephone (see Table 3.2 for list of interviewees).

Case study of the RLW at Luton Town

Why did Luton become a RLW employer?

The decision to introduce the RLW was the club chief executive's moral vision:

> We did it with, effectively, a mission or a mantra of fairness, or a set of cornerstones, if you like, which were not just only based around football success, but actually about our community engagement, our charitable engagement as well, and effectively, what

we did was see there was not just a duty or responsibility in effectively using the club crest, or the authority of the football club in its environment, but actually an opportunity to use the club's authority to do some good.

[CEO]

The decision to implement a RLW was pioneering for the club – the first ever football league club to do so, despite no Premier League club having done so at that time.

When making this commitment, we hoped it would have a knock-on effect across the leagues, which it has slowly done. When looking at the pros in being a Living Wage employer, it is one of the easiest decisions the business has ever made. It mystifies us that clubs – especially in the Premier League – do not commit to this scheme. Comparatively, Luton Town's yearly turnover is significantly dwarfed by that of any team in the top tier.

[CEO]

Given the enormous wealth of Premiership clubs compared to Luton, the CEO was adamant that other wealthier clubs should follow suit:

There is absolutely no excuse across the EFL and the Premier League not to be involved in such an excellent scheme[Living Wage accreditation] , yet a majority of clubs in the top four tiers are still not accredited employers – in fact, there are only four in the Premier League.

[CEO]

The decision was to develop as a 'model employer' by adopting the RLW. The club was aware of its local community and national position and acts as a leading pioneer to combat low pay, in-work poverty and be a role model for other employers and football clubs:

We are proud to differentiate as a business in a positive way in this sense. However, we would much rather see every single club in professional football become an accredited employer, if it meant there were fewer people living below the poverty line. The second thing that we want after prosperity for the football club is prosperity for our team, and region. So, if we can persuade other local companies to adopt the real living wage, too, then that is a benefit, indirectly. We've been involved in providing advice for other organizations locally.

[CEO]

It was significant in itself that LTFC was registered as a Living Wage Foundation employer four years before the local council, although the council is now a Living Wage Employer.

Implementation/practicalities of the RLW

The club secretary explained that the RLW was the base hourly pay for lowest-paid staff over 18 years of age. Essentially the RLW is the base pay, but since other workers were on higher pay bands based on effort, skill and responsibility and financial performance, there is a graded pay system with pay differentials:

I would say, effectively about 90 per cent of our staff, we now have a living wage plus 10 per cent band. Well, not a band, that's the wrong word, level, and a living wage plus 20 per cent, and a living wage plus 30 per cent [pay] bracket. Bracket's the word I'm looking for. So, every time the living wage goes up now, those people move up with it.

[Club Sec]

For example, Ellen (Commercial Sales employee) outlined that she has an annual pay rate calculated on the RLW rate increase, plus a 25 per cent annual hourly pay rise. Consequently, not only lowest-paid staff receive a pay rise if the RLW increases but other staff also receive a pay differential rise. This ensures differentials are maintained in all job roles, providing guaranteed pay rises for all employees except senior executive roles.

However, there are some age differentials in pay rates. All staff aged 18 years receive the RLW, but staff aged 17 receive 90 per cent and 16-year-olds receive 80 per cent of the RLW. These rates are still quite a bit higher than the NMW, especially for apprentices. In comparison, 16–17-year-olds elsewhere would only be paid £4.55 on the NMW rate, and apprentices not employed by Luton Town would only be paid £4.15 on the NMW apprentice rate. This was confirmed by two respondents: apprentice Jens, and under 17 years old events worker Jay confirmed their friends in other employments were only earning NMW rates. Table 3.3 provides a comparison of pay differences between Luton's RLW rates compared to NMW/NLW rates set by the government and the Low Pay Commission as of 2020 (before the most recent rises in April 2021).

It is significant that the club also insists that employment agencies used by the club also pay temporary agency staff the Luton RLW rate instead of the agency rates of the basic NMW/NLW, which the Head of Catering Operations (HCO) commented on:

They used to pay their staff national minimum wage and when I talked to them that I pay my staff the voluntary living wage, they automatically upped that rate without

Table 3.3 Pay differences between Luton real living wage (RLW) rates and national living wage (NLW) hourly comparative rates 2020

	Club Hourly Rate (RLW) (2020)	NLW Hourly Rate (2020)	Increase in NLW Rate	Increase Pay (35 hours) From NLW Rate (week)	Increase for Average 3 x 4-hour shifts events per Month (12 Hrs) Month
RLW Adult Rate (Hour)	£9.30	£8.72 (over 25)	+6%	+£20.30	+£6.96
Club Hourly Rate 18+	£9.30	£7.70 (over 21–under 25)	+20%	+£56	+£19.20
Club Hourly Rate 18+	£9.30	£6.45 (18–20)	+44%	+£99.75	+£34.20
Club Rate 17–under18 (90% RLW)	£8.37	£4.55	+83%	+£133.70	+£45.84
Club Rate 16–under 17 (80% RLW)	£7.44	£4.55	+63.5%	+£101.15	+£34.68
Apprenticeship Rate 18+	£9.30	£4.15	+124%	+£180.20	N/A
Apprentice Rate 17–under 18	£8.37	£4.15	+101.5%	+£147.70	N/A
Apprentice Rate 16–under 17	£7.44	£4.15	+79.5%	+115.15	N/A

charging me the premium, which was good of them and I said, 'It can only strengthen the relationship', because if you're looking after your staff, that's good because that's what we want as a club as well.

[HCO]

Fit with inclusive 'People Strategy' and CSR

There was evidence that the RLW was part of a broader inclusive 'People Strategy' at Luton, as well as a CSR element. For example, clauses were inserted into renewed/renegotiated contracts with external suppliers and agencies to ensure all staff delivering services are paid at least the RLW. Essentially the RLW is fitted into a wider 'People Strategy', ensuring all staff get a 'fair deal':

Ethically, we want to be an inclusive company, and it would it be wrong on a fundamental level to label ourselves as inclusive if staff were being paid an amount that sees them struggle to make ends meet.

[CEO]

Managing the flexibility of staffing can be challenging. This is especially so for match days, according to the Catering Hospitality Manager (CHM), as there is a higher level of younger workers in kiosks serving food and refreshments, and bar staff have to be over 18, with hospitality staff aged 18–23. Recruitment is continuous, and younger staff have usually been retained for the past three to four seasons.

Regarding employee voice and representation, the playing football staff are all members of the Professional Football Association (PFA) and individually represented by agents. Academy junior football apprentices are encouraged to join the PFA on gaining a contract, and the PFA Youth Advisory service offers advice to Academy players, trialists and parents and carers. However, the non-football staff are not organized in a trade union. This provides a clear background of an organization with little trade union involvement in the real living wage (see Heery et al., 2018:321).

Academic research suggests that while workers benefit from the real living wage, it's not an automatic fix as a people management strategy. Higher hourly pay does not necessarily translate into a better standard of living if working hours are too low. The problem is that there are large concentrations of part-time living wage jobs in the UK economy with people underemployed with few hours. Small income increases are offset by rising costs of living. This factor underpins the Living Wage Foundation's 'living hour's campaign' (2020). At Luton, for example, full-time staff have sufficient working hours, but some external agency staff work relatively few hours and many rely on more than one job to make a living.

The Catering and Hospitality Manager (CHM) highlighted the challenges of only being to offer limited hours (three to four hours) for three matches per month for a football season lasting nine months, compared to other employers (bars/pubs, restaurants, fast-food employers, hotels). However, the key incentives for recruitment and retention at the club include a range of factors. The CHM identified the wage differential for younger workers at Luton receiving the RLW as an incentive, comparing Luton's wages favourably with alternative employers locally:

Yes, so let's say they're going to get another job, a shift off in the pub, it's a six-hour shift, they'll be getting £7.70 an hour or possibly £7.85, they'd rather come here and do a four-, five-hour shift, they will be getting £9.30, they will be pretty much the same and they're working less hours. I think I've got a couple of benefits on top of other employers, because a lot of my employees, they're Luton Town supporters.

[CHM]

In addition to better wages, many workers are also LTFC supporters, which is a big incentive to work at the club in itself for many, according to the Catering and Hospitality Manager (CHM):

Yes, it's just the atmosphere is great on a match day, because we're going through great momentum as well. There is a lot of factors that contribute to that, and I think that being able to offer them a better [pay] rate is just a cherry on top of the cake, if you know what I mean, so it just completes the package and makes it more interesting for them.

[CHM]

The RLW was also linked to a responsible employer and community inclusivity philosophy, with the stadium located in a deprived local community:

Our work in being an inclusive business within the community doesn't stop there – our partner charities over recent years such as Chums and Level Trust help different people from different backgrounds. We invested a lot of time during our links with these charities and it proved incredibly fruitful, notably, the money we raised helped Level Trust open up a fantastic uniform exchange shop in the Town centre. We hope to reach the same level of success with Luton Food Bank this year.

[CEO]

Most senior executives and staff are Luton supporters, and this is critical to the local community ethos of the club, still located in the historical original site, Kenilworth Road. Corporate governance has been problematic in English professional football clubs (Michie and Oughton, 2005). Rather than have a simple shareholding model, corporate governance at Luton is different. Corporate governance arrangements encompass board nominees by the supporters' trust and the Community Trust. The Community Trust elects a member to the Luton Town Board and has grown since its formation in 2009. The Luton Town Supporters Trust elects an independent member to promote supporter representation on the club's board. Major financial decisions such as the move to the proposed new stadium and investment must have been approved by the board, with Football Trust and Community Trust approval.

The new stadium plans are also geared towards developing the community and the town. *The Independent* (2019) stated:

The club have drawn up plans for a 23,000-seater stadium in central Luton, hoping that a bigger ground would help to unlock the obvious potential of the area, including Luton's Asian community. We genuinely want to be more inclusive to the people of Luton. The architecture and design of the stadium will allow us to do that. We will have a banqueting suite that will hold over 1,000 people, which would open up opportunities for us within the Asian community. We will have a multi-faith prayer room included within the stadium, which physically we are unable to do within Kenilworth Road.

This inclusive community strategy was highlighted by the club secretary:

> We've got now planning permission for the stadium, in the heart of the town, and that's another question. People say, why have you chosen the heart of the town? Your other site, which is out by junction ten of the motorway, surely that makes much more sense? No, we want to be at the heart of the community. If you put it out there, people don't use it. They'll come to a game, but will they use it any other time? No, they won't. So, that's in the middle of the town, we've got another piece of land out at junction ten, which we want to turn into a mixed use retail, housing, office, hotels and investments.
>
> [Club Sec]

However, the concept of CSR is not explicitly used:

> The corporate social responsibly isn't something, I don't think […] It's not a real phrase I've ever heard usually here, but we do it, but we don't do it because there's a blueprint which says a good CSR is to do this, this, this and this, we actually do it because it makes sense for us to do it.
>
> [Club Sec]

Benefits, outcomes, employee experiences

When asked about the concrete benefits and outcomes of the RLW, the CEO stated: firstly, higher wages and improved standard of living for employees and their families, especially match-day staff. One example was of how RLW employees can now afford a mortgage, which was previously out of reach. Secondly, and relatedly, higher disposable income for staff has a multiplier effect and feeds into the local economy – 75 per cent of all staff (100 per cent of match-day staff) live locally. Thirdly, the RLW has improved staff retention – and around 20 staff have been employed on the living wage and then moved to other roles to develop their careers within the club. Finally, the CEO and board all believe that Luton Town has an improved reputation as an ethical employer locally and nationally.

The Catering and Hospitality manager identified both a moral and a productivity-related business case for a RLW:

> I think it's both, to be honest with you. I think, morally, you should pay it. I mean, I think I said to you earlier, I'm a firm believer that if you find the right people, you should treat them right. Treating them right by paying them a sensible wage is the way forward, definitely. So, I get that. Morally, yes, I certainly get that, but again, if you've got the right workforce that are motivated, that are sensibly paid, I'm sure the productivity at the end of it is worthwhile.
>
> [CHM]

A central aspect of the research was to assess employee experiences of the RLW. To test this, we interviewed and observed full-time and event staff, asking about their experience of working at Luton and, in particular, if the RLW had made a difference to their lives. The respondents reported that the RLW was a welcome base for pay and rewards at the club.

Jens, an apprentice chef, compared his current Luton apprentice wage rate of £7.44 per hour to that of his friends on apprenticeships elsewhere earning the NMW apprentice rate of £4.30. When asked if he thought this made a difference to his life, and affinity with the club, Jens stated:

> Yes, I do. I save quite a lot of my money up for the future, and that, and I'm saving up for a car, as well. [...] and I can help my mum pay rent, and that [...] Then, I've got my own bits of money whenever I go out with my mates and that. Well, because I've been a season ticket holder since I've been five, I've always supported Luton, but I never knew any of the players, obviously, when I was a season ticket holder, but now I'm close with all the players, the management staff. It's just nice to see another side of the club, instead of just sitting down, watching them run around the field.
>
> [Jens]

Staff on a full RLW rate of £9.30 (in 2020) have also noticed a difference compared to the lower NMW rate. For example, Will, who joined the club 20 years ago as a car park attendant, commented:

> In the security industry, mostly people are working on [national minimum wage] locally [...] But you feel [Luton] they look after the lower waged. They know that some people in this club are on a lower wage, they're struggling, so the club [...] try to help them to improve their lives. That's the main thing. I think the concern about their employees.
>
> [Will]

Two (female) cleaners, Jenny and Alison, have both worked full-time at the club for over ten years. Alison commented:

> I've not found more money in Luton for a cleaner (compared to here).
>
> [Alison]

Mary, in laundry, is originally from a Baltic state and moved to work in the UK. She worked at a banana sorting factory, then for an agency in a school canteen. She had an interview with Luton and started at the club as a laundry-kit assistant. Mary irons, washes and repairs players' kits. She has worked at the club for 14 years full-time. When asked if the RLW was enough for her as a full-time worker to live on she replied:

> It is enough. It's not big [...] of course, it's not big money but we live with [it]. Recently there have been very bad bills, but what I'm paid, everything is all right. If it's not, my son now he's starting for a few months [with] (an)other job in Amazon.
>
> [Mary]

Joe is a full-time general maintenance employee. He started as a volunteer fan at the club, having been previously employed in the electronics industry:

> It all started off about 11 years ago when they wanted the pitch cleared of snow and they asked for volunteers, so I come down and helped, and then I started volunteering in the summer. They offered me a season ticket for doing a couple of months' work, so, you know. I'd been doing electronics for 40-odd years and I was getting fed up

with it, I was looking for something else to do. To be honest with you, when I left my last job, I didn't realize the state of the industry. There's nothing in electronics in this country anymore virtually. I'd have to commute to London and I'm not a fan of commuting, and to get a job I'd have had to go to London or outside of Luton, there was nothing around Luton.

[Joe]

Joe highlighted how this RLW made a difference by enabling him to participate more in the local community:

It's basically about getting out in the community more, get out and go to the pub or for a meal, something like that. I've been a supporter since I was a lad, so for me it's a privilege to be here in a way. I quite enjoy it, I do it because I enjoy it.

[Joe]

All full-time interviewees, but not part-time event staff, were invited to the club's promotion celebration in May 2019, together with the football team and CEO, directors and so on. All staff interviewed (including Mary, Jenny and Alison) mentioned that they were invited with a family guest to the presentation of the Division 1 trophy in the Town Hall.

We also observed an induction session for new part-time events staff. They are casual agency staff, who only work four hours per match. The induction outlined the roles and training for sessions (kiosks, hospitality lounges, recruitment communication for the matches for availability and so on). A key theme for the induction was the club's policy on paying the voluntary living wage. What was highlighted were club pay rates compared to the NMW/NLW rates and the commitment to local employment and the community. The researchers gained contacts to interview and asked if inductees were aware of differences between the higher club rates and lower NMW/NLW rates prior to induction. Most inductees were aware of the NMW/NLW, having also worked for other employers. In the follow-up interviews four months later, events worker Jay, aged 17, contrasted his pay rate at Luton with other jobs available:

Yeah, it's good because there's a big difference of what you earn compared to other jobs that pay minimum. Ah, I think at Luton I get £7 an hour [...] now when I get paid, I can go out and buy my own clothes if I need them, or new shoes. I pay like £20 a month to the family and because if I was earning like £5 (hourly), I wouldn't really get enough like to help. I worked at like a corner shop near where I live, and I think I was only getting like £5 an hour, so I was like, 'Oh this is too long for the amount of money I'm going to earn'. I think there is a chance, well if you work hard enough, you can become supervisor so then you earn more money and you do more hours.

[Jay]

When pressed about the choice of working at the club, in addition to the pay, Jay mentioned the opportunity to be associated with Luton plus the open communication style:

I started working there because my mate told me it was good and like I do support Luton myself and I watch football regularly. I like the way things are done. If we did have anything to say, we'd probably tell our supervisor who's working on the shift and he'll go and tell [XX], the manager.

[Jay]

Conclusion

There is a lack of research on the voluntary RLW in the sector context of football, hence the contribution of the research which this chapter draws on. Few football clubs pay their low-paid staff a RLW. Luton Town FC was the first professional football club in the UK to do so, becoming an all too rare 'good employer' exemplar in the sector context of football; hence our interest in conducting a qualitative case study of the club's living wage initiative. In particular, we were keen to learn about the moral underpinnings of the RLW at Luton, and whether it had made a discernible difference to employees' lives at work and beyond. We identified several pertinent research themes for the case study.

Firstly, why did Luton Town decide to become fully accredited employers with the Living Wage Foundation, and pay all their staff at least the RLW? Discussions with the CEO and other senior club executives revealed a moral underpinning based on fostering greater workplace inclusivity, as well as extending inclusion into the local community and acting as a social catalyst to address low pay in the club and also locally. The decision to register with the Living Wage Foundation was instigated by the recommendation by the CEO to act in a positive way to resolve poverty not just for the club but also locally and nationally.

Secondly, Luton made a decision to be a positive club and a pioneer, one of the few football clubs that have established Living Wage Foundation accreditation, committing themselves to pay all staff the RLW rate, including part-time and agency subcontracted staff on match days.

Thirdly, what, (if any), are the implications of a RLW for other related (internal) employment and human resource management (HRM) policies and (external) community (CSR) policies in Luton Town? Firstly, at present HRM functions are administered by the club secretary and pay policy is based on a minimum of RLW 'plus rates'. Every annual increase in the Living Wage Foundation rates means an automatic pay increase for all staff. This means their pay policies include an enhanced calculation of minima rate of the RLW-plus rate for all full-time staff and part-time events staff. It is noteworthy that employment agencies dealing with the club must ensure agency staff are paid the respective Luton rate (according to age) as part of their procurement contract with the club. There are slightly lower rates for those under 18 and apprentices. But they nonetheless provide younger people with far higher pay rates relative to the statutory NMW rates for younger workers and apprentices. However, the RLW is not without challenges, notably providing people with sufficient 'living hours', which is difficult in a seasonally focused sector like football. Although the club does not (understandably) explicitly refer to corporate social responsibility, their CSR policy is proactive and illustrates why the club is committed to the RLW and to acting as a positive local and national role model to promote fairness at work.

Fourthly, the strategic outcomes identified by the CEO and club secretary were community oriented and focused towards an ethical strategy to resolve poverty locally and act as an ethical leader in football clubs. The RLW not only contributes to a higher disposable income for staff individually but exerts multiplier effects by collectively feeding into the local economy. There are indirect positive outcomes as adopting the RLW has improved staff morale, productivity and retention – and also career development and promotion of staff have been enhanced. The challenges include increasing annual labour costs as rolling out a RLW means differentials in non-footballing staff are maintained annually as a RLW-plus pay policy is maintained. The economic effects of the RLW were important to provide additional income, but a sense of 'family', pride and commitment to working at the club was also an emerging outcome for staff personally affected by and experiencing the RLW.

Further research is required on the RLW in sectors like sport, especially scholarship considering the experiences of low-paid workers.

Acknowledgements

Note: The authors wish to thank British Academy/Leverhulme Small Grant Funding SRG1819/190788 for their sponsorship of this research. We would also like to thank all research participants for so generously sharing the insights and time with us.

References

Annual Survey of Hours and Earnings (ASHE) (2017–18). *Annual Survey of Hours and Earnings (ASHE) – Estimates of the number and proportion of employee jobs with hourly pay below the living wage, by work geography, local authority and parliamentary constituency, UK, April 2017 and April 2018.* ONS Government Statistics. Downloaded 6/8/2020.

Breitbarth, T., and Harris, P. (2008). 'The role of corporate social responsibility in the Football business: Towards a conceptual model', *European Sport Management Quarterly*, 8(2):179–206.

Cominetti, N., and Slaughter, H. (2020). *Low Pay Britain 2020*, Resolution Foundation.

Deloitte (2020). *Eye on the Prize: Football Money League*, Deloitte LLP: London.

Dobbins, T. (2019). 'National living wage is not enough to fix Britain's low-pay problem – here's why'. *The Conversation*, 8 April. https://theconversation.com/national-living-wage-is-not-enough-to-fix-britains-low-pay-problem-heres-why-114867

Dobbins, T., and Prowse, P. (2017). 'How football's richest clubs fail to pay staff a real living wage'. *The Conversation*, 30 March 30. https://theconversation.com/how-footballs-richest-clubs-fail-to-pay-staff-a-real-living-wage-74347

Fifka, M. S., and Jaeger, J. (2020). 'CSR in professional European football: an integrative framework', *Soccer & Society*, 21(1): 61–78.

GMB (the union) (2016). *End Foul Pay*, GMB End Foul Pay campaign.

Heery, E., Hann, D., and D. Nash, (2017). 'The Living Wage campaign in the UK', *Employee Relations*, 39(6): 800–814, https://doi.org/10.1108/ER-04-2017-0083.

Heery, E., Hann, D., and Nash, D. (2018). 'Trade unions and the real Living Wage: survey evidence from the UK', *Industrial Relations Journal*, 49(4): 319–335.

Hirsch, D. (2017). 'Contemporary wage floors and the calculation of the Living Wage', *Employee Relations*, 39(6): 815–824.

Independent (2019). 'Luton's fight for the future: how the League One club is planning to save itself and its community', *The Independent*, 1 February. www.independent.co.uk/sport/football/football-league/luton-town-new-stadium-latest-redevelopment-fight-for-the-future-league-one-championship-a8757026.html

Jenkins, H., and James, L. (2013). *It's Not Just a Game: Community Work in the UK Football Industry and Approaches to Corporate Social Responsibility*. ERSC Centre for Business Relationships, Accountability, Sustainability & Society, Cardiff University: Cardiff.

Johnson, M., Koukiadaki, A., and Grimshaw, D. (2019). 'The Living Wage in the UK: testing the limits of soft regulation?', *Transfer: European Review of Labour and Research*, 25(3): 319–333.

Linneker, B., and Wills, J. (2016). 'The London living wage and in-work poverty reduction: Impacts on employers and workers', *Environment and Planning C: Government and Policy*, 34(5): 759–776.

Living Wage Foundation (LWF) (2021). 'Living Wage Employers'. Retrieved on 1/6/2021 from www.livingwage.org.uk/accredited-living-wage-Employers.

Michie, J., and Oughton, C. (2005). 'The corporate governance of professional football clubs in England', *Corporate Governance*, 13(4): 517–531.

Noy, C. (2008). 'Sampling knowledge: The hermeneutics of snowball sampling in qualitative research', *International Journal of social research methodology*, 11(4): 327–344.

Plows, A. (2018). *Messy Ethnographies in Action* (ed). Vernon Press: Wilmington, DE and Malaga.

Prowse, P., and Fells, R. (2016a). 'The living wage-policy and practice', *Industrial Relations Journal*, 47(2): 144–162.

Prowse, P., and Fells, R. (2016b). 'The living wage in the UK – an analysis of the GMB campaign in local government', *Labour & Industry*, 26(1): 58–73.

Prowse, P., Fells, R., Arrowsmith J., Parker, J. and Lopes, A. (2017a). 'Editorial: low pay and the Living Wage: an international perspective', *Employee Relations*, 39(6): 778–784.

Prowse, P., Fells, R., and Lopes, A. (2017b). 'Community and union led Living Wage campaigns – a comparative analysis', *Employee Relations*, 39(6): 825–839.

Walters, G., and Panton, M (2014). 'Corporate social responsibility and social partnerships in professional football', *Soccer & Society*, 15(6): 828–846.

Williams, S., Abbott, B., and Heery, E. (2017). 'Civil governance in work and employment relations: how civil society organizations contribute to systems of labour governance'. *Journal of Business Ethics*, 144(1): 103–119.

4 Outsourcing and the Real Living Wage

Evidence from the United Kingdom

Edmund Heery, Deborah Hann and David Nash

Introduction

In an earlier commentary, Jane Wills connected the UK's campaign for the living wage to what she described as 'subcontracted capitalism' (Wills 2009: 442). For Wills, the fight for a living wage was an essential response to an 'emblematic' feature of contemporary capitalism, its reliance on subcontracting, which dissolved once integrated employing organizations into a nexus of service and supplier contracts. In this chapter, ten years after Wills' commentary, we return to the question of the link between the living wage and outsourcing and in doing so explore two broad themes. First, we examine what effect the Living Wage campaign has had on the frequency of outsourcing and, in particular whether campaigners have persuaded employers to bring work back in-house. Second, we consider whether the campaign has provided an effective response to the problems of low earnings, which Wills and others identify as characteristic of outsourced service employment (Grimshaw et al. 2014). In pursuing this second theme, we present original, empirical evidence on the extent to which employees on outsourced contracts have benefited materially from the living wage.

In exploring the first of these two themes we focus on the objectives of the UK's Living Wage campaign. Wills' view, very definitely, was that the Living Wage campaign should seek to reverse the trend towards outsourcing and, where possible, ensure that previously outsourced workers rejoin the direct workforce. As a community activist at Queen Mary University of London (QMUL), she campaigned successfully for this outcome herself, helping restore the previously outsourced cleaning workforce to direct employment. Others, since have followed this lead and the campaign for the living wage has been repeatedly attached to a secondary demand that the contracting out of support services be brought to an end. New 'indie unions', such as the Independent Worker's Union of Great Britain (IWGB) and United Voices of the World (UVW), for instance, have campaigned both for the living wage and for the 'in-housing' of outsourced cleaning, catering, portering and security services at hospitals, universities and other public service organizations in London (Peró 2020; Shenker 2019).

While seeking to reverse outsourcing is one route that living wage campaigners can follow, attempting to ameliorate the conditions of outsourced workers without changing their employer is another. Much of the growth of private voluntary regulation in the global economy over the past three decades has attempted to effect change of this kind. The development of private labour codes and standards of good practice, such as those promoted by Social Accountability International and the Ethical Trading Initiative are directed at improving labour conditions within supplier companies along global supply

DOI: 10.4324/9781003054078-4

chains (Bartley 2018). These attempts at private regulation have encompassed efforts to promote the living wage. The Ethical Trading Initiatives of Denmark, Norway and the UK have issued joint advice to member companies on how they can best implement living wages within global value chains (Joint Ethical Trading Initiatives 2015). Those advocating private regulation tend to emphasize the role of economic incentives in sustaining private regulation, with brands protecting and enhancing their value through adherence to ethical practice while their suppliers maintain their participation in global supply (O'Rourke 2006). Reflecting this reliance on economic incentives, the surrounding rationale for private regulation stresses the 'business case' for good labour standards. For the Joint Ethical Trading Initiatives, ensuring a living wage is paid can help resolve a number of significant problems, including 'high labour turnover and restricted skills development, limiting product quality [...] increased risk of labour unrest and [...] reputational damage from exposés about goods produced by chronically low-paid workers' (2015: 6).

Much of the literature on private regulation within global supply chains is sceptical about its effectiveness in improving wages and other conditions of employment. It has been shown that improvement is restricted to issues that can be addressed at limited cost, that supplier firms often cycle in and out of compliance with standards and that measuring compliance is fraught with problems of manipulation and evasion (Locke 2013). It has also been shown that the level of effectiveness of private regulation is variable according to context. Certain types of business may be susceptible to pressure to raise labour standards, particularly those with valuable but also vulnerable brands providing goods and services to affluent consumer markets (Vogel 2010). Accounts of international private regulation often focus on global brands in clothing, footwear, sports equipment, electronics and food production (Bartley 2018; Locke 2013). The business membership of the UK's Ethical Trading Initiative is composed largely of companies of this type and also includes general retailers, such as Aldi, Morrison's, Tesco and ASDA. These issues of the level and context in which regulation is effective take us to the heart of our second theme, dealing with the impact of the living wage on contract workers. Below we present original data on the extent to which contracted workers have gained from the living wage in the UK and identify in which economic sectors, industries and types of business indirect workers have been most likely to benefit.

The research evidence that we use in pursuing these themes takes a number of different forms. At its heart is a programme of more than 90 semi-structured interviews with Living wage campaigners, employers that have adopted the living wage and trade unionists. This programme of interviews has been supplemented by the collection and analysis of material from websites and news outlets, much of which focuses on particular campaigns to secure the living wage. This archive material has furnished cases of attempts to link the living wage to the return of outsourced jobs in-house. Sitting alongside this qualitative evidence are two bodies of quantitative data. In late 2016 we surveyed organizations that had been accredited as paying the living wage by the Living Wage Foundation. The questionnaire used in this survey contained items on outsourcing and whether the decision to become accredited had led to changes in outsourcing policy. More than 800 employers provided data via the survey (30 per cent) and responses were broadly representative of the survey population in terms of size, sector and geographical location. The other body of quantitative data is a database of all organizations that have been accredited by the Living Wage Foundation since the system of accreditation was introduced in late 2011. This dataset contains information on more than 8,300 Living Wage Employers, which collectively employ more than 2.5 million UK workers. The dataset also contains information on the types of employees who have benefited materially from Living Wage accreditation by receiving a pay increase. These data on living wage beneficiaries include information on the number of indirect workers employed by contractors, who have gained from the living wage and the types of organization they work for. The combination of qualitative and quantitative evidence, we feel has made the study more robust and allowed us to examine different aspects of the link between contracting and the Living Wage.

Campaign objectives

Adoption of the second route outlined above, seeking to regulate rather than abolish outsourcing, has characterized what might be considered the 'official' Living Wage campaign run by the Living Wage Foundation. The Foundation is the organization that calculates the living wage, promotes it to employers and accredits those businesses that agree to implement the standard. It is a 'business-friendly' organization that seeks to elicit the voluntary cooperation of both client firms and their contract suppliers in its goal of raising wages for the low-paid. The alternative objective, of driving contractors out of the employment relationship and linking the living wage to a demand for 'in-housing', has effectively been abandoned by the Foundation. This second route is now largely the preserve of indie unions and their supporters and has been followed separately from the main Living Wage campaign (Peró, 2020).

The Foundation's regulatory purpose is readily apparent in the living wage commitment that it seeks to obtain from employers. To become an accredited Living Wage Employer (LWE), a business must not only ensure that the directly employed workforce are paid the living wage but also that indirect workers employed by contractors are paid the rate. The terms of accreditation state that, provided a contract or agency worker is employed to work at the premises of the employer for two hours a day and for a minimum of eight weeks, then they should be paid the living wage. It is permissible to phase in this requirement, implementing the living wage for contract workers at the point that service contracts with suppliers are renegotiated, which in some cases means that accredited employers do not become fully compliant for a number of years after they have made their initial living wage commitment. This provision to pay the living wage to indirect workers is intended to reverse the downward pressure on the earnings of low-wage employees, which has often been the result of outsourcing (Grimshaw et al. 2014). While the nexus of outsourcing contracts remains in place, private regulation has been designed to offset the negative consequences for cleaners, catering staff, security personnel and other contract workers who are co-located with the direct workforce.

Further evidence of the Foundation's commitment to the regulation of outsourcing can be seen in the development of a supplementary standard for facilities management companies. Recognised Service Providers (RSPs) are businesses that provide outsourced services to clients and which give an undertaking, firstly, to ensure that their head office staff are paid the living wage, and, secondly, to always include a bid that incorporates the cost of the living wage alongside a market rate whenever they tender for work. RSPs are also asked to report annually on the number of contracts that specify the living wage and the number of workers covered, and many have adopted a business plan aimed at increasing the proportions of both over time. The objectives of the service provider standard are twofold: to use contractors to promote the living wage to their clients by informing them of the Living Wage and of the cost of paying it to outsourced workers, and to ensure that there is a supply of contractors that will cooperate in paying the living wage if this is the policy of the client. The service provider standard has been successful in recruiting some of the UK's largest facilities management companies, including ISS, OCS and Sodexo, as well as many smaller cleaning, security and catering businesses. Essentially, it seeks to use commercial relationships between these contractors and their clients as a tool for diffusing the Living Wage within the 'subcontracted' economy.

Underpinning pursuit of this regulatory purpose are systems of accreditation for LWEs and RSPs, through which businesses commit to the standards developed by the Foundation and which require the payment of an annual subscription. In return for the latter, businesses can use the Living Wage logo and promote themselves as accredited supporters of the living wage. If they do so, the Foundation contends, then they will reap a series of benefits, including enhanced reputation, improvements in employee recruitment, retention and performance, and the ability to win contracts or funding from other organizations that support the living wage. The Foundation's website prominently features research findings that support the business rationale for the living wage and contains case studies of successful businesses, such as Brewdog and IKEA, which attest to the business benefits (www.livingwage.org.uk/). The promotional material released by the Foundation frequently contains testimonials from business owners and managers about the positive effects of the living wage.

To reinforce the business case for the living wage, the Foundation has tried to develop economic incentives for accreditation. In the manner of Fairtrade, it has sought to create a Living Wage consumer brand. The Foundation's website contains an interactive map, through which individuals can identify Living Wage businesses, including bars, cafés, restaurants and retail outlets in their local area, and it promotes consumer goods and services produced by Living Wage Employers at Christmas, Valentine's Day and other gift-buying points of the year. Another feature of the campaigning repertoire of the Foundation is its use of business 'champions' to recruit both peers working in the same industry and clients and contractors along supply chains. The accountancy and consultancy practice KPMG has been particularly prominent in this work, organizing Living Wage events for its client businesses and using its trainee consultants to help smaller firms adjust to paying the living wage. Other businesses have acted in the same way. Mother Ivey's Bay Holiday Park is an accredited LWE in Cornwall, which sought to identify a caravan supplier that would commit to paying the living wage, eventually identifying ABI, a manufacturer in Humberside, which has also become accredited. Living Wage champions of this kind are recognized in an annual award ceremony, which both celebrates and seeks to reinforce the commitment of employers that have supported the living wage. Award ceremonies of this ilk are a common feature of attempts to raise labour and other business standards through private regulation, used by a broad range of other civil society organizations (Williams et al. 2011). The Living Wage Foundation has drawn from an established repertoire of business-supporting campaign techniques to promote its standard to employers, all of which draw upon a 'business-case' rationale.

Impact on outsourcing

The survey of Living Wage Employers provided evidence on the empirical relationship between outsourcing and the adoption of the Living Wage standard. It found that, while outsourcing is common, it is far from ubiquitous amongst accredited organizations. Over 330 employers (40 per cent of the sample) reported that they used contractors, 'whose staff members work regularly on your premises and who are eligible for the Living Wage'.

These employers tended to be larger, more long-established and to be located disproportionately in the public sector though an absolute majority were private businesses.

Table 4.1 shows the types of changes that these organizations have made to their
contracting arrangements as a result of Living Wage accreditation. The most striking
finding is that very few organizations report that they have brought work back in-house.
On this evidence, the 'official' Living Wage campaign has disappointed the hope expressed
by Wills that it be used to combat 'subcontracted capitalism'. It is important to note,
however, that the survey was conducted in late 2016 when the campaigns of IWGB and
UVW were at an early stage and before the collapse of outsourcing giant Carillion in
2018, which has led some organizations to review their outsourcing policies. Both of
these developments have prompted a number of LWEs to bring work back in-house.
Nationwide Building Society, a living wage champion, for example, transferred cleaning
and maintenance workers to direct employment following the ending of its supply contract with Carillion, while the London School of Economics restored direct employment
for cleaners in 2017 under pressure from UVW. However, the extent to which these
actions have been reproduced in other organizations is uncertain: it may be that they are
relatively unusual cases and that the pattern seen in the table, of most LWEs retaining their
contract arrangements, remains broadly accurate.

Moreover, Table 4.1 indicates that in a small number of cases, Living Wage accreditation has stimulated, not reversed outsourcing. We encountered some examples of this
kind in our interviews. An educational charity, for instance, reported that following the
adoption of the living wage, it had outsourced a number of support services, claiming that
guaranteeing the living wage demonstrated that this decision was based on an operational
and not a cost-cutting rationale. We were also informed that the adoption of the living
wage had helped resolve a long-running dispute between the National Gallery and the
Public and Commercial Services Union over the outsourcing of gallery attendants. In
these cases, it seems, requiring contractors to pay the living wage served to reduce opposition to outsourcing.

Stronger evidence can be seen in Table 4.1 of Living Wage accreditation stimulating
the revision of subcontracting arrangements. More than half of employers report that
they have renegotiated contracts with suppliers to allow the living wage to be paid,
about one in seven have replaced contractors and twice that proportion have contracted

Table 4.1 The impact of the Living Wage on contracting

	Number	Per cent
Renegotiation of contracts with existing contractor(s)	187	57
Replacement of existing contractor(s)	47	14
Contracting with a Living Wage Recognised Service Provider(s)	96	29
Bringing work previously contracted back in-house	15	5
Extending contracting to activities that previously were in-house	7	2
Encouraged contractor(s) whose employees do not work normally on your premises to also pay the Living Wage; e.g. a contractor providing an occasional service to your organization	172	53
Encouraged contractors to adopt other good employment practices in addition to the Living Wage; e.g. offering greater job security, increasing training	117	36

Source: Survey of Living Wage Employers, 2016.

with a Living Wage service provider. The findings attest to private regulation leading to the reform of contracting arrangements. There is also evidence of some employers seeking to go beyond the requirements of the Living Wage standard in reconstituting their relationships with suppliers. Just over half of surveyed employers report that they have encouraged contractors to pay the living wage even when workers are not located on the client's premises, while just over a third state that they have encouraged contractors to adopt other good employment practices. Initiatives of these kinds can be seen particularly in the public sector where employers have introduced procurement policies that encourage all suppliers to pay the living wage and which promote the latter alongside equality and diversity initiatives, the employment of local people on public contracts, the offer of apprenticeships and steps to counter the abuse of zero-hours contracts. National governments in Scotland and Wales, regional authorities such as those in London and Greater Manchester, and large local authorities, such as Cardiff, Sheffield and Birmingham, have launched good employment charters and procurement codes, which seek to diffuse the living wage in their areas of jurisdiction and along their supply chains, together with other ethical employment practices (Heery et al. 2020). All of this evidence, we believe, indicates very firmly that the Living Wage campaign has primarily been associated with attempts to regulate, not abandon, outsourcing.

Impact of the living wage on contract employees

It was noted above that international private regulation of employment is often perceived as ineffectual, failing in its declared objective of raising workplace standards. In this section we present evidence on the effectiveness of domestic private regulation, assessing the extent to which outsourced workers have benefited materially from the Living Wage campaign. To complete this assessment we present evidence on: (1) the scale of impact measured in terms of the number of outsourced workers receiving a pay increase; (2) the characteristics of outsourced workers receiving the living wage, including their occupations and whether they work full-time or part-time; and (3) the characteristics of organizations which have paid the living wage to outsourced workers, measured in terms of their size, sector and industry.

Scale of impact

The Living Wage Foundation collects information on the number of contract employees benefiting from accreditation from two sources. LWEs are asked to provide data on the number of workers that have received a pay increase at the point of accreditation, with separate counts for direct and contract employees. The second source are RSPs who are asked to provide a headcount figure for the number of workers receiving the living wage on contracts with client companies both at the point of accreditation and on the anniversary of their accreditation date. These two sets of data are not perfect. There are a substantial number of missing values, accredited organizations sometimes make mistakes in completing the return and there is no independent check on the accuracy of the information. Despite these shortcomings the evidence gathered from accredited organizations offers a unique record of the redistributive impact of the Living Wage campaign. It supplies quantitative information for assessing the effects of private regulation.

Between 2011 and mid-September 2020, 7,632 LWEs provided a breakdown of the numbers of employees who had benefited directly from the living wage, including those working for contractors. In total these employers employed a direct workforce of just over two million and reported that about 204,535 workers had received a pay increase at the point of accreditation. Only a minority of 1,741 of these employers (23 per cent) reported that contract workers had benefited from the living wage, but the total number of contract workers benefiting was nevertheless substantial. The returns indicated that 70,800 contract employees had had their pay increased as a result of Living Wage accreditation, 35 per cent of all who had benefited. It should also be noted that these data are collected at the point of accreditation, and that the terms of the latter allow contract employees to be brought onto the living wage at a later date at the point of contract renewal. The figure of 70,800 therefore probably underestimates the number of contract workers who have gained from the living wage.

The accreditation scheme for RSPs began in 2012 and by September 2020 had recruited a total of 165 facilities management and other contracting companies. In combination, these businesses employed more than a quarter of a million workers, virtually all of whom provide outsourced services to client firms. A total of 159 Service Providers submitted baseline data to the Living Wage Foundation at the point of accreditation, which indicated that 91,199 contract employees were working on contracts with a minimum rate set at or above the living wage. By September 2019, this figure had increased to 93,944, with a third of service providers reporting that the number of covered workers had increased over time.

It is not possible to add the estimates of contract workers receiving the living wage from LWEs and from RSPs to obtain an accurate total estimate because of the risk of double-counting: returns from clients and from contractors can include the same employees. Whichever estimate is used, however, it is apparent that the campaign has benefited a substantial number of low-paid workers on outsourced contracts. Private regulation has not been ineffectual and has often delivered substantial wage increases to tens of thousands of employees. It is nevertheless important to place this achievement in context. According to the Resolution Foundation, more than 6.5 million jobs were paid below the living wage in April 2018 (Cominetti et al. 2019). The estimated number of contract workers who have benefited from the living wage is equivalent to just over 1 per cent of this figure, indicating the scale of the challenge that living wage campaigners continue to face.

Characteristics of contract employees benefiting from the living wage

There are also two sources of information on the characteristics of employees benefiting from the living wage. The first of these is the return that LWEs make at the point of their accreditation, which asks for the number of living wage recipients who are full-time and part-time and who have received the UK and the London living wage. These data are provided for both direct and contract employees. The returns indicate that more than half of benefiting contract employees (54 per cent) work part-time, a pattern which is echoed amongst direct employees and which suggests that a majority of those benefiting from the living wage have been women, as women are still much more likely than men to work part-time. The returns also indicate that a substantial proportion of contract employees have received the higher, London living wage. More than a third of contract workers (37 per cent) were reported to be London-based compared with only a quarter of direct employees. The Living Wage campaign began in London, seeking to obtain pay justice for outsourced workers like those at QMUL who were supported by Jane Wills. The evidence from Living Wage Employer returns is that many thousands of these employees have benefited from the campaign in the intervening period.

The second source of data on employee characteristics is the employer survey, which asked Living Wage Employers to list the 'five main jobs carried out by staff members who are paid the Living Wage in your organization'. Separate lists were requested for direct and contract employees. Employers provided the names of 948 jobs of direct employees and 227 jobs performed by contract employees, which were matched to job titles in the Standard Occupational Classification. The most frequently mentioned contract job by far was that of cleaner, listed by 111 employers, while security guards and kitchen and catering assistants were also relatively common, listed by 20 and 19 organizations respectively. Cleaners were also commonly listed as gainers amongst direct employers, listed by 97 employers, as were kitchen and catering assistants (40), administrative assistants (157), receptionists (37), care workers and home carers (39), sales and retail assistants (38) and elementary storage occupations (38). What is notable about these frequently mentioned jobs, with the possible exception of care workers, is that they have the quality of ubiquity: they are broadly spread across the economy and are not confined to industries characterised by low-wage employment. This ubiquitous quality is obviously true of cleaners, receptionists and junior administrators but it is also arguably true of sales and catering assistants who are concentrated in low-wage hospitality and retail but are also found in many high-wage industries. Universities, for example, often employ catering and retail workers either directly or through contractors.

Further information on the jobs reported to have benefited from the living wage is shown in Table 4.2. The table shows frequency distributions of jobs reported to have gained from the living wage by official counts of the gender composition of these jobs. The table attests firstly to the extent of horizontal job segregation within low-paid occupations. Jobs largely performed by women have gained from the living wage, such as cleaner, receptionist, housekeeper, nursery nurse and care assistant, as have jobs largely performed by men, such as labourer, gardener, van driver, caretaker and warehouse assistant. The overall pattern displayed in the table, however, indicates that benefit from the living wage has been skewed towards female-dominated occupations. This pattern is particularly true for jobs performed by contract workers, with more than half of all benefiting jobs having a female participation rate of more than 75 per cent. These data, like those on part-time employees, suggest that the living wage has been of particular benefit to women workers and especially to women workers in contract employment.

Table 4.2 Gender composition of occupations benefiting from the Living Wage

Percentage of women in occupation across UK	Occupations of direct employees N = 925	Occupations of contract employees N = 227	Occupations of all employees N = 1152
Below 35%	23	25	23
35–49%	6	3	5
50–74%	27	14	25
75% and above	44	58	47
Total	100	100	100

Sources: Survey of Living Wage Employers, 2016; Annual Population Survey 2017.

Characteristics of employers with workers benefiting from the living wage

It was noted above that the literature on international private regulation has reported that receptive organizations tend to be found amongst large, private sector organizations with extended supply chains rooted in low-wage economies in the Global South. A particular susceptibility has been observed amongst branded companies in retail and consumer goods industries that are particularly vulnerable to campaigning activity that might tarnish corporate reputation. It is companies of this type that feature prominently in the membership of the Ethical Trading Initiative and other programmes to promote good labour standards. In this section, we use evidence from the dataset of Living Wage Employers to establish whether the characteristics of accredited organizations follow this international pattern.

The evidence is presented in Table 4.3, which contains data from accredited Living Wage Employers and shows the percentage of contract, direct and all employees who have benefited from the living wage broken down by different employer characteristics. Unlike schemes of international private regulation, the living wage has recruited many small and medium-sized employees: only 6 per cent of employers accredited under the scheme directly employ 500 or more people. These large employers, however, account for the bulk of living wage impact. Two-thirds of direct employees who have received a living wage pay increase are found within these organizations, and this figure leaps to more than 80 per cent for contract employees. Large organizations with relatively extended supply chains may constitute only a minority of Living Wage Employers but they account for the majority of impact.

It is not the case, however, that these organizations are overwhelmingly found within the private sector. The table shows that less than half of impact is concentrated in the private sector and that there are disproportionately high percentages of benefiting employees in the not-for-profit and public sectors. The importance of the public sector in generating pay increases for outsourced workers is particularly apparent from the table. There are a number of possible reasons for the relatively high level of living wage impact in the public sector. Trade union strength is concentrated in the public sector, and though unions have not generally played a major part in diffusing the living wage, they may nevertheless have been influential in the public sector and particularly in local government where accreditation is concentrated (Johnson 2017; Prowse et al. 2017). In addition, public sector support for the living wage may be internally generated, arising from the long tradition of seeking to act as a 'good employer' (Bewley 2006), of which living wage accreditation has become the latest manifestation. Public sector organizations have traditionally offered relatively good employment to manual workers and they have often sought to extend these standards in their areas of jurisdiction and amongst their suppliers. The evidence of high levels of impact amongst employees working for public sector contractors indicates that this latter policy continues to have effect.

The evidence of impact across industries further affirms the importance of public sector and other public service employers. It shows that there is a broad spread of impact across all industry divisions but that the highest concentration for both direct and contract employees is found in public administration. There is also substantial impact in education, where many universities have adopted the living wage and extended it to cleaning and other suppliers, in healthcare, where a number of NHS Trusts and NHS Boards are accredited, and in real estate, where accreditation is concentrated amongst providers of social housing. Impact in

Table 4.3 Characteristics of employers with contract employees gaining from the Living Wage

	Direct employees[1] %	Contract employees[2] %	All employees[3] %
Size of organization			
0–9	4	4	4
10–49	10	4	8
50–249	13	6	11
250–499	7	3	5
500+	66	83	73
Sector			
Private	45	49	46
Not-for-profit	24	14	20
Public	31	37	34
Selected Industries			
Manufacturing	5	3	4
Wholesale & retail	10	4	8
Transport & storage	2	6	3
Accommodation & food services	2	0	1
Information & communications	3	2	2
Finance & insurance	4	16	8
Real estate	2	2	2
Professional services	2	5	3
Administrative & support services	4	6	5
Public administration	27	31	28
Education	12	9	11
Health & social work	15	6	13
Arts & entertainment	4	7	5
Other industries	8	3	4
Industry pay relative to UK hourly median			
–20% or lower	27	16	23
Below 0–20%	7	5	6
0–20% above	25	23	25
20–40% above	31	37	32
More than 40% above	10	19	13

Source: Dataset of Living Wage Employers, including all employers accredited from 2011 to September 2020.

Notes:
a Estimates based on 129,722 employees;
b Estimates based on 70,800 employees;
c Estimates based on 204,535 employees.

the industries affected by international private regulation, in contrast, appears relatively modest, particularly if one focuses on impact amongst outsourced employees. A number of global manufacturing companies have signed up to the living wage, including Astrazeneca, GSK and Nestlé, but manufacturing as a whole contributes little to the positive impact of the scheme relative to its size in the UK economy. The same is true of consumer-facing industries, such as retail and hospitality, which record few benefiting employees, relative to size, especially amongst contract workers. It was noted above that branded, consumer-facing businesses dominate participation in schemes like the Ethical Trading Initiative. Only three of 99 corporate members of the latter, Burberry, Marshalls and Union Hand-Roasted Coffee, however, have signed up to the living wage, while a fourth, Oliver Bonas, was accredited but has subsequently withdrawn. IKEA is the only major retail chain that has signed up to the living wage. The partial exception to limited impact within consumer industries comes from the entertainment sector, which accounts for 7 per cent of impact amongst contract employees and 5 per cent of total impact. Public service organizations, such as galleries, theatres, museums and libraries, have contributed to this effect but so too have professional football teams. Amongst the ranks of benefiting contract employees are match-day attendants, security and catering employees working for Chelsea, Crystal Palace, Everton, Hearts, Liverpool, Luton and West Ham (see Chapter 3).

The place that retail, clothing and electronics companies occupy in systems of international private regulation has been taken by other types of business within Living Wage accreditation. Prominent among the latter are businesses providing financial and insurance services. Most of the major banks in the UK are accredited Living Wage Employers, as are several building societies and insurance companies and specialist financial institutions such as Lloyd's of London and the London Stock Exchange. Together, these organizations are responsible for more than 11,000 contract employees who have gained from the living wage. There are two noteworthy characteristics of these accredited organizations in finance. First, while some maintain a presence on the high street and serve a consumer base, many do not and are focused on providing financial services to other businesses and to government. This characteristic is shared with accredited organizations in administrative and professional services, which are also responsible for substantial living wage impact, and represents a departure from the pattern found within international private regulation. The Living Wage campaign is distinctive in that it has recruited organizations engaged in business-to-business relationships, which are relatively invisible to consumers. The second characteristic is that finance is on average the highest-paying industry in the UK and does not have an extensive low-wage workforce.

Direct evidence of the link between industry wage rates and living wage impact is presented in Table 4.3. The table shows that the Living Wage campaign has raised pay for employees in low-wage industries: about 30 per cent of benefiting employees are employed in industries with an hourly median rate below the UK median. The table also shows, however, that the majority of beneficiaries are employed in relatively high-wage industries and that this is particularly so for contract employees. More than half of contract employees gaining from the living wage are found in industries with wage rates 20 per cent or more above the UK median, and a fifth are found in industries with wage rates that are more than 40 per cent higher. The evidence indicates that many of the beneficiaries of the Living Wage campaign are low-wage workers working in high-wage industries, that is, workers who are performing the generic, broadly distributed jobs identified above, such as cleaners, security guards, administrative assistants and receptionists. What this evidence suggests is that the voluntary nature of the Living Wage standard has skewed take-up towards higher-paying industries, such as finance, professional services, higher education, utilities and information technology, where it can be more readily afforded. The large retail, hospitality, food service, coffee and entertainment chains, which employ large numbers of low-paid, customer-facing workers, have largely remained aloof.

Conclusion

This chapter has examined the relationship between the Living Wage campaign and outsourcing along two broad avenues of inquiry. Along the first avenue, we have examined the extent to which the living wage has led to the reversal of outsourcing and the return of jobs in-house, in the manner suggested by Jane Wills and currently advocated by indie unions like UVW and IWGB. Along the second, we have assessed its effectiveness in producing material gains for outsourced low-wage workers, testing the propositions that private regulation of labour standards is both generally ineffectual and largely restricted to large private-sector employers selling branded goods and services to consumer markets.

The evidence we have assembled on the first theme indicates strongly that the Living Wage campaign has not led to widespread abandonment of outsourcing. In a minority of cases jobs have been brought back in-house, and it remains to be seen if the campaign of indie unions to secure the in-housing of contract jobs alongside payment of the living wage expands further and achieves greater success. To date, however, these developments have been marginal to the main campaign for a living wage, which has pursued the regulation, not reversal of outsourcing. The Living Wage campaign emerges from the evidence as a quintessentially reformist enterprise leading to piecemeal change in existing economic arrangements – the commercial relationships between client and contract businesses and the employment relationship between the latter and their employees – rather than their overthrow. In this regard, it embodies a core principle of the community organizing movement, which gave birth to the campaign, which has prioritized securing immediate, often modest improvements that are nevertheless of value to those affected by the campaign. Sometimes this focus is described as 'cutting issues from problems' (Walls 2015); for example, securing immediate pay increases for contract employees as a contribution, but not the ultimate solution, to the problems of low pay and working poverty.

Our evidence also indicates that this piecemeal change has yielded substantial cumulative gains for outsourced employees. Thousands of businesses have been recruited to the Living Wage standard, tens of thousands of low-wage workers have received a pay increase and millions of pounds have been redistributed to those on low pay. The evidence also suggests that there has been redistribution by sex, with part-time workers and workers in female-dominated occupations benefiting particularly from the living wage. The living wage is an example of a relatively soft form of private regulation, and scepticism is often evinced by commentators with regard to regulation of this form (Johnson et al. 2019). The evidence, however, demonstrates that the campaign has had a substantial positive effect and cannot be deemed ineffectual.

However, the evidence also points to the limits of the Living Wage campaign, particularly in the pattern of impact across different types of employers. The latter is skewed towards employers in relatively high-paying industries, such as finance, information technology and professional services, and in the public services. A voluntary form of regulation, like the Living Wage standard, has diffused most readily in parts of the economy with relatively few low-wage workers, where costs can more readily be accommodated. Employers in low-wage industries have supported the scheme: most notably the cleaning, security and facilities management businesses that have signed up to the Service Provider standard. The main large employers in the UK's core low-wage industries, however, such as hospitality, retail, entertainment and social care, have largely avoided committing to the scheme. In this regard, employer acceptance of domestic regulation differs from that for international private regulation. Businesses that have supported the Ethical Trading Initiative and similar programmes are largely absent from the ranks of LWEs. An important policy lesson, we feel, can be drawn from the skewed distribution of living wage impact. Voluntary regulation of the kind promoted by the campaign, while impactful, cannot be the primary method for reducing low pay. Rather, it should be viewed as a welcome supplement to other measures. The latter must rely upon action by government, be enforceable by law and should be targeted directly at low-wage industries.

References

Bartley, T. (2018). *Rules without Rights: Land, Labor, and Private Authority in the Global Economy*. Oxford: Oxford University Press.

Bewley, H. (2006). 'Raising the standard? The regulation of employment and public sector employment policy', *British Journal of Industrial Relations*, 44/2: 351–372.

Cominetti, N., Henehan, K., and Clarke, S. (2019). *Low Pay in Britain 2019*. London: The Resolution Foundation.

Grimshaw, D., Cartwright, J., Keizer, A., Rubery, J., Hadjivassiliou, K, and Rickard, C. (2014). *Coming Clean: Contractual and Procurement Practices*. Manchester: Equality and Human Rights Commission.

Heery, E., Hann, D., and Nash, D. (2020). 'Political devolution and employment relations in Great Britain: the case of the Living Wage', *Industrial Relations Journal* 51/5: 391–409.

Johnson, M. (2017). 'Implementing the Living Wage in UK local government', *Employee Relations*, 39/6: 840–849.

Johnson, M., Koukiadaki, A., and Grimshaw, D. (2019). 'The Living Wage in the UK: testing the limits of soft regulation?', *Transfer*, 25/3: 319–333.

Joint Ethical Trading Initiatives (2015). *Living Wages in Global Supply Chains: A New Agenda for Business*. Copenhagen: JETIs.

Locke, R.M. (2013). *The Promise and Limits of Private Power: Promoting Labor Standards in a Global Economy*. Cambridge: Cambridge University Press.

O'Rourke, D. (2006). 'Multi-stakeholder regulation: privatizing or socializing global labor standards?', *World Development*, 34: 889–918.

Peró, D. (2020). 'Indie unions, organizing and labour renewal: learning from precarious migrant workers', *Work, Employment and Society*, 34/5: 900–918.

Prowse, P., Lopes, A., and Fells, R. (2017). 'Community and union-led Living Wage campaigns', *Employee Relations*, 39/6: 825–839.

Shenker, J. (2019). *Now We Have Your Attention: The New Politics of the People*, London: Bodley Head.

Vogel, D. (2010). 'Taming globalization? Civil regulation and corporate capitalism', in D. Coen, W. Grant, and G. Wilson (eds), *The Oxford Handbook of Business and Government*, Oxford: Oxford University Press, 472–494.

Walls, D. (2015). *Community Organizing*. Cambridge and Malden MA: Polity Press.

Williams, S., Heery, E., and Abbott, B. (2011). 'The emerging regime of civil regulation in work and employment relations', *Human Relations*, 64/7: 951–970.

Wills, J. (2009). 'Subcontracted employment and its challenge to labor', *Labor Studies Journal*, 34/4: 441–460.

5 Employer experiences of the living wage in the higher education, hospitality and construction sectors

Calum Carson

Introduction

This chapter explores the experiences of three separate case study employers across the UK in both their initial decision to adopt the living wage, and the consequences of doing so for their organizations and workforce. A key focus is placed on the decision-making processes within each firm which led them to become accredited Living Wage Employers (LWEs), and the organizational ripple effects that this decision created through a series of internal and external impacts for the employers in question. It examines both the benefits and the challenges of implementing the living wage for each, determined in part by the geographical and industry-related circumstances that each operates within, and the wider ramifications of the implementation process for both individual workers and fellow organizations within each accrediting employer's orbit. The chapter concludes with a discussion of what the decision-making processes of these organizations, and their experiences of implementation of the living wage, tell us about the ways and means in which ethically led organizational change occurs and progresses across the British employment landscape in the twenty-first century.

The chapter defines the 'living wage' as the voluntary-based 'real living wage' accreditation scheme promoted and facilitated by the Living Wage Foundation (see Chapter 2), which provides oversight across their network of each individual organization that has made the decision to become a formally accredited 'Living Wage Employer' with the Foundation. There is a distinct difference between the non-mandatory nature of this scheme and the legal requirement for employers to pay the 'National Living Wage', the legal minimum-wage rate of pay for all workers over the age of 25 across Britain.

Established in 2011, the Living Wage Foundation has to date formally accredited over 7,000 separate UK-based organizations as part of their independent employer network (Living Wage Foundation, 2021). This network ranges widely across a large number of separate sectors and industries, from city councils to law firms to graphic design agencies, and has a heavy concentration of small and medium-sized enterprises (SMEs), with nearly three-quarters of accredited Living Wage Employers consisting of SMEs with fewer than 50 employees (Johnson et al., 2019). The SME-heavy nature of the accreditation network at present is discussed in greater detail in Chapter 7.

Rather than seeking to provide an extensive overview of the wider accreditation network and the organizations within it (covered in Chapter 2), this chapter instead focuses on three separate case study employers within the higher education, hospitality and construction sectors, and their own individual experiences in adopting and implementing the living wage.

DOI: 10.4324/9781003054078-5

This chapter is structured as follows. Some background details on each of the case study employers under investigation is provided, along with an explanation of the wider research project that has yielded this series of insights into the employer experience of the living wage in the UK. Discussion then moves on to an analysis of the initial awareness of each employer about the living wage (and the campaign promoting it), and the processes and individual actors involved in facilitating the measure's adoption at each organization. An exploration of the various organizational impacts for each firm following the implementation process of becoming a LWE then follows, ranging from external and internal impacts to the wider ripple effects for other organizations within their own supply chain networks. The chapter concludes with a series of reflections on the continued evolution of the campaign for the living wage in the UK, and the likely ways in which future employers will decide to become accredited members of this civil regulatory network.

The contextual landscape

The insights discussed within this chapter are taken from a wider research project exploring the impact of the living wage on the employment landscape of the UK, from the motivations behind the decisions of individual employers to become accredited with the campaign, to the organizational ramifications of these decisions, to the impacts on workers themselves as the ultimate recipients of these higher rates of pay. This project adopted a case study approach to exploring these multilevel impacts, utilizing the experiences of three separate case study employers within the higher education, hospitality and construction sectors.

Case study employer one (or CSE1) is a holiday park in the south-east of England, providing seasonal caravan stays and year-round camping grounds, and became an accredited LWE in 2014. The park and its director have a long-established and extensive record of corporate social responsibility initiatives in other areas, including sustainability and ethical tourism, and pride themselves on being a responsible employer within their own region of the UK.

The organization remains one of only six holiday parks accredited as an LWE in the UK at the time of writing (Living Wage Foundation, 2021), with the hospitality sector as a whole possessing very few LWEs in contrast to other sectors. With a workforce of under 100, it is the smallest of the organizations explored within this chapter, presenting a clear contrast with the other case study employers and the opportunity to ascertain the similarities and differences in decision-making processes and post-accreditation outcomes when the Living Wage is adopted by organizations of different proportions.

Case study employer two (CSE2) is a university based in the west of the UK. The university became accredited with the Living Wage Foundation in 2014, following a concerted effort by a local Citizens UK chapter and the organization of elements of the university's own workforce in publicly pressuring them to do so. To date, the UK higher education sector has a remarkably low number of LWEs, with fewer than 10 in operation across the UK at the time of this case study's own accreditation, and only 35 universities accredited at the present time of writing (Living Wage Foundation, 2021).

Numerous campaigns for individual universities to accredit, conducted by a mixture of traditional trade unions, social movements led by Citizens UK chapters, and the internal mobilization of workers themselves, are currently in existence across a number of British universities. The diversity of these campaigns demonstrates the wide variety of actors involved in the wider living wage landscape, beyond Citizens UK and the Living Wage Foundation themselves (Lopes and Hall, 2015; Prowse et al., 2017).

Case study employer three (CSE3) is a multipurpose construction firm, based in the north-east of England. The organization was the first in both its sector and its region to become an officially accredited LWE, and has since taken a firm lead across the north-east in extolling the benefits of Living Wage accreditation to other potentially interested employers. In a similar fashion to CSE1, CSE3 was not the recipient of any targeted industrial relations action or civil society Living Wage campaign extolling it to become accredited, but did so through their own voluntary initiative. As with each of the other case study employers discussed within this chapter, the organization also operates within a sector with a comparatively low level of Living Wage accreditations to date (Living Wage Foundation, 2021).

The insights discussed below have all been derived from the experiences of these three case study employers, through the utilization of in-depth, semi-structured interviews with the key individuals at each organization involved in the decision to adopt the living wage, and/or involved in the process of implementing both the measure and the wider stipulations that come with official accreditation status with the Living Wage Foundation. Interviews took place from January 2018 to April 2019, with the focus of each varying depending on the individual interviewee's own expertise, experiences and position within the case study employer in question.

The selection criteria for each case study employer were the exploration of the experiences of organizations that had become accredited LWEs from 2012 to 2015, and which were operating within sectors that still had a low density of accredited LWEs as a whole. The rationale for these criteria was that those involved in the decision to accredit were still accessible to be interviewed, and that the living wage had been fully embedded within the firm for long enough that longer-term ramifications could be seen; to ascertain why such organizations had taken a decision which was against established conventional wisdom in the sector that they operate within; and finally, to understand more fully the consequences and reaction to their choice to accredit among their own individual supply chain networks and immediate competitors, and whether or not their example had led to other employers in that sector following their example.

The decision was also made to explore the experiences of both employers who had been the focus of specific Citizens UK/Living Wage Foundation pressure to accredit, and those who had chosen to do so without any form of external public pressure. The variety of these experiences was ascertained not only through the primary case study employers selected, but also via insights derived from in a separate number of non-case study expert interviews conducted.

It was decided early in the research design process not to select cases on the basis that they were of similar size, sector, geographical location and/or were alike in any other ways to each other. Given the sheer breadth of variety among the employers officially accredited in 2016 when this project was constructed, from independent breweries with fewer than five staff members to multisite enterprises with a workforce of thousands, it was (and still is) not possible to determine what a representative or 'ideal' UK LWE looks like; therefore, it was deemed of more importance to focus on their common experiences and interaction with the living wage and the Foundation itself, more than any other common characteristics between them.

Nevertheless, and as can be seen throughout the findings discussed in this chapter, extensive comparisons and contrasts can be made between organizations of vastly different size, scope and sector upon their adoption of the living wage, without their extensive differences rendering such judgements unfeasible. Equally, the established literature on the cross-sectoral impact of the living wage, particularly that conducted by Heery et al. (2017) and Werner and Lim (2016), was instrumental in deciding to select cases for this project based on criteria separate to their defining characteristics of size/sector/operations. All interviews adhered to standard research ethical guidelines, with all respondents remaining anonymous, and the transcriptions of each interview was coded and analysed in NVivo utilizing a thematic analysis approach (Braun and Clarke, 2012). The following sections explore the insights derived from each case study employer, followed by a discussion of the implications of these findings.

The decision to adopt the living wage: exploring employer motivations

This section explores the project's case study employer's initial awareness and interaction with the concept of the living wage, as well as their awareness of the specific campaign for the measure led by Citizens UK and the Living Wage Foundation. There is no universal experience of how organizations first interact with the campaign, and of how they experience civil society encouragement for them to voluntarily raise their wages to compensate for the limitations of legal minimum-wage rates, as prior knowledge of both the movement and the principle of living wages differs considerably from person to person, and employer to employer. Additionally, the degree to which an organization experiences specific external pressure to pay the measure varies widely between the employers currently accredited with the Living Wage Foundation: a Premier League football club is much more likely to be campaigned at directly to pressure them to pay it than a social care firm, for example, given the disparities in profit and wealth between them (See Prowse and Dobbins in Chapter 3 of this volume).

Many employers become aware of what the living wage is, and what the UK campaign for the living wage is promoting, through either their own relationships with other organizations, or through being targeted by the campaign itself. A consistent thread throughout data collection efforts for this project was that employers who became aware of the living wage and the voluntary nature of the movement through non-campaigning circumstances reacted much more positively to becoming a part of it, and that 'shaming' organizations into becoming accredited was in some instances counterproductive.

For CSE1, awareness of the existence of a campaign advocating the voluntary adoption of a higher minimum rate of pay came about through sheer circumstance by the park's director 'reading about it in an article in The Guardian', rather than any specific external or workforce demands for action in this area, with the initial thinking behind deciding to adopt it focusing upon the fact that beyond the positive impact for the park's workforce, 'for a few extra pennies, I could have a brand that was going to improve my corporate social responsibility'.

Of particular interest in these remarks is the clear awareness of the business case for becoming an accredited LWE as an initial reaction, specifically of the reputational benefits that could be enjoyed by adopting the measure as part of the park's 'brand' (Coulson and Bonner, 2015). In the vast majority of other firms spoken to, awareness and experience of the organizational benefits of living wage adoption were something that came to be seen more clearly over time, rather than initially at the outset (Carson, 2020). CSE1, in contrast, presented an interesting case of the director of an organization having both a strong passion for corporate social responsibility in its own right, and a keen sense of the strategic advantages to the company that could be accrued through advocating socially responsible policies and positions.

Having made the decision to support the living wage, the park's director then approached the organization's board to sanction this recommendation, who 'were surprised at how little we were paying [...] so the board said, 'if the park can afford to, we want to do it'. One board member additionally stated that within his own firm, his unionized workforce was all operating on wages above and beyond the living wage rate of pay already. The park was subsequently accredited as a LWE in 2014.

Two particularly salient points emerge from these remarks, the first being the first example within this project's findings of employers who have successfully adopted the living wage having an individual or a team that is particularly passionate about its implementation arguing for it internally. The need for internal advocacy can perhaps be understood through the lens of the difficulty of changing the mindsets of organizations to considering the Living Wage as an opportunity rather than a cost.

The second point is the highlighting of the surprise that one of the board members present at the meeting expressed at the low rates of pay the non-unionized workers of the park were receiving. There is a strong body of evidence that demonstrates that decades of weakening trade union influence and membership numbers have diminished the capacity of workers to collectively demand higher wages, and that workers operating within workplaces without a trade union presence at all are at a particular disadvantage (Millward et al., 2000; Simms and Charlwood, 2010; Bornstein, 2019). Indeed, the emergence and continued existence of the Citizens UK Living Wage campaign itself could be argued to be a direct symptom of the weakened ability of trade unions to secure wage rises to rates that enable workers to afford a decent standard of living, alongside the regulatory failure of legal minimum-wage rates to accurately and consistently reflect the present cost of living in the UK on an annual basis.

In contrast to the relatively straightforward decision-making process of CSE1, CSE2 became aware of the living wage and the campaign itself in a more direct way. The university became accredited with the Living Wage Foundation in 2014, following internal support for the living wage from key individuals within the university's management team, and a concerted joint effort by the local Citizens UK chapter and the university's own cleaners in publicly campaigning for them to do so.

This journey towards accreditation occurred in a piecemeal fashion, with the initial public campaign for the university to begin paying the living wage succeeding first in raising the rates of core university staff, then subcontracted staff, and finally resulting in the full accreditation of the university as part of the Living Wage Foundation's accredited employer network itself. A critical component in ensuring that each of these decisions followed the other was the continuation of the campaign by the local Citizens UK chapter and members of the university (both staff and students) in raising awareness of the existence and impact of the living wage thus far, and the measure's importance for university workers. Video testimony involving individual university cleaners discussing the difference it had made to their lives was produced and shared widely, and a public celebration was launched to celebrate the university's initial move towards paying its own staff and subcontracted cleaners Living Wage rates, to encourage it to then move towards accrediting as a LWE. This campaigning approach, and the specifics of the strategies utilized in service of this approach, follow the community-focused, worker-organizing model that Citizens UK has utilized as a model in promoting the living wage across Britain, among other issues (Wills, 2001; Wills, 2009).

The importance of this approach to the ultimate success of the campaign at CSE2 was highlighted by a number of those interviewed for this project, most notably the university's HR director, who argued that 'one of the powerful ways that Citizens approaches it, is that they bring it back to the individual, to the individual's story', and that reminding the university's decision-makers of their 'civic mission' was a critical part of changing their mindsets and convincing them to support adoption of the living wage. Another member of the university executive board, which ultimately took the decision to adopt, argued that:

> when I saw the videos, what was a theoretical exercise at first became something very different, and I think if you get those people and you get those messages in your head, all the rest about costs and everything don't go away, but they seem surmountable.

A number of these individuals also had both financial and organizational concerns about the implications of accreditation, with one expressing concern that their opposition stemmed from the fact that 'we can't give an external organization control of our wages policy'. Another argued that the reputational risks of publicly committing to an independent accreditation benchmark were as large as the benefits that such a commitment could accrue, arguing that:

> the bad press of leaving, of no longer being an accredited member, is obviously much more damaging than if we'd had a much more low-key approach of matching, and then at some point that match didn't work.

This touches on Johnson et al.'s (2019) criticisms of the public nature of the Living Wage Foundation's accreditation structure as being an 'important but partial' solution in tackling in-work poverty in the UK, particularly given the limited scope of the measure in working in conjunction with other wage-setting mechanisms within Britain. It may also explain why more employers have not become fully accredited members themselves, despite already fitting the criteria of the Foundation's guidelines for organizations.

Eventually, however, strategic thinking began to move towards full accreditation as a means of ensuring that payment of the living wage was universal across the institution, with the argument summarized by the HR director, that, 'for the university it was just, we just want to make this quite clear: absolutely everyone gets it, so the Vice-Chancellor can go out when he wants to and say that quite easily'. The inherent logic within this decision was a recognition of the reputational risks that an employer calling itself an 'official Living Wage Employer' was vulnerable to if it was publicly found that there were gaps within this coverage. These concerns reflect the inherently hazardous nature of an employer publicly committing itself to any externally enforced accreditation scheme, and that the potential for reputational benefits through such moves also carries with it a distinct level of risk that an organization's public image could be damaged rather than enhanced.

Given the similarities in size and the lack of a concerted campaign encouraging them explicitly to accredit, the decision to adopt the living wage at CSE3 has similar undertones to that of CSE1: namely that the decision was made by an executive board broadly supportive of the idea, after being made aware of what the living wage was and why it was considered beneficial to the firm by one individual passionate about the idea within the organization (in this case the firm's finance director). The organization's director described a situation where the board members were in broad agreement over the living wage from the first meeting, followed by a process before formally adopting it of planning how exactly it would impact the company at separate organizational levels. He argued that the finance manager:

> brought it up, we discussed it, and we all thought it was a positive in the first meeting [...] and then we went back and just looked through the numbers, the impacts, how to use it, how to develop it, how would we communicate it through the business.

The firm's managing director also alluded to the broader business case of the measure being a means of investing greater resources within an organization's workforce, arguing that:

> you've got to be commercially responsible, and have to view how it impacts on your business [...] but we measured that with not so much the direct commercial impact, but more just what you get in terms of your valued workforce, and the additional responsibilities they then feel that they're becoming part of your business.

The organization's finance manager reiterated the moral case for adoption while placing the decision in a wider ethical stance to operating a business, arguing that:

> you can't have the Living Wage in isolation, it needs to be part of a demonstration of your responsibility as human beings, and as businessmen.

Another member of the firm's board expressed disappointment that so many other employers that they had spoken to about accreditation could only perceive the decision to pay the living wage from a narrow commercial perspective, and that 'everyone's just looked at it purely as a commercial issue, and made their decisions in a negative way based on the commercial impact on the business', rather than as a means of providing longer-term benefits to an organization. These comments further underline one of the central themes of this chapter, namely the need for internal advocacy for the living wage within an organization in order for it to ultimately take the decision to accredit.

Adoption of the living wage by UK employers, then, cannot be said to be guided by a typical and uniform process, but varies widely depending on both the specific internal decision-making processes of an organization, and the existence and actions of certain individuals within them who are supportive of becoming a LWE. This is perhaps even more essential for a decision such as voluntarily deciding to raise wage rates, a choice that for some organizational decision makers may be seen as an unnecessary and expensive course of action, and where the costs of adopting the living wage may be more apparent than its benefits.

To counter internal opposition to accreditation within organizations which are considering the measure, dynamic individuals who can put forward the moral and business cases for adoption can help change mindsets. Rossiter and Lilien (1994: 68) have argued that 'the production of high-quality creative ideas can be regarded as essential to the survival of most companies and organizations', and the inclusion of employees who possess the ability to see decisions and paths forward in different ways, and crucially are also in positions where they can influence these decisions, are invaluable to employers.

These differences in mindsets do not appear to be a simple split between the moral and business case arguments for the living wage, but in many cases a lack of strategic awareness of the longer-term benefits for an organization that adoption could potentially provide, beyond existing as a clear and present wage-setting mechanism that can help ethically minded employers alleviate in-work poverty rates across the UK and within their own workforce. These include a consideration of the potential for an improvement in recruitment and retention rates, for example, or an external reputational boost for the employer, rather than simply being concerned about a higher wage bill.

The park manager for CSE1, for example, argued that:

> it is about mindsets, it is about you seeing wages not just as a cost, there will always be a cost, but they're actually a good cost and they're an investment.

Similarly, CSE2's HR officer stated that other employers who have not accredited 'just don't look at the benefits properly'. Without dynamic individuals in place with the insights and influence to offer a different point of view, then, alongside a diffusion in organizational decision-making processes that allows alternative voices and arguments to be heard, it is less likely that other individual organizations will also decide to voluntarily adopt the living wage.

The organizational impacts of adoption and implementation of the living wage: employer experiences

Each case study employer reported a wide range of both internal and external organizational impacts of their decision to become a fully accredited LWE. For CSE1, the park's finance officer made a direct link between the impact of the living wage as a tool for investing in a high-quality workforce, and the commercial benefits that result from having such a workforce, arguing that:

> so much of our income and staff is from repeat business, and to get repeat business, you've got to be selling a good service. And if you're selling a good service, you've got to have good staff.

One particular strand of the business case reasoning for adopting the living wage that came through in interviews at CSE1 was that an extra investment in workers is less of a cost, and viewed more as an opportunity to improve the business, and that this reasoning had consequently been demonstrated post-implementation. A number of comments were made about the organizational improvements that the park has enjoyed by investing in their workers, and having that investment returned in kind to them via increased rates of retention and a higher standard of work. The park's bookings director suggested that the key to an organization's success is 'about getting our investment as workers', arguing that actions like voluntarily adopting the living wage and other non-financial attempts at team building help create an organizational culture where workers feel more invested both in their own work and in the wider employer's success:

> everybody is invested in this business, and you can see that [...] they almost feel a personal involvement in the business.

Those spoken to argued that the park had received a significant reputational boost among both ethically minded consumers, with repeat bookings increasing year-on-year since implementation of the living wage, and among the park's uniqueness as a LWE within the local region. A wide number of interviewees and the director of the park themselves also expressed a strong sense of surprise and even confusion at the lack of other holiday parks in their local area deciding to become accredited LWEs themselves, as it provides their own organization with what one member of the senior management team called 'a clear run' at being seen as a socially responsible destination for potential customers to holiday, and an almost-unique means of attaining both a higher profile in the public consciousness as well as an enhanced level of attractiveness to jobseekers within the park's local labour market. The park's HR officer argued that 'it was crazy' that local competitors had not seen the reputational benefits that could be enjoyed by deciding to accredit,

In a similar vein, for CSE2, one of the most marked benefits came in terms of providing a strong public defence for the university when challenged on the high pay levels of their vice chancellor and senior management team, with one member of the HR team arguing that accreditation provides them with the capacity to say:

> that yes, there is that, but we also support our lower-paid, we have the Living Wage, we're accredited, we implement it, we've made a commitment to this. That kind of acts like a balance, in terms of those two ratios.

The university's HR officer also added that:

> it is such a strong statement of look we're a really good employer, we do this for our directly employed people, and even ensure that our contracted cleaners get the living wage, and we have a proper way of managing pay.

In terms of internal impacts, following implementation of the living wage at CSE2, tensions arose among the workforce concerning the issue of wage differentials, with workers one or two grades above those being paid at living wage rates of pay expressing frustration that they were not paid sufficiently enough more to reflect their higher roles and levels of responsibility. One worker argued that 'it's not so much about the top, it's got to be the middle, for the people who are not happy because they're thinking that they can't be bothered to do this or not bother doing that because of it', and that because of this, adoption of the living wage can be 'really demotivating' for other workers. Another argued that in some instances these differentials were as little as 30p per hour, and that while 'it is a great thing for the staff, obviously, it's just not perfect (yet)'. One member of the university's management team also expressed concerns of specific examples in which well-qualified individuals had been 'put off' applying for roles advertising as paying the living wage, because the higher rate of pay had signalled to them that they were not skilled enough to take up such a position. These issues reflect the complexity of successfully embedding a measure such as the living wage within the pre-existing structure of an organization, and that even ethically led initiatives can result in a series of separate HRM challenges for an employer.

For CSE3, one of the most marked organizational impacts of adoption of the living wage came from their decision as part of becoming accredited to extend payment of living wage rates to their apprentices, something not specifically required by Living Wage Foundation accreditation guidelines. The firm's finance manager argued that this was a decision made to ensure that apprentices also felt like a central part of the organization, regardless of age or experience, and that their choice to do this created a virtuous cycle where the firm experienced a reputational boost for treating their apprentices with respect, which then translated into regularly attracting a higher quality of candidate at the interview stage for both apprenticeships and other roles. He argued that this extension of the living wage 'means that we've become an employer of choice, and we get well known, and, we get people coming to us'. Another member of the senior management team argued that their adoption of the Living Wage had given the organization 'a distinct USP' (unique selling point) among the local labour market, which consequently resulted in making the firm a much more attractive option as a desirable place to work for local jobseekers.

Beyond apprenticeships, these reputational and recruitment benefits from adoption of the living wage also extended to other elements of the organization's workforce. Because of the firm's (and wider construction sector's) commonplace policy of hiring third-party employment agency builders on an ad hoc basis to work on particular construction projects and support their core workers, and that given that agency workers in the local labour market had the choice between opting to work for different construction firms, attracting them to CSE3 specifically was crucial. The organization's managing director explained that once their decision to pay the living wage had become embedded as common knowledge among the local employment agencies and the workers that found work through them,

> automatically you had a lot of candidates that gravitated towards us because of us, so automatically you got that cream of the people straight away […] And then word got around, I want to work for them.

These reflect some of the recruitment benefits that can be enjoyed by a LWE upon accreditation.

Interviewees at CSE3 also linked the higher quality of candidate achieved through becoming a desirable employer in the local labour market to a rise in workforce retention rates, a particularly important issue within a sector such as construction. The firm's director cited this post-implementation rise in retaining reliable workers as a 'common sense' motivation for adopting the living wage, arguing that:

> the longer we can keep people, the more productive we can make them, the less we have to pay on training, the less we have to pay on recruitment. So, to us it's just common sense to pay it.

These insights further underline that the choices of individual employers in deciding to adopt the living wage cannot be neatly divided between those with ethically minded motivations for doing so, and those with more strategic reasoning for making such a choice: for many, there is a conflation of the two, among other factors.

Discussion

The previous two sections have explored the initial decision of three separate employers to become formally accredited 'Living Wage Employers', and the consequences for both their organization and their workforce of doing so. These insights demonstrate that voluntary adoption and implementation of the living wage by UK employers can only be fully understood not just through the influence of external actors and institutions such as the Living Wage Foundation, but through a comprehensive analysis of both the personal and business-oriented standpoints of the key individuals involved in making such decisions internally within an organization. They suggest that adoption of the living wage is contingent on internal support for the initiative by those individuals in a position to influence an employer's decisions, that the specific role and position of said supportive individuals within a firm varies on a case-by-case basis, and that without this critical source of internal support an organization is unlikely to commit to paying the living wage.

These insights also demonstrate that there is no uniform process by which an organization decides to become a LWE: while some experience a concerted, civil society and/or worker-driven public campaign to put pressure on them to accredit, others do so out of the independent initiative of ethically minded individuals within an organization, while others do so as a strategic decision to maintain important financial relationships: and, more often than not, the motivations of employers include both moral and strategic considerations. While it is central to understand the role of civil society institutional actors such as Citizens UK and the Living Wage Foundation in promoting organizational change, it is of equal importance to analyse and understand an employer's internal power dynamics alongside this analysis, to demonstrate how and why such decisions are made, and how ethically-led voluntary organizational change occurs.

This chapter also explores the numerous organizational impacts that can occur following an employer's decision to adopt the living wage. These can range from broadly external impacts, such as the enrichment of an employer's public image in the eyes of the wider public and ethically motivated consumers, to internal consequences, such as challenges within the workforce in mediating tensions over wage differentials. In many instances, the external benefits of accreditation can directly impact on the internal effects of the measure, too. This can be seen in the case of CSE3, for example, and the firm's ability to attract a larger number of higher-quality candidates at the recruitment stage through an enhanced public reputation within the local labour market, which then translates into the recruitment and maintenance of a higher-motivated workforce.

The organizational impacts of the living wage on the case study employers that this chapter is concerned with also demonstrate that formal accreditation as a LWE is not an operational decision that is made by individual firms in isolation from the wider workings of an organization, and that while such initiatives can have good intentions and ultimately be targeted at improving the financial security of low-paid workers, they do not also come without their own challenges. Implementation of the measure can impact on aspects of an employer's operations in areas as varied as public reputation and recruitment and retention rates, and both help resolve some workplace tensions while in some instances creating new ones, as well as creating wider ripple effects among an organization's local labour market.

It is also the case that, as with the motivations of individual employers in making the initial decision to adopt the living wage, there is no uniform or conclusive set of organizational impacts that can be predicted when a firm becomes accredited: the ramifications of this decision will depend on the individual circumstances of the employer in question, from the sector in which they operate to the region (or regions) of the UK that they reside within.

Concluding remarks

This exploration of the experiences of three case study employers in deciding to voluntarily adopt the UK Living Wage, and the organizational ramifications of these decisions, have demonstrated the complexity of both making and implementing ethically led organizational change across the British employment landscape in the twenty-first century. These findings make a significant contribution to the existing literature on why organizations make the choice to become accredited LWEs, alongside a contribution to the wider corporate social responsibility literature surrounding the voluntary adoption of higher wages and stronger working conditions by organizations across the world. With the Citizens UK/Living Wage Foundation campaign for the living wage continuing to evolve, grow and consistently add more employers to their accreditation network on an annual basis, insights into this increasingly important aspect of the civil regulation of the UK labour market are crucial.

To summarize the insights discussed within this chapter, then, it is clear that employer experiences of both the decision to adopt the living wage and the organizational impact of these decisions extend beyond a one-size-fits-all story of net gains for both employer and employee following implementation. Each case is different, depending of the decision by the organisation as to how to most effectively implement the process of becoming a LWE, and decisions which in and of themselves are impacted by the specific sectoral and financial considerations of each individual firm.

These insights also help reinforce a series of wider discussion points within the wider academic literature surrounding the UK living wage, most notably around the broad consensus on the moral and business case motivations of employers' motivations in deciding to adopt the living wage, and the resultant organizational impacts on areas such as reputation, recruitment and retention rates. They also underpin the wider themes of this chapter, specifically that those employers who typically decide to implement the living wage contain dynamic individuals within their workforce who are passionate about it, and can help drive it forward; that such organizations tend to already have a pre-established foundation of corporate social responsibility strategies in place; and that the means and motivations by which the living wage comes to be adopted by individual firms vary widely depending on their own decision-making processes, the influence (or not) of external actors/institutions such as Citizens UK and the Living Wage Foundation, and the geographical and sectoral characteristics which determine what kind of organization it is.

References

Bornstein, J. (2019). 'Employees are losing: Have workplace laws gone too far?' *Journal of Industrial Relations*. 61(3): 438–456.

Braun, V., and Clarke, V. (2012). 'Thematic analysis'. In Cooper, H. (ed.), *APA Handbook of Research Methods in Psychology*, vol. 2. Research Designs, American Psychological Association: Washington, DC, 57–91.

Carson, C. (2020). *The UK Living Wage Campaign: Experiences of Employers, Workers, and Advocates*. PhD thesis, University of Leeds.

Coulson, A. B., and Bonner, J. (2015). *Living Wages Employers: Evidence of UK Business Cases*. [Online]. [Accessed 17 January 2021]. Available from: www.livingwage.org.uk/sites/default/files/BAR_LivingWageReport%20cropped%2021%2001.pdf

Heery, E., Nash, D., and Hann, D. (2017). The Living Wage Employer experience. Cardiff: Cardiff Business School.

Johnson, M., Koukiadaki, A., and Grimshaw, D. (2019). 'The Living Wage in the UK: testing the limits of soft regulation?' *Transfer: European Review of Labour and Research*. 25(3): 319–333.

Living Wage Foundation (2021). *Accredited Living Wage Employers*. [Online] [Accessed 15 January 2021]. Available from: www.livingwage.org.uk/accredited-living-wage-Employers

Lopes, A., and Hall, T. (2015). 'Organising migrant workers: The Living Wage Campaign at the University of East London'. *Industrial Relations Journal.* 46(3): 208–221.

Millward, N., Bryson, A., and Forth, J. (2000). *All Change at Work?* Routledge: London.

Prowse, P., Lopes, A., and Fells, R. (2017). 'Community and union-led Living Wage campaigns'. *Employee Relations.* 39(6): 825–839.

Rossiter, J. R., and Lilien, G. L. (1994). 'New "Brainstorming" principles'. *Australian Journal of Management.* 19(1): 61–72.

Simms, M., and Charlwood, A. (2010). 'Trade unions: power and influence in a changed context'. In Colling, T., and Terry, M. (eds.). *Industrial Relations: Theory and Practice.* John Wiley & Sons: Chichester, West Sussex, 125–148.

Werner, A., and Lim, M. (2016). *Putting the Living Wage to Work: Strategies and Practices in Small and Medium Sized Enterprises (SMEs).* Middlesex University: London.

Wills, J. 'Identity making for action: the example of London Citizens'. In Wetherell, M. (ed.). *Theorizing Identities and Social Action.* Palgrave Macmillan: Basingstoke, 157–176.

Wills, J. (2001). *Mapping Low Pay in East London.* Queen Mary University: London.

6 What about care work and in-work poverty? The case of care workers in the UK

Julie Prowse, Peter Prowse and Jeremé Snook

Introduction

The social care sector in the United Kingdom (UK) has experienced numerous changes over the last 30 years that culminated in the problems experienced during the Covid-19 pandemic of 2020 (Cominetti et al. 2020). At the same time, care workers are heralded as 'heroes' and essential workers. This accolade does not necessarily fit with the experience of care workers who for many years have been a neglected and ignored workforce. This chapter presents research examining the work and experiences of care workers employed in care homes in the social care sector across a single region in Yorkshire, UK. Initially, a brief overview of the history of community care is presented to explain the context, and this is followed by an outline of the research methods and the main findings and discussion.

The rise of mixed-care provision

The history of social care in the UK is complex and to some extent mirrors the political persuasion of successive governments and the move towards a neoliberal stance. A post-war consensus of political parties saw the role of the state as to directly provide social care and if necessary, to fund it (Farnham and Horton 1996). The advent of Thatcherism in the 1980s marked a break in this cross-party consensus and a move to a more public and private mix in the provision of social care that continues now and will now be briefly outlined.

Throughout the 1980s a series of social care reviews were commissioned by the Conservative Government, with a particular remit to look at care funding. The Griffiths review (1988) of community care noted the fragmentation, at both the local and central government level, of the responsibility for social care, and that perverse financial incentives had encouraged local authorities to place older people unnecessarily in residential care. To address this, Griffith's recommended that local authorities should be responsible for assessing local community care needs, setting priorities and objectives, and arranging what was called 'packages of care'. The Government's response to the Griffiths report (1988) was included in the White Paper, *Caring for People* (DH, 1989) and the subsequent Community Care Act (DH 1990). A key change was that Local Authorities were no longer directly responsible for the provision of social care; rather, they now commissioned care from a range of providers mainly independently run care homes. However, a few local authorities continued to directly provide social care.

DOI: 10.4324/9781003054078-6

A series of further reforms of community care were implemented, the most recent being the Care Act (DH 2014). This was intended to introduce reforms in the way social care is organized and delivered; however, parts of this Act have been delayed for over six years by successive Governments. On election to office in 2019 the UK prime minister, Boris Johnson, in his maiden speech, promised to 'fix the crisis in social care once and for all'. How this will be achieved is yet to be determined but illustrates the ongoing complexity of social care provision and the context in which care workers are working.

The organization of social care

Between 2009/10 and 2018/19, the number of people in England aged 65 and over grew by 21 per cent, while the population aged 75–84 and 85 plus increased by 13.6 per cent and 20.2 per cent respectively (NHS Digital 2018: 12). Consequently, this growth in the elderly population is reflected in the demand for adult social care. This service covers a wide range of activities and is designed to help people who are older or living with disability or physical or mental illness to live independently and stay well and safe (Kings Fund 2019a). The social care services provided includes the following: support in people's own homes (home care or 'domiciliary care'); support in day centres; care provided by care homes and nursing homes ('residential care'); 'reablement' services to help people regain independence; provision of aids and adaptations for people's homes; provision of information and advice; and provision of support for family carers (Kings Fund 2019a).

Social care funding comes from different sources and may be a payment by individuals, local authorities (based on needs assessment) or a mixture of the two. In practice the National Audit Office (2018) estimates that most social care is unpaid and provided in the home informally by friends and family, equating to between £62–£103 billion pounds per year. This is followed by publicly funded care (£22bn) and self-funded residential care (£11bn). As a result of the Community Care Acts most adult social care services are provided by independent sector home care and residential care providers. These are mainly private for-profit companies but also include some voluntary or charitable organizations, and a few local authorities who continue to provide care services directly themselves (Kings Fund 2019a). In 2014, approximately 60 per cent of residential care home places were funded by local authorities. However, LaingBuisson (2019) notes that austerity measures and tighter budgets have meant that local authorities negotiated lower fee levels, leading to on average a 5 per cent reduction in income over the period 2010 to 2016. The concern is that cost savings can only be achieved by changing the wages or terms and conditions of care workers.

The social care workforce

The social care workforce is predominately employed by the private sector. Figures published in 2019 highlight that the adult social care workforce is comprised of 1.49 million people, amounting to 1.62 million jobs (Oung et al. 2020). Care workers employed in the adult sector are the most common job role with an estimated 865,000 roles being carried out in 2019–2020 (Skills for Care 2020, p31). The qualifications required for a care worker are varied, and historically many learnt on the job and have no formal qualifications. The introduction of the Care Certificate in 2015 by Skills for Care was intended to standardize training across the social care sector. However, since 2015 only 40 per cent of the total adult social care workforce had achieved or were working towards the Care Certificate and 60 per cent had not started or were not engaged with the certificate (Skills for Care 2020:97).

Between 2009/10 and 2018/19, the number of jobs in the independent sector rose by 29.7 per cent, while care staff directly employed by local authorities fell by 37.4 per cent, due to in the outsourcing of adult social care services (Fenton et al. 2018). Approximately half of the adult social care workforce work on a full-time basis and the remaining are part-time (Skills for Care 2020:40). The Living Wage Foundation (2019) launched a campaign targeted at 'living hours' work with the aim of tackling work insecurity. Their research found that one in six workers across all sectors was in insecure or low-paid work.

Pay in the social care sector

Historically, social care is a low-pay sector and is an area the Low Pay Commission (LPC) focuses on. Briefly the LPC was formed in 1997 with the remit to advise government on what rates the different minimum wages in the UK should be. Following its creation, the LPC recommended pay increases known then as the national minimum wage (NMW) for apprentices, workers aged under 18, 18–20 years and over 21.

In November 2015, the Conservative government introduced the 'national living wage' (NLW) for adults aged over 25 years of age. They retained the national minimum wage (NMW) rates for workers aged under 25 years of age and apprentices. The age rate for adults was amended to aged under 23 (in 2021) and the adult rate will be changed to ages over 21 in 2024 (LPC, 2020). This rate of pay is in contrast to the real living wage (RLW) proposed by the Living Wage Foundation. The RLW is calculated on the cost of living and is voluntary (for a detailed discussion, see Howard (2021) (Chapter 2). In practice this means different rates of pay are proposed. As an example, from 2021, the NMW is £8.36, NLW £8.91 and RLW £9.50 (£10.85 in London) (Living Wage Foundation, 2021). A survey by Skills for Care (2021: p.10) found that although pay was increasing for most care workers, there are fewer earning a wage that meets the cost of living (according to that set by the Living Wage Foundation). Around 29 per cent of care workers were paid on or above the RLW in March 2020. Hourly pay rates for care workers are amongst the lowest 10 per cent of earnings in the UK. Data show that the median hourly rate for a care worker in the independent sector was £8.50 in March 2020 and there was a clear north-south regional divide, with the highest average hourly pay rates recorded in London (£9.00) and the south-east (£8.82), and the lowest in the north-west (£8.37) and the north-east (£8.33) and Yorkshire and Humber (£8.38) respectively. The average care worker was better off, in real terms, by 90p per hour in March 2020 than they were in September 2012 (Skills for Care 2021: p.1).

This issue of low pay was identified in the First Report of the Low Pay Commission (1998) and all subsequent reports to date. Consequently, the LPC expressed concern that government reductions in Local Authority funding following austerity measures would affect paying the NMW to care workers (LPC 2015: p.216). The LPC (2017) recommended to government that low-paid workers should be awarded a 4 per cent rise. However, to fund this pay rise, some employers reduced workers' hours and did not offer additional hours to make up any shortfall (ASHE, 2017). Although the introduction of the NLW resulted in an increase in average pay for care workers from £6.78 an hour to £7.89 in March 2018, in practice the average hourly pay for care work is still below the basic rate paid employees in most UK supermarkets (Kings Fund 2019b). In order to meet the NLW commitments, social care providers have had to hold down the overall pay bill in other ways. An increasing proportion of the workforce is now paid at or around that minimum level, and the pay differential between care workers with less than one year of experience and those with more than 20 years of experience has reduced to just £0.15 an hour (Kings Fund 2019b). Finally, Johnson and Jaehrling (see Chapter 9) outline UNISON's voluntary code, introduced in 2012, that recommends contractors increase pay to employees, but this still needs to be acted upon by employers and local authorities who are transferring care homes to the independent sector.

Data for 2017 shows that the average national weekly pay for care workers is £285, with pay disparities existing between women and men. Regionally, different areas have an influence on low pay. For example, some sectors in Yorkshire and Humberside, such as Sheffield, calculate that one in six employees is earning the lowest wage as set by the LPC national living wage (Clarke, 2017). Table 6.1 compares the earnings of care workers in Yorkshire and Humber by gender and employment status and shows that the average earnings, based on 35 hours working, is £279 a week for a care worker and £320 for senior care workers. However, earnings are rising faster for male full-time and part-time workers compared to women.

Reasons for low pay in the social care

There are a number of reasons why low pay persists in the social care sector, which will now be considered. Acker (1990) suggests that gender segregation of work is complex and requires a wider analysis of organizations and the comparative worth of the job hierarchies operating in them that leads to lower grades of work being dominated by women. This notion fits with the care sector where historically, care work is regarded as 'women's work'. Acker (2006: p.446) argues that inequality and stereotyping of jobs results in men's work being seen as a priority with managerial potential, while women are described as a, 'party of outsiders who do not belong'.

As a consequence, what is termed 'inequality regimes' result in the creation of inequalities in work and wage settlements leading to lower levels of pay awarded to women across all occupations and roles (Acker 2006: p.431). As women predominate in the care sector, this results in this work being undervalued in terms of pay, job choice and care workers considered as a less economically valued workforce. One reason suggested for why low pay continues to persist in the care sector is the wage penalty and gender bias applied. This refers to care workers receiving less pay than other occupational sectors based solely on the job they do, and the low societal value (cost) placed on caring (England 2005). Palmer and Eveline (2012) found that employers stereotyped women workers with children as the 'ideal' care workers. This stereotyping envisaged a care worker as a mother and second wage earner, who required little or no professional skills, as these had been acquired through caring for a family (England et al. 2002). Gender bias means that care work is paid 5–10 per cent less than male occupations even when levels of education, skill and working conditions are comparable (England 2005: p.382). In later studies, England (2010: p.153) found little cultural or institutional change in the care sector had occurred, with the devaluation of traditional female roles and occupations continuing and women still receiving less pay than workers in male-dominated occupations. This is further compounded by social care work being undervalued by the public, who have a poor understanding and negative perceptions of the sector and see the jobs as low status (Kings Fund 2019b). Similarly, Becker (1985) argued gendered occupations, such as care work, are valued less in society, which reflects in lower pay. Crowding into certain occupations, less training, lower skills,

Table 6.1 Yorkshire and Humberside gross weekly pay for care workers and senior care workers in UK 2017

	Yorks and Humber All	Male	Female	All Full Time	All Part Time	Male Full Time	Male Part Time	Female Full Time	Female Part Time
Care Workers									
Av. weekly Pay £	56,000	9,000	47,000	27,000	29,000	6,000	3,000	21,000	25,000
	£279.10	£312.80	£272.50	£372.20	£192.80	£389.90	£195.20	£367.70	£192.50
Annual % rise	+8.3%	+18.7%	+5.9%	+7.2%	+5.5%	+10.8%	+29.5%	+6.2%	+2.7%
35 hrs/17.5	£7.97	£8.91	£7.77	£10.63	£11.07	£11.04	£11.15	£10.54	£11.00
Senior Care Home workers	6,000	1,000	5,000	4,000	2,000	1,000	1,000	3,000	1,000
Av. weekly Pay £	£320.50	£392.80	£308.80	£361.80	£173.00	£361.80	N/A	£362.50	£173.00
Annual % rise	-5.1%	+10.2%	-7.2%	-4.7%	-16.2%	-4.7%	N/A	-7.4	-16.2%
35 Hrs/17.5	£9.15	£8.93	£11.22	£10.33	£9.88	£10.33		£10.35	£9.88

Source: ASHE (2017)

lack of promotion opportunities, the balancing of caring commitments and the lower valuation and discrimination placed on women's work all account for lower pay (D'Arcy 2018). Budig and Misra (2010) concur and argue cross-national inequality regimes place care work in the lowest-paid global occupations. Mueller's (2019: p.19) study examined 20 European Union countries and found care home workers were over 80 per cent female and earned below the 50 per cent median wage.

Another explanation cited for low pay is the emotional attachment that develops between care workers and the resident, termed fictional kinship (Dodson and Zincavage 2007). This phrase refers to a situation in which employers promote a 'commodification of intimacy', with a subculture developing in which the care worker becomes a substitute for the residents family until they leave (or dies) and the bond of kinship ceases, known as 'disenfranchised grief' (Doka 1989 see also Folbre and Nelson 2000). A consequence of this for care workers is the development of a genuine emotional attachment to residents, job satisfaction and intrinsic reward, but leading potentially to unpaid labour and work exploitation. Examples cited included running errands, buying items for residents, making unpaid visits and baking birthday cakes. Palmer and Eveline (2012: p.272) suggest that employers believe that care workers gain intrinsic rewards from their work, including emotional reward and recognition of the high quality of care delivered. However, despite this, employers' ingrained perception of the wider societal and cultural undervaluing of care reinforces low pay in the care sector and accounts for its persistence (Palmer and Eveline 2012: p.272). Hebson et al. (2015) also suggest that low pay in the care sector is balanced by care workers high levels of job satisfaction and that to some extent this can mitigate low pay.

To summarize, the evidence shows that care workers are subject to gender bias, their work is less valued, and women are paid lower wages compared to male-dominated occupations.

Research methods

The aim of the research was to examine care workers' work and their experiences and understanding of pay and conditions A qualitative approach was adopted for the study and involved interviewing care workers working in residential care homes across one region in England. The fieldwork took place between 2016 and 2017, with access to care workers initially facilitated by the GMB Union. The GMB was undertaking a recruitment drive to encourage care workers to join the GMB, and the researchers were invited to attend these sessions, to explain the research and recruit volunteers for the study. Care workers who were interested in participating contacted the researchers directly, with no managers aware of their participation. An information pack was sent out explaining the research aims, what consent and participation involved and that a respondent could withdraw from the study at any point, with a reassurance that their anonymity would be maintained. Care workers who agreed to be interviewed provided written consent. The project was approved by the University ethics committee.

In total, 29 respondents agreed to participate and included two managers, a team leader, 3 night managers, a senior care worker and 23 care workers from 15 different care homes. Over a three-month period, telephone interviews were conducted and these lasted between 30 minutes and an hour. This method suited care workers shift patterns and ensured the interviews were private as they were conducted in respondents' homes. All the care workers agreed to be recorded. Following transcription of the tapes, the major themes were identified using colour coding, then manually sorted and categorized into main themes and sub-categories, with appropriate quotes to support them. These categories were continuously revised to ensure that all significant issues had been captured. Using these techniques, data saturation was achieved (Strauss and Corbin 1998).

The following section presents the findings and is organized around the themes of care workers' roles and work, issues of pay and conditions, and their experience and knowledge of low pay and conditions. Initially, the biographical data is presented.

Biographical data

The 15 homes were all privately owned, registered care homes, varying in size from 30 to 60 beds and providing long-term care for elderly residents. The smaller homes tended to be owner managed, whilst the larger homes were part of a national chain of care homes. Seven homes recognized unions, but overall union membership density was below 20 per cent. All the care workers were female, predominantly white (n = 27) and aged between 18 and 70 years. Employment status varied from full-time (n = 18), to part-time (n = 10) to zero-hours (n = 1), with no respondents reporting working in any other jobs. The average hours worked were 30 hours per week. Job titles varied from duty manager/ nurse (N = 2), night shift manager (N = 3), night care assistant (N = 5), care assistant (N = 16), activities co-ordinator (N = 1), cleaner (N = 1), and kitchen assistant (N = 1). Approximately 90 per cent of respondents had caring roles outside of work for children, parents and grandparents.

The nature of the job

Care workers provided detailed descriptions of their job and the broad range of skills needed to meet the personal and social needs of residents, which changed as they became older, more dependent and less mobile. All the care workers cited the needs of their residents as their main priority and stated that, 'You've got to want to do the job'. Respondents expressed a deep commitment and job satisfaction with caring for residents, who were described, 'as family'. When asked, 'what would improve your work here?' the main factor identified was to improve their residents' care and was unanimously rated more important than a pay rise. Care workers noted:

> I love caring and I do enjoy it, but I find it more and more frustrating. The biggest problem for me is not having enough staff. If I have more staff, I have more time to do the care that I want to do and that's the biggest thing.
>
> [Night Care Assistant, Respondent 22]

A care worker explained:

> It's difficult because in 12 hours a day they are like your second family. You spend half of your life with them (residents).
>
> [Night Worker, Respondent 24]

Incisive comments included care workers acting as advocates for residents:

> Care staff in our building have been there for years, we do not have a big turnover of staff. We will not have agency staff because they don't know our residents and it will affect their routine. Because people with dementia they're very fragile, so for

people to turn around and say, 'Well, leave', and you're only arguing your point for the resident's well-being is wrong. They won't listen to you. You've got nursing staff that don't listen to you, but they don't actually know the residents because they don't work with them, they just do paperwork, they don't understand.

[Night Care Assistant, Respondent 23]

Despite care workers' commitment to the job and the residents, they were aware of how the nature of the work resulted in tensions and dissatisfaction. Increased fatigue among care workers was frequently mentioned due to the long shift hours and the physically and emotionally demanding aspects of their work. Many cited being frustrated and wanting to see improvements, but were overwhelmed with the documentation required, resulting in less direct contact time with residents and was described as, 'a lack of time to do the job properly'. Lack of staff was also mentioned as a key issue that not only impinged on the ability to provide care but also the capacity to have breaks or get off work on time. One care manager remarked that if they had more staff:

I would able to let them take their time on their job, so they would hopefully feel better with their jobs, which will then make me have more time to do my job properly.

[Night Manager, Respondent 18]

Broader recognition of their caring role and that 'it's actually a hard job' was also cited by many [n = 24], who felt their work was not fully acknowledged or valued by the public. Care workers compared their work to other occupations and believed it was undervalued and they were underpaid and often described it as, 'just getting by':

I think people just look at us and think, they're the lowest of the low. I think you find yourself, thinking, 'I'm just a carer'. I don't think that people really understand what it entails, I don't think anybody does. I think for some people they think that caring means you go and sit with little old ladies and do their knitting, and chat about the Second World War, but that's not the nitty-gritty.

[Night Care Assistant, Respondent, 22]

However, care workers also realise they are exploited by employers:

They expect everything out there, but don't give you nothing in return. And because you care about the residents, they're using it as an excuse to me as blackmail.

[Care Worker, Respondent, 28]

Respondents' views about pay and conditions

As part of the study, we asked care workers about their pay, working conditions and understanding of pay rates such as the NLW. Care workers' experience of work was shaped by a constant sense of job insecurity and low pay. Care homes were bought and sold by companies to either other companies or private owners, while local authorities transferred the care homes they managed and the staff to the new employers. Approximately 65 per cent of respondents, in 14 different care homes, reported they had been transferred from local authority employment to private care homes and subsequently these homes sold to new owners. This change had serious consequences for both their pay and conditions. All respondents previously employed by local authorities expressed concern about pay reductions following care home transfers and explained that, after a review by the different care homes, their pay and conditions were changed. As a result, the protected conditions or enhancements, which also included special payments, were stopped. This meant that although basic hourly pay rates remained the same, additional pay (enhancements) in the form of overtime, night allowances, holiday entitlement and bank holiday rates were reduced to the statutory minima. Consequently, the pay and conditions for 17 respondents were affected, including night managers and deputy managers. These changes reduced overall pay rates, in some cases significantly, and one care manager explained, 'Well I am going to lose approximately £3,500 a year plus five days reduced holidays' [Night Manager, Respondent 4]. Another night care manager, [Respondent 10] identified the loss of pay enhancement as £63 per week for night allowance and double time at weekends:

> I mean it will make me feel less valued. I'll be going in and doing the same job for less pay. It'll affect my family life because my husband can't work because he's really poorly. I'm the breadwinner. I might have to sell the house and everything. It's going to affect my life.
>
> [Night Manager, Respondent 10]

A care worker explained:

> They're trying to get us onto their new contract. This is why we've got the union in. For 24-hours shift we were paid a single enhancement of £18.05. That's for working these shifts like 5–10 p.m. But they're cutting that out and they're proposing to stop that. This means over a month that £18.05 [less] for me. I think all changes work out at nearly £2,000 a year.
>
> [Shift Care Assistant, Respondent 7]

The researchers asked the newly employed care workers about their rates of pay and conditions compared with existing staff. Over the past 24 months, ten new staff had been recruited to the care homes but were on different contracts and not paid the enhancement that previously employed local authority care workers had received. Despite new employees working the same shifts and performing the same job, they were paid at a lower rate. The data showed 28 per cent actually received a reduction in their current rate for working additional hours, 62 per cent were paid the same rate for additional hours and only a single respondent received an additional premia rate.

Low pay and in-work poverty

Low pay was an issue that led to care workers leaving and a belief that their work was not valued, despite the NMW. One respondent noted, 'I actually earn the same amount now that I did ten years ago' [Care worker, Respondent 18]. Care workers indicated that their pay rates per hour were either exactly the same rate as the NLW hourly rates in 2017 [£7.50] or lower for under-25-year-olds. This may be explained by employers offering part-time contracts and restricting new female care workers to minima rates and reductions in terms and conditions for senior care workers. The plight of under-25-year-olds illustrates some of the anomalies this group of care workers face with regard to pay and in-work poverty, as one young care worker explained:

> Because I'm only 20, I get a lot less money. My relation works for the same company, as a cleaner, but gets £7.50 and I'm a care assistant and I get, I think it's £6.70. But what I don't understand, obviously, it's because of different ages, but I live on my own as well, I also pay bills as well, so just because of different ages, like we have the same bills to pay – like me and my relation, you know – same bills, but just because we're different ages, I get less money.
>
> [Care Assistant, Respondent 26]

Another respondent commented:

> I know a couple that work in the care home. One works in the kitchen and one is in care work and they're hand-to-mouth every week. They're not making ends meet at all.
>
> [Night Care Assistant, Respondent 24]

A night care worker who started on a rate of £7.50 per hour in November 2016 and had experienced minimum pay rises stated, 'Whoever thinks people can live on £7.50 an hour obviously doesn't live in the real world' [Night Care Assistant, Respondent 23]. An issue identified even before TUPE was that part-time workers in 15 of the private care homes were paid less after their guaranteed TUPE rate for any additional contractual time worked.[1] As part of the transfer, it was determined that pay rates for any additional hours worked were only at the national living wage rate of £7.50, and this was a lower rate than the local authority paid.

Changes in ownership of the care homes resulted in staff not being replaced and led to a more stressful environment for care workers and ongoing changes in terms and conditions. All staff confirmed they were no longer eligible for a company sick pay scheme. Respondents also reported they had been threatened with reductions in their pay rate, holiday pay and required to individually contribute more into their pension schemes, with many stating they could not afford this. There was a consensus about the image of care homes as being low-paid and challenging work environments. Care workers compared their job with cleaners, and one noted:

> The cleaners do four shifts a week, but they're only four hours shifts, and they get the same amount of money and it's a lot less work than we have to do and it's a lot easier work. Like, you know, ours is hard work going in and trying to treat these residents as humanely as possible. It's physical work and it's emotional work. And then I don't think that it's right the cleaners get the same amount of money as us.
>
> [Care Assistant, Respondent 26]

Respondents' knowledge of the Living Wage Rates

Responses to the question about whether care workers understood the living wage rate led to mixed results, with some having an awareness, but many not being clear. As one noted, 'I have heard of it, well it's like £7.21 and the rest, and that's what people need to earn an hour to live on' [Care Assistant, Respondent 23]. Respondents also referred to what hourly rate they could live on, and 90 per cent estimated £10 per hour with no deductions. It must be noted that no respondents had knowledge of the voluntary real living wage (RLW) rate, which at the time of the study was £8.75 per hour.

Care workers were asked if they knew what the legal hourly rate of pay was, and only five respondents (17 per cent) could name the correct rate of the NLW, while 24 said they trusted their employer to inform them of any increases introduced . There was some scepticism about how statutory increases in the living wage were implemented, and a respondent explained her experience:

> When this new fellow took over the care home, the first thing he did was give us a rise. So, a lot of us we said, 'Well, he's only giving us a rise because he's got to give a rise [by law]' And the younger people perhaps don't realize they think, 'Oh, it's wonderful. He's giving us a rise', so immediately you're really pleased. But the older ones of us who know he's just doing it because in a few months' time he's got to do it.
>
> [Care worker, Respondent 22]

Opportunities to improve pay

Care workers were asked what opportunities would improve their pay. All stated being able to work full-time and for overtime to be paid. The ten care workers who were part-time cited that they would have preferred to work full-time, but this was not available. Only one care worker who worked shifts on a weekly basis had chosen a zero-hours contract as this work pattern fitted with their caring commitments. All respondents were paid for one hour to undertake online training (often mandatory) at home, but none mentioned training at work or as a means to more pay. Most of the care workers worked long shifts and had personal caring commitments, and so were unable to do other jobs to raise their income. As one noted:

> I'm really in a catch-22 situation. Even though I don't do very good financially, I'm always skint. I can't work more hours because I'm only able to earn a certain amount while I am my Nan's carer.
>
> [Domestic Cleaner, Respondent 25]

Discussion

This study provides an insight into the neglected area of care workers' work, pay and conditions. The classic explanations for low pay in the care sector argue that female-dominated employment sectors suffer low pay, underdeveloped skills and less mobility (D'Arcy 2018). This study has highlighted wider issues and some key findings. Firstly, all care workers enjoy their job and caring for their residents but identified some key challenges. Secondly, care workers identified pay as an issue but stressed that more staff and more time to do the job are equally as important. Thirdly, there is a lack of clarity about the voluntary RLW and what it is. Fourthly, long working hours and inadequate staffing levels were significant factors affecting care workers' roles. Fifthly, there are few opportunities to increase their pay, and additional hours worked were not always paid at an overtime rate and wages had been eroded despite the NLW. Finally, job satisfaction can be enhanced by increasing staffing levels and recognition that pay rises will be a factor to attract and retain care workers.

The findings show that since 2016/17, there was a dual paid workforce in the different care homes studied. Staff transferring from local authority to private sector care homes were paid initially on protected local authority terms and conditions (TUPE). Overall, pay rates for ex-local authority care workers were higher and conditions such as additional rates for shifts, weekends and bank holidays more beneficial. These conditions were changed to basic hourly rates for working shifts, bank holidays and weekends, resulting in them earning lower rates of pay. In contrast, new care worker recruits after 2016 received NLW rates or hourly rates just above the NLW hourly rates and were paid at lower hourly rates than ex-local authority staff and received no premia rates for additional hours (shifts, weekend and bank holiday rates).

The research found that care workers with similar qualifications, training and experience working in the same care home received different rates of pay. This finding concurs with Burns et al. (2016) who found employers were introducing cuts to services, increasing unpaid work and reducing terms and conditions, leading to increased in-work poverty. Care workers expressed high levels of job satisfaction, despite low pay. This balance between job satisfaction and low(er) pay neglects the fact that, from this study evidence, care workers all expressed a trend towards increasing working poverty. This 'race to the bottom' in gross pay means retaining staff at all levels will be a challenge and supports the thesis of inequality regimes in labour markets continue despite high turnover in the sector (Acker 2006).

This regional study found that the frequent turnover of ownership of care homes was a key factor underpinning changes in care workers terms and conditions; associated with a distinct market approach of private care homes selling and transferring ownership. As a result, the majority of recently recruited care workers, since 2016, would have preferred to work more hours, but employers only offered part-time hours and additional hours at short notice to cover sickness. These care workers were only paid legal minima hourly rates for unsocial hours, weekends and the terms and conditions offered were less, this was despite having previous work experience, training and qualifications, they were not paid additional grade premia. The junior managerial staff grades (night managers, deputy home managers) all reported significant reductions in terms and conditions, and all were established staff with 17–24 years experience.

Conclusion

This regional study in Yorkshire, UK, identifies that the trend towards increasing in-work poverty for care workers is mainly due to the marketization of adult social care and the increasing trend to reduce both employment security and pay premia rates. Care workers are predominantly women, working part-time (but in this research not through choice) and balancing caring commitments. This study outlines the effects of reducing terms and conditions and the lived experience of care workers and increased in-work poverty. Care workers are dedicated to their residents and enjoy their job, but the value of the work is not recognized in their pay or by the wider society.

Acknowledgements

The authors would like to gratefully acknowledge Louise Foster-Wilson of the GMB, without whom this project would not have been possible.

The authors would like to gratefully acknowledge Sheffield Hallam University's Higher Education Innovation Fund (HEIF), which funded and supported this project. We would also like to thank all research participants for so generously sharing their insights and time with us.

Note

1 TUPE stands for the Transfer of Undertakings (Protection of Employment) Regulations and its purpose is to protect employees if the business in which they are employed changes hands.

References

Acker, J. (1990). 'Hierarchies, jobs, bodies: a theory of gendered organizations'. *Gender and Society*, 4:2. 139–158.

Acker, J. (2006). 'Inequality regimes: gender, class, and race in organizations'. *Gender and Society*, 20:4. 441–464.

ASHE (2017). *Annual Survey of Hours and Earnings-Gross Weekly Pay in UK*, Table 15.1a.

Becker, G.S. (1985). Human capital, effort, and the sexual division of labor, *Journal of Labor Economics*, 3:1. 33–38.

Budig, M.J., and Misra, J. (2010). 'How care-work employment shapes earnings in cross- national perspective', *International Labour Review*, 149:4. 441–460.

Burns, D.J., Hyde, P.J., and Kilett, A.M. (2016). 'How financial cutbacks affect the quality of jobs and care for the elderly', *Industrial Relations and Labor Review*, 69:4. 991–1016.

Clarke, S. (2017). *Forging Ahead or Forging Behind? Devolution and the Future of Living Standards in the Sheffield City Region*, Resolution Foundation Report, January.

Cominetti, N., Gardiner, L., and H. Slaughter (2020). *The Full Monty: Facing Up to the Challenge of the Coronavirus Labour Market Crisis*. The Resolution Foundation. June.

D'Arcy, C. (2018). *Low Pay Britain* 2018, Resolution Foundation Report. Accessed 24/11/20, https://www.resolutionfoundation.org/app/uploads/2018/05/Low-Pay-Britain-2018.pdf.

Department of Health (1989). *Caring for People: Community Care in the Next Decade and beyond*. Cmnd. 849, London: HMSO

Department of Health (1990). *Community Care Act*. London: Department of Health.

Department of Health (2014). *Care Act*. London: Department of Health.

Dodson, L., and Zincavage, R. (2007). '"It's like a family" – caring labor, exploitation, and race in nursing homes', *Gender & Society*, 21:6. 905–928.

Doka, K.J. (1989). *Disenfranchised Grief: Recognizing Hidden Sorrow*. Lexington, MA: Lexington Books.

England, P. (2005). 'Emerging theories of care work', *Annual Reviews of Sociology*, 31: 1. 381–399.

England, P. (2010). 'The gender revolution: uneven and stalled', *Gender & Society*, 24: 2. 149–166.

England, P., Budig, M., and Folbre, N (2002). 'Wages of virtue: the relative pay of care work', *Social Problems*, 49:4. 455–473.

Farnham, D., and Horton, S. (1996). *Managing People in Public Services*. London: Macmillan Press.

Fenton, W., Polzin, G., Arkseden, J., and McCaffrey, R. (2018). *The Size and Structure of the Adult Social Care Sector and Workforce in England*. London: Skills for Care.

Folbre, N., and Nelson, J.A. (2000). 'For love of money – or both?' *Journal of Economic Perspectives*, 14:4. 123–140.

Griffiths, R. (1988). *Community Care: Agenda for Action*. HMSO: London

Hebson, G., Rubery, J., and D. Grimshaw. (2015). 'Rethinking job satisfaction in care work: looking beyond the care debates'. *Work, Employment and Society*, 29:2. 314–330.

Howard, D. (2021). 'The Living Wage Foundation's 'Real Living Wage' Campaign', in Dobbins, T. and Prowse, P., *The Living Wage: Advancing a Global Movement*, Routledge: Oxon. Chapter 2.

Kings Fund (2019a). Key facts and figures about social care. Accessed 23/7/2020. www.kingsfund. org.uk/audio-video/key-facts-figures-adult-social-care

Kings Fund (2019b). Average pay for care workers: is it a supermarket sweep? Accessed 15/10/20. www.kingsfund.org.uk/blog/2019/08/average-pay-for-care-workers

LaingBuisson (2019). *Care Homes for Older People: UK Market Report*, 29th edition, May.

Living Wage Foundation (2019). Living hours campaign launched to tackle work insecurity. Accessed 15/10/20. https://www.livingwage.org.uk/news/living-hours-campaign-launched-tackle-work-insecurity

Living Wage Foundation (2021) Explaining UK Wage Rates. Accessed 3/6/21. https://www. livingwage.org.uk/what-real-living-wage

Low Pay Commission (1998) T*he National Minimum Wage. First Report of the Low Pay Commission.* Cmnd 3976. HMSO London

Low Pay Commission (2015). *National Minimum Wage: The Low Pay Commission Report 2015*, March, Cmnd. 9017, HMSO. London.

Low Pay Commission (2017). *Non-compliance and Enforcement of the National Minimum Wage*, pp. 31–32. London.

Mueller, T. (2019). *She works hard for her money: tackling low pay in sectors dominated by – from the health and social care sector*, European Trade Union Institute. Working Paper 2019.11.

National Audit Office (2018). *Adult Social Care Briefly*. London. Accessed 3/6/21. https://www. nao.org.uk/report/adult-social-care-at-a-glance/

NHS Digital (2018). *Health Survey for England 2017: Adult Social Care*. London: NHS Digital.

Oung, C., Schlepper, L., and Curry, N. (2020). What does the social care workforce look like across the four countries? Nuffield Trust. Accessed 15/11/20. www.nuffieldtrust.org.uk/news-item/ what-does-the-social-care-workforce-look-like-across-the-four-countries

Palmer, E., and Eveline, J. (2012). 'Sustaining Low Pay in Care Work', *Gender, Work & Organization*, 19:3. 254–275.

Skills for Care (2020). *The State of the Adult Social Care Sector and Workforce in England*. London.

Skills for Care (2021) *Pay in the adult social care sector: Skills for Care analysis of National Minimum Data Set for Social Care (NMDS-SC)*. London.

Strauss, A., and Corbin, J. (1998). *Basics of Qualitative Research*. Thousand Oaks, CA: SAGE.

7   Making the living wage work in SMEs

Evidence from accredited employers in the UK hospitality sector

Andrea Werner

Introduction

The voluntary or real Living Wage (RLW) accreditation scheme in the UK, which commits employers to paying their direct and indirect employee hourly living wage (LW) rates based on 'basic living costs' as opposed to (lower) legal minimum–wage rates, has at the time of writing accredited over 6,500 organizations (Living Wage Foundation (LWF) n.d.), and the number keeps growing. One of the surprising facts about the scheme is that about half of the accredited organizations are small and medium-sized enterprises (SMEs) operating in the private sector, with a substantial number of accredited SMEs operating in so-called low-wage sectors, such as retail, hospitality, and social care.

The fact that there is a significant number of SMEs among LWF-accredited employers could be considered astonishing because SMEs are usually perceived as having fewer resources available (Carland et al. 1984) and facing severe competitive pressures (Barrett and Rainnie 2002), and thus as being less able to afford paying higher than legally required wages to their staff. On the other hand, certain characteristics of SMEs such as their social embeddedness (Curran and Blackburn 2001: 6–7), the coinciding of ownership and control (Spence 1999), and a belief that certain benefits might accrue to them due to being a LWF-accredited employer (Heery et al. 2017; Werner and Lim 2016a), may make SMEs open to adopting the RLW. The high proportion of SMEs among LWF-accredited organizations in the UK, and the fact that SMEs collectively account for about 60 per cent of all private sector employment (DBEIS 2019a), and as such influence the working and living conditions of millions of workers, point to SMEs' potential to contribute to a transformation of the economy towards more fairness and social equity.

This chapter provides evidence on how SMEs make RLW implementation work in their organizations from a pioneering in–depth empirical study of voluntary LW adoption in UK SME employers across a range of sectors including hospitality, care, retail, construction, and manufacturing (Werner and Lim 2016b). The focus will be on case studies of LWF-accredited SMEs from the hospitality sector. The hospitality sector has been chosen for analysis because, as a sector notorious for its low wages, adoption of the RLW has significant implications for employers, as the LW would influence the pay strategy for companies' core employees, not just for ancillary staff. Furthermore, the case studies selected exhibit a range of rationales and implementation strategies and thus can be seen as a kind of microcosm of how SMEs engage with the RLW. The insights gained by this study contribute to a better understanding of the drivers and motivators for the decision to adopt the RLW in SMEs, a segment of the economy which, despite its huge contribution to the economy, has remained under-researched, and its potential for contributing to a fairer

DOI: 10.4324/9781003054078-7

society under-recognized. This study identifies the benefits and challenges employers face when implementing the RLW within their organizations. Last, but not least, this study paves the way for a better understanding of the potential and limitations of LW adoption in SMEs, and subsequent implications for policy and practice.

This chapter is structured as follows. After giving some background information about the SME and hospitality sectors, a description of the research method is provided, and the case studies are set out. Subsequent discussion draw out the range of SMEs' motivations for signing up to the RLW, the multitude of benefits of LWF accreditation for these SMEs, challenges regarding the implementation of the RLW, as well as some industry-related issues. The chapter concludes with some reflections about the implications of RLW adoption in SMEs for individuals, businesses, and the economy; and about the prospects and conditions for future growth of RLW accreditations among SMEs, in particular in low-wage sectors.

The SME context

SMEs, that is, private sector organizations that employ up to 249 employees, collectively make a huge contribution to the UK economy (DBEIS 2019a), and in economies elsewhere around the world (Spence 2016). In 2019, UK SMEs contributed £2.2 trillion to the UK economy (52 per cent of GDP), employing over 16.6 million people (DBEIS 2019a).

Due to their relatively small size, however, SMEs are perceived, by some, to be limited in how they can engage in social responsibility (e.g. Carland 1984), such as paying voluntarily higher than legally required wages. Limitations are thought to arise from SMEs' exposure to market pressures and especially from the fact that SMEs may compete against, or have terms and conditions specified by, more powerful businesses (Barrett and Rainnie 2002). By contrast, others hold that structural market forces do not so much *determine* the actions of SMEs, as present them with constraints as well as opportunities, constituting the setting for differentiated strategic responses (Ram and Edwards 2003). Others again would add that SMEs are not just able to engage in differentiated strategic responses, but that the values and ethics of those owning and running the business have the potential to make a significant impact on how the company is run and what gets prioritized (Egels-Zandén 2017), including the decision to engage in profit-satisficing rather than profit-maximization (Spence and Rutherfoord 2001). Furthermore, due to their size and set-up, SMEs are considered to be rather strongly embedded in the sociocultural contexts in which they operate (Curran and Blackburn 2001: 6–7), and may therefore be responsive to emergent norms and expectations from their sociocultural environments, such as those promoted by the LW movement, not least to enhance their legitimacy and reputation. A final reason why an SME might engage in social responsibility, in particular in relation to their employees, is the low social, and thus moral, distance between SME (owner-) managers and their stakeholders (Spence 2016). Employees are generally considered an important moral stakeholder within SMEs, with employers developing caring relationships with employees given their close reliance on them (ibid.). In summary, both strategic and ethical reasons may play a role in SMEs' decision to positively engage with the LW.

The hospitality context

The hospitality sector is an important industrial sector in the UK. Comprising accommodation and food service activities, the sector in 2019 contributed £110bn to the economy, 55 per cent (or £60.5bn) of which was contributed by SMEs. The sector employed close to 2.4 million people, with close to 60 per cent (1.4 million) working for SMEs (DBEIS 2019b). At the same time, it was an industry with the highest incidence of low pay in 2019: 66 per cent of workers in hotels and restaurants were paid below the RLW, which constituted 17 per cent of the total UK workforce paid below the RLW, the second-largest industry group after wholesale and retail (26 per cent), with health and social care ranking third (14 per cent) (Cominetti et al. 2019). Furthermore, it is known to be an industry with poor working conditions and high staff turnover, leading hospitality managers to face ongoing challenges with regards to the recruitment, development, and maintenance of a committed workforce (Walmsley et al. 2019). The high incidence of low pay in the sector may be explained to some extent by the casual, part-time nature of a large number of jobs (Ignite Economics 2018; Walmsley et al. 2019), but there seems to be an endemic industry culture which is reluctant to reward employees with better pay. The introduction of a higher minimum wage in 2015 for people aged 25 and over – termed confusingly the 'national living wage' by the then-UK chancellor – has been regarded as one of the main 'pressures' or threats facing the industry (Ignite Economics 2018). A possible downside to (higher) minimum wages in the hospitality industry is the potential for some businesses, in particular small firms, to enter the informal sector, as was previously observed in studies that examined the impact of national minimum wages when they were first introduced (Ram et al. 2001). Another potential downside is the substitution of younger for older workers to exploit lower-level youth minimum wages (Walmsley et al. 2019).

Absolute numbers of LWF accreditations in hospitality businesses may initially appear low: at the time of writing about 5 per cent (or about 200) out of the 4,400 accredited private sector LW Employers are from the hospitality sector (LWF, n.d.). This is, however, two-thirds higher than the proportion of the number of *all* hospitality businesses in relation to the total number of businesses in the UK (3 per cent) (DBEIS 2019b). These figures bear testimony to the fact that there is both the will and the capacity among hospitality businesses to implement the RLW. They also raise the rather interesting question of what motivates these hospitality businesses to be involved with the LW and how they make it work in their day-to-day business operations.

Methodology

This chapter reports from a qualitative interview-based part of a mixed-method study (Creswell 2009) carried out to explore RLW adoption among SMEs (Werner and Lim 2016b), which consisted of a survey and semi-structured interviews. The initial sample frame consisted of 250 private sector SMEs, which were selected from the membership database managed and owned by the LWF, the organization that awards and manages RLW accreditation. Primarily companies from sectors in which the prevalence of low-wage workers was assumed to be likely (care, hospitality, retail, cleaning, manufacturing, construction) were included in the sample, as it was expected that LW adoption had more implications in such companies. Care was taken to ensure that the sample largely reflected the overall composition of SMEs contained in the LWF database in terms of geographical regions, and size groups (up to 10 employees, 11–50, and 51–250 – set by the LWF). A Qualtrics survey was sent out to the sample companies, which apart from gaining initial insights into how SMEs engage with the LW, was used to recruit respondents for the research interviews. In total, 60 responses were received (7 of which came from hospitality employers), and 38 respondents indicated their willingness to grant an interview. From these responses, 23 companies were selected to be interviewed (4 of which were from the hospitality sector). Interviews took place between May and August 2016. Interviews lasted between 25 minutes to an hour and a half, with an average interview time of about 40 minutes. The respondents were in one or more of the following categories: founder/ owner/managing director/functional director (HR, marketing, and so on). In a few cases the interview was conducted as a group interview, with the initial interview partner inviting other company directors to participate to provide additional perspectives. The interviews focused on motivations, benefits, challenges, and strategies around RLW adoption as broad topics for exploration, using a semi-structured format and thus allowing the views and voices of SMEs to emerge naturally (Wengraf 2001). The main ethical issue arising in interviews is linked to the fact that talk is a rather uncertain phenomenon, and therefore insights into actual motivations, attitudes, and behaviour might be limited (Alvesson and Karreman 2000). However, the aim of the present study was to identify the *range* of stated views existing among LWF-accredited SMEs, and as the findings yielded a sampled range of stated views, the interview accounts can be treated as 'uncertain, but often interesting clues for the understanding of social reality and ideas, beliefs, values and other aspects of "subjectivities"' (ibid.). The interviews followed standard research ethics protocols, assuring confidentiality and anonymity to the respondents. All interviews were fully transcribed for analysis. Interview transcriptions were coded in NVivo10 using a thematic analysis approach (Braun and Clarke 2012).

The findings presented in this chapter comprise three hospitality case studies from the study's interview sample. The case studies were selected on the grounds that they reveal, and enable discussion of, emergent issues with regards to RLW adoption in SME hospitality businesses (Yin, 2014). The following sections will set out the three case studies and discuss their findings.

The case studies

PIZZABAR

The first case, *PIZZABAR*, is located in a bustling area in a large UK city, employs 13 people – a mix of full-time and part-time staff – and offers a drinks and mainly pizza-based food service, including the hosting of birthday parties. It caters in the main to customers from within a five-mile radius, although due to good transport links, it also gets customers from further afield.

PIZZABAR became a LWF-accredited employer when the owner-director did a tour of a local company that was LWF-accredited and thought that this would be a good idea for her business, too. She emphasizes that since the inception of her business, which happened five years prior to the interview taking place, she had always paid her staff above the LW, so LWF accreditation was for her a way to get recognition for already paying progressive wages. When asked what motivated her to pay above minimum wages to her staff, she responds that she has worked in hospitality a lot herself and knows 'how hard it is'. She adds that in the cultural context she comes from (outside of the UK), working in hospitality is seen as a career and paying decent wages to bar staff is considered the norm, and this is something she seeks to reflect in the way she runs her business. At the same time, she is aware that paying decent wages is bringing her a lot of benefits. She mentions that paying good wages enables her to 'keep people happy', to keep good staff and to reduce her overall staff turnover. She also believes that in a cash business, such as hers, paying a LW keeps theft by staff low. Overall, she thinks that paying the RLW is a net benefit rather than a net cost:

> If you add up all of the hours that you spend in training people, in advertising for people to work for you, in theft, in all these things, I think that at the end of it all actually paying staff more you're going to come out on top anyway.

In addition, she mentions the benefit that paying a LW as an owner-manager gives her from a personal morality point of view:

> I work really directly with the staff so I have a fairly direct benefit in that it makes me feel better to know they're paid reasonably. We don't have staff coming in who can't pay their rent and can't afford to get the bus to work, things like that.

Finally, when asked whether LWF accreditation had any surprising effects, she mentions that *PIZZABAR* gained a lot more acceptance from 'a different sector of customer', people who would be familiar with the LWF logo and who thought that it was a 'really positive thing' *PIZZABAR* was doing.

Whilst *PIZZABAR* did not have to make any adjustments regarding the payment of wages on becoming an RLW employer, the question remains how the business manages to survive and thrive in the marketplace. The owner-director explains:

> We've got a combination of factors which mean that we can afford to pay our staff more. I think really it's a combination of me being sole owner, so we don't have shareholders or anyone like that that we need to keep happy, and we look to have quite a high turnover in terms of our sales and we keep our prices really low and we aim to exceed people's expectations a little bit which means that we're often pretty busy.

She adds that 'another really key thing is that our staff are really friendly', and that because of the flat hierarchy she runs in her bar, her employees take on a greater level of personal responsibility within their role than would be the case in a lot of other bars.

PIZZABAR's owner-director is aware that she is an exception in the industry, which is why she felt it was important to get recognition for her approach through LWF accreditation 'in part so that our customers know, but also in part so that more people in the industry recognize the importance of paying people reasonable wages'. She uses public platforms to talk about the benefits the RLW provides, but also to challenge her industry, in particular with regards to the informal economy practices occurring in hospitality, which she thinks is one of the main barriers to people being paid a LW rate. Asked about her plans to continue with the RLW in the future, she is adamant that 'we actually pay more than the LW, and there's no way we'd ever pay less'.

EVENTSAGENCY

EVENTSAGENCY is an events management and hospitality company which provides bar staff, waiters, and event managers to both individuals who want staff to host dinner parties or other big events as well as to companies which need hospitality staff for events.

The company also runs its own events as well as a theatre bar. *EVENTSAGENCY* runs events all over the UK, as well as abroad. The company was founded by its owner-director, who owns all the shares of the business. It employs a small team of four permanent staff, and has over 580 part-time staff on its books – people looking to earn an income through casual jobs, ranging from actors and musicians who are between professional engagements to housewives seeking to earn some extra money.

When asked what triggered his decision to adopt the RLW, the owner-director responds that becoming a LWF-accredited employer was 'instant alignment' of his beliefs in being an ethical employer. He says that, at the time that he sought LWF accreditation, he was already paying his staff above the RLW, and he saw accreditation as a 'public acknowledgement of what we're trying to do with staffing'. He added that he 'do[es]n't believe that anybody should be paying less than the RLW [...] the minimum you need to live off'. This, he acknowledges, sets him at odds with the majority of the hospitality industry, as, he says, 'there is a lot of resistance to paying what they see as junior staff at a decent rate'.

For the owner-director, paying (at least) the RLW is at the core of his business strategy. He says that for the type of service *EVENTSAGENCY* seeks to provide, he needs people who 'got loads of experience [...] [and] choose to come back to us every time they are available', and the existence of his business is 'one hundred per cent dependent on [him] being able to attract and recruit and retain the best staff in the industry'. He tries to achieve that by being flexible, offering his staff work that suits their lifestyle, and creating a nice working environment. But he adds that he cannot retain staff if he does not pay them properly, so the RLW is the starting salary in his business, and they get often paid more. The owner-director strongly believes that why they 'win clients and why [they] keep clients is the fact that [they] have better motivated, happier, more experienced staff', and that LWF accreditation helps him differentiate his business from his low-wage competitors' in the marketplace.

The owner-director enumerates a long list of benefits that paying a LW brings to his business, based on his ability to attract and retain good staff. He believes that having experienced staff at hand means that *EVENTSAGENCY*'s service is more efficient. For example, a job could be done by his staff in less time or with fewer people, compared to using less experienced people. Also, his staff are more likely to turn up on time, and he says that the event drop-off rate (that is, people turning up late to events and 'no-shows') in his business is significantly lower than in competitor businesses, up to 400 per cent, and that this saves him and his clients the need to book any back-up staff. He further says that, because people stay with him, he has a good relationship with them and this makes it also easier to communicate any bad news to his staff, such as sudden cancellation of events.

To accommodate the RLW, the business pays a higher proportion of the money it gets from contracts to its staff. Thus, the owner-director accepts a smaller margin, and he also cross-subsidizes the RLW from *EVENTSAGENCY* doing its own events. This enables the business to stagger any price increases that arise from the annual increases of the RLW rate, and not having to immediately pass them fully through to *EVENTSAGENCY*'s clients.

The owner-director reflects that, while *EVENTSAGENCY*'s business model is still an exception in the industry, there is a growing appreciation among its clients of *EVENTSAGENCY*'s business model. At the same time, he would welcome it if the RLW were to become a mandatory minimum-wage rate. He said that this would put him at an advantage over his competitors, as being an LWF-accredited employer has forced him to streamline his operations: 'I'd suddenly have the biggest margins in the industry because I've already got more efficient processes'. But until this happens, he will regard LWF accreditation as a good tool for 'selling' his approach of doing business to his clients and customers.

COMMUNITYPUB

Located in a mid-sized city in the UK, *COMMUNITYPUB* is a popular local pub, which had built up a reputation as a live alternative music venue for more than 20 years. When the previous, private, pub owner wanted to sell up, patrons of the pub were worried that the place would lose its 'edginess' or be turned to different use. An initiative was started to buy the pub as a community venture. *COMMUNITYPUB* now has more than 500 local shareholders, who have between £500 and £20,000 invested in the business, and the pub runs as a cooperative. The pub employs 23 part-time staff, all on zero-hours contracts, and a full-time general manager. It is overseen by a board of directors consisting of local businesspeople and professionals who have an affinity to the pub and for whom this is a pro-bono role.

The adoption of the RLW was triggered by a discussion at an annual general meeting, at which a number of *COMMUNITYPUB* shareholders, who are described by the board of directors as 'kind of left-wingish', demanded that the pub become an LWF accredited employer. They felt that people working for the pub should be treated well, which also included concern about the zero-hours contracts that staff are employed on. A decision was made by the board not to touch the 'zero-hours contracts' issue, as, so the board directors state, these contracts were drawn up with the employees' agreement, as the flexibility coming with these contracts suited their employees' lifestyles. There was a debate among the board directors as to what to do about the RLW. A few board directors had some reservations, as, so they argued, one should 'get a service for as little as [one] can pay for it' and that there was no need to pay the LW. In the end, however, the majority of the board voted to adopt the RLW for *COMMUNITYPUB*.

This decision was assisted by the fact that adoption of the RLW was almost cash neutral for *COMMUNITYPUB,* although changes to the pay structure had to be made. The previous pay structure contained a significant performance-related element – a bonus for avoiding stock losses – and this, together with an allowance for free staff drinks, added up to the RLW rate. The performance-related element was now taken away, as well as the free staff drinks, and replaced by the fixed RLW rate. The removal of the staff drinks allowance was, so the board directors explained, also part of a drive to improve health and safety, and to make the pub run more professionally.

The reaction to the implementation of the RLW among staff has been mixed. On the one hand, it was felt that it made the pay structure fairer to those few employees who do the accounts for the business and could not benefit from the perks for those who work in the bar. On the other hand, bar staff were perceived to be initially suspicious about the new pay structure, with some being aggrieved over the removal of the drinks allowance. Board directors had to work hard to explain to them why the RLW was a good thing and to get staff to accept the new pay structure. At the same time, the board directors noticed that stock losses had increased – which was of some concern to them and which they hoped would be addressed with the introduction of smart tills in the future. The board of directors also state that the pay increase to the RLW had no effect on staff turnover, as it was extremely low even prior to implementation of the RLW.

More unambiguous were the effects of LWF accreditation on shareholders, who were pleased that *COMMUNITYPUB* had signed up to the RLW. Board directors also felt that becoming an RLW employer fitted well with the pub's image, enabling them to get 'a better balance amongst the stakeholders', which in their view a cooperative was expected to do: a business 'extending care and consideration to customers, shareholders, employees, and the broader world'. One director added that they also relished 'bask[ing] in the pleasure of knowing that we've done it'. With regards to their future commitment to being a LWF accredited employer, the board directors explained that they would not want to take the 'bad PR hit of withdrawing it', and that in the future some minor price increases would help meet any RLW rate rises.

Discussion

The three case studies above provide some interesting insights into why SMEs seek LWF accreditation, what they perceive to be the benefits of being an RLW employer, and the challenges of implementation. They further raise a range of industry-related issues with regards to the hospitality sector.

Motivations

The findings show the wide range of motivations for why SMEs adopt the RLW, encompassing moral, strategic, and political reasons. *PIZZABAR*'s example provides a good illustration of the low social, and thus moral distance, between managers and their staff that we may find in SMEs (Spence, 2016). The owner-director explains that her personal experience of having worked in the industry influenced her decision as to how much she ought to be paying her employees. *EVENTSAGENCY* illustrates how ethical values of owner-managers (Egels-Zandén 2017), in this case the owner-director's belief in 'being an ethical employer', can shape a business' decision to adopt the RLW. An interesting variant of this can be found in *COMMUNITYPUB*, where it was the shareholders who demanded that management adopt the RLW, based on political convictions. The *COMMUNITYPUB* case is a good illustration of the embeddedness of SMEs in specific sociocultural contexts (Curran and Blackburn 2001) which may make them responsive to issues such as the LW.

What is interesting to note in the cases of *PIZZABAR* and *EVENTSAGENCY* is that they had already paid LW rates prior to their accreditation. Thus, a motivation in seeking LWF accreditation was the ability to gain recognition for their progressive pay practices going hand in hand with an ability to use it for strategic positioning of the business, which *EVENTSAGENCY* exploits in particular (see below), or an ability to raise industry-related issues in the public sphere, as is especially the case with *PIZZABAR* (see below).

Benefits

As with motivations, the findings also show a range of benefits attached to LW adoption and accreditation for SMEs. Both *PIZZABAR* and *EVENTSAGENCY* mention a number of HR benefits related to the decision to pay staff at least a LW (Werner and Lim 2016a). *PIZZABAR,* in particular, emphasizes the recruitment and training costs savings made through better staff retention; whilst *EVENTSAGENCY* highlights the fact that through the capacity to attract and retain 'the best staff in the industry', it is able to benefit from highly experienced staff, who in turn are able to carry out their jobs in a highly professional and efficient manner. A remarkable finding here is that the owner-director believes that efficiency gains from more productive employees may offset to a large extent the higher wage costs attached to LWF accreditation. Noticeable is also *EVENTSAGENCY*'s owner-director's perception that paying the LW improves employee relations in such a way that it is easier to communicate 'bad news' to staff. Interestingly, *COMMUNITYPUB* does not mention any tangible HR benefits, but this is likely related to how the RLW was introduced in the business (see below).

All the case study businesses emphasize the positive reputational and brand effects (Heery et al. 2017) of LWF accreditation: something that enhances *COMMUNITYPUB*'s image of a caring business attached to its cooperative model; that attracts a new clientele to *PIZZABAR*, people who are familiar with the LWF logo and seek to reward such businesses with their custom; and that enables *EVENTSAGENCY* to clearly differentiate itself from low-wage competitors in the marketplace.

Finally, there are personal moral and emotional benefits attached to LWF accreditation for the SME's directors. For example, *PIZZABAR*'s owner-director talks about how LWF accreditation 'makes [her] feel better to know [her employees] are paid reasonably', whilst a *COMMUNITYPUB* director talks about their basking 'in the pleasure of knowing that we've done it'; showing that for LW adoption, not just rational arguments count, but that moral emotions play an important role too (Ten Bos and Willmott 2001).

Implementation

Two out of the three case studies, *PIZZABAR* and *EVENTSAGENCY*, had no RLW implementation costs as they already paid LW rates and above when they sought accreditation. This is a finding that is replicated in the wider SME study (Werner and Lim 2016b), which found that more than half of the LWF-accredited SMEs surveyed already paid the RLW rate or above to all or most of their staff prior to accreditation, demonstrating that paying the LW is to a large part a business choice. The accounts of *PIZZABAR* and *EVENTSAGENCY* imply that it is their overall service orientation that helps them make the RLW work in their business. This is coupled with a willingness to accept smaller profit margins, an attitude that can be found among SMEs more generally (Spence and Rutherfoord 2001). The challenge of accommodating annual LWF rate rises, however, remains a challenge, and *EVENTSAGENCY* in particular demonstrates how this can be done smartly through cross-subsidization, in addition to an overall approach of keeping operations streamlined.

In comparison, *COMMUNITYPUB* highlights how implementation of RLW into a business can present a significant challenge. Whilst RLW adoption was largely 'cash-neutral', *COMMUNITYPUB*'s management encountered suspicion and some resistance from staff, as the RLW replaced an incentive-based pay structure. The company also encountered some unintended negative consequences for the business in the form of stock losses, as avoidance of stock loss was formerly part of the incentive structure. This example highlights that any implementation of the RLW that comes with organizational changes, be it changes in workload, or in this case, changes in pay structure, needs to be done very carefully and go hand in hand with extensive communication efforts as well with some organizational measures to counteract any unintended negative consequences (in the case of *COMMUNITYPUB*, the introduction of smart tills).

Industry-related issues

Whilst the three cases mentioned motivations, benefits, and implementation challenges that can be observed in SMEs across industries (Werner and Lim 2016b; Werner and Lim 2017) they also raise some interesting industry-specific issues. It is interesting to note that *PIZZABAR* and *EVENTSAGENCY* see themselves as an exception in their industry and refer to employer resistance in the hospitality sector to paying higher wages, whilst *COMMUNITYPUB* itself went through some struggle among its board directors to achieve a breaking away from the usual industry practice of paying as little as one can get away with.

There are some indications that *PIZZABAR* and *EVENTSAGENCY,* with their LWF accreditation, may contribute to a transformation of their industry: *PIZZABAR*'s owner-director, using the accreditation to highlight and critique poor industry practice in public forums – and in particular critiquing the informal nature of many businesses – and *EVENTSAGENCY* by explicitly and strongly promoting a business model that is significantly different to the low-wage models prevalent in the industry. It appears that LWF accreditation helps professionalize the industry and raise overall standards: that *EVENTSAGENCY*'s approach of doing business introduces the notion of a high-quality, highly professional service; and that *PIZZABAR*'s campaigning for the RLW seeks to reduce the 'off-the-books' perceived to occur in the hospitality sector. Even *COMMUNITYPUB*'s organizational changes, made or planned: the aligning of the employees' pay structure with health and safety directives, and the introduction of smart tills, point to a professionalization in how the pub is run.

At the same time, the case studies also show that LWF accreditation does not necessarily address the issue of income security, and that there are limitations in this regard, especially in the hospitality sector. *COMMUNITYPUB* and *EVENTAGENCY*'s workforce is a casual one and the jobs provided are described as 'lifestyle jobs' that people fit around other commitments. So, these businesses will not feel responsible for securing a full living income for their staff, although the commitment to paying an RLW rate means that their workers are not being exploited.

Conclusion and outlook

This analysis of three cases has highlighted the potential, and limitations, of SMEs' engagement with the RLW. The case studies highlight that paying a LW is possible for SMEs – even in low-wage sectors – and that, if implemented in the right way, can yield a multitude of different benefits for them. Thus, LWF-accredited SMEs may play a small, yet significant, role in transforming their sectors, and the economy, towards more fairness and social equity. The case studies highlight, however, that it is not just 'business case' arguments that will inspire SMEs to adopt the RLW – personal moral values and moral emotions of business-owners will play a significant role, too. At the same time, LW accreditation alone is unable to enable people to secure a living income unless they are employed on stable full-time contracts. This is particularly difficult to achieve in sectors such as hospitality, which was examined here, due to the casual, part-time nature of many jobs in the industry and the lack of guaranteed hours. When the wider study on which this chapter draws was conducted, the UK economy was thriving, services such as hospitality sector providers were in high demand, and there was also a steady influx of workers willing to work even in low-wage jobs in various industries (due to European Union immigration). A few years on, and the UK economy (as well as most other economies around the world) have had to face the 2020 Covid-19 crisis, which has threatened the survival of many businesses, and confront the prospect of a drying up of the flow of free movement of labour from abroad due to the nature of the UK's exit (Brexit) from the EU. Interestingly, the demand of businesses to become RLW employers has not stopped, however. The changed employment situation due to Brexit may partly be responsible for this, although at the same time the economic crisis emanating from the coronavirus pandemic could be thought to have put a stop to employers seeking to voluntarily commit to paying higher wages, and to focus on their survival instead.

At the time of writing, the three hospitality companies analysed in this chapter are still in business and still LWF accredited, although the hospitality industry has been hit particularly hard during the Covid-19 crisis. Maintaining LWF accreditation may be easier if this does not include the commitment to providing guaranteed hours to employees, but overall it is an encouraging sign that the RLW has not fallen casualty to the current public health crisis, as the overall rising number of LWF accreditations also attests. Indeed, it could be companies which have pioneered successful LW adoption in their business may lead the economic recovery, in the spirit of the UK government's motto of wanting to 'build back better'. Continued commitment to the LW also requires growing awareness and recognition from clients, that LWF-accredited businesses will be rewarded for their ethical pay policies – as highlighted by two of the case study companies. This also requires government policies that recognize the potential for RLW commitment of businesses, including small employers, and provide appropriate incentives and support, in particular during times of economic crises. But it will be the convictions of LWF-accredited employers that a better way of doing business is possible that will continue to challenge 'business as usual' in the years to come.

References

Alvesson, M., and Karreman, D. (2000). 'Varieties of discourse: On the study of organizations through discourse analysis'. *Human Relations* 53(9): 1125–1149.

Barrett, R., and Rainnie A. (2002). 'What's so special about small firms? Developing an integrated approach to analysing small firm industrial relations'. *Work, Employment and Society*, 16(3): 415–431.

Braun, V., and Clarke, V. (2012). 'Thematic analysis', in Cooper, H. (Ed.), *APA Handbook of Research Methods in Psychology, vol. 2: Research Designs*. American Psychological Association: Washington, DC, 57–91.

Carland, J., Hoy, F., Boulton, W., and Carland, J.A.C. (1984). 'Differentiating entrepreneurs from small business owners: A conceptualization'. *Academy of Management Review*, 9(2): 354–359.

Cominetti, N., Henehan, K., and Clarke, S. (2019). *Low Pay Britain 2019*. Resolution Foundation: London.

Creswell, J.W. (2009). *Research Design: Qualitative, Quantitative, and Mixed Methods Approaches*. SAGE: Los Angeles.

Curran, J., Blackburn, R. (2001). *Researching the Small Enterprise*. SAGE: London.

Department for Business, Enterprise, Innovation and Skills (DBEIS) (2019a). *Statistical Release – Business Population Estimates for the UK and Regions 2019*. https://assets.publishing. service.gov.uk/government/uploads/system/uploads/attachment_data/file/852919/Business_ Population_Estimates_for_the_UK_and_regions_-_2019_Statistical_Release.pdf. Accessed 19 October 2020

Department for Business, Enterprise, Innovation and Skills (DBEIS) (2019b). *Business Population Estimates for the UK and Regions 2019: detailed tables*. www.gov.uk/government/statistics/ business-population-estimates-2019. Accessed 19 October 2020

Egels-Zandén, N. (2017). 'The role of SMEs in global production networks: A Swedish SME's payment of living wages at its Indian supplier'. *Business and Society*, 56(1): 92–129.

Heery, E., Hann, D., and Nash, D. (2017). The Living Wage campaign in the UK. *Employee Relations*, 39(6): 800–814.

Ignite Economics (2018). *The Economic Contribution of the UK Hospitality Industry* www.ukhospitality.org.uk/page/EconomicContributionoftheUKHospitalityIndustry2018. Accessed 12 October 2020

Living Wage Foundation (LWF) (n.d.). *Accredited Living Wage Employers*. www.livingwage.org.uk/accredited-living-wage-employers. Accessed 19 October 2020

Ram, M., and Edwards, P. (2003). 'Praising Caesar not burying him: What we know about employment relations in small firms'. *Work, Employment and Society*, 17(4): 719–730.

Ram, M., Edwards, P., Gilman, M., and Arrowsmith, J. (2001). 'The dynamics of informality: Employment relations in small firms and the effects of regulatory change'. *Work, Employment and Society*, 15(4): 845–861.

Spence, L. (1999). 'Does size matter? The state of the art in small business ethics'. *Business Ethics: A European Review*, 8(3): 163–174.

Spence, L. (2016). 'Small business social responsibility: Expanding core CSR theory'. *Business and Society*, 55(1): 23–55.

Spence, L., and Rutherfoord, R. (2001). 'Social responsibility, profit maximization and the small firm owner-manager'. *Journal of Small Business and Enterprise Development*, 8(20): 126–139.

Ten Bos, R., and Willmott, H. (2001). 'Towards a post-dualistic business ethics: Interweaving reason and emotion in working life'. *Journal of Management Studies*, 38(6): 769–793.

Walmsley, A., Partington, S., Armstrong, R., and Goodwin, H. (2019). 'Reactions to the national living wage in hospitality'. *Employee Relations*, 41(1): 253–268.

Wengraf, T. (2001). *Qualitative Research Interviewing*. SAGE: New York.

Werner, A., and Lim, M. (2016a). 'The ethics of the living wage: A review and research agenda'. *Journal of Business Ethics*, 137(3): 433–447.

Werner, A., and Lim, M. (2016b). *Putting the Living Wage to Work: Strategies and Practices in Small and Medium Sized Enterprises (SMEs)*. Barrow Cadbury Trust: London.

Werner, A., and Lim, M. (2017). 'A new living contract? Cases in the implementation of the Living Wage by British SME retailers'. *Employee Relations* 39(6): 850–862.

Yin, R. (2014). *Case Study Research: Design and Methods*. 5th ed., SAGE: New York.

Part 2

The living wage in international comparative contexts

8 The living wage and the European Union

John Hurley

Introduction

The revival of living wage campaigns since the 1990s is noteworthy in that it has largely occurred in certain English-speaking developed countries – the UK, New Zealand, Canada, and the USA. These are distinctive in having liberal market economies with residual welfare states. In the European Union (EU), following the departure of the UK as a member state in 2020, only one country – Ireland – has an active living wage campaign. The lack of living wage campaigns in other member states should not however be taken to indicate indifference to the living wage idea. The concept is alive even if practical examples are few on the ground. Indeed, policymaking in relation to minimum wages, both at the national level and within the EU institutions, is increasingly informed and motivated by the concerns with income adequacy for the low-paid that are at the heart of the living wage project.

In this chapter, we will introduce in outline alternative approaches to conceiving what a living wage is and how it can be estimated taking account of national tax and benefit systems which are important sources of income support to low-pay households. We then discuss the policy background to the more active recent engagement with minimum wage policy, both at the EU and the member state level, including fair wage commitments framed in typically living wage terms in the EU's European Pillar of Social Rights (European Commission, 2017). Using recent EU and Organization for Economic Cooperation and Development (OECD) data, we assess existing national minimum-wage levels against one emerging living wage benchmark (60 per cent of median pay) and also estimate the share of EU-27 workers by sector earning under this level, and who would in principle benefit were minimum wages to be raised in this way. The Irish living wage campaign is presented in order to understand how such an initiative is mounted and sustained and the extent to which it relates to national minimum-wage policy. Related recent initiatives in other member states are also presented – not always bearing the 'living wage' banner but with similar objectives of boosting pay for those at or near minimum-wage earnings. We conclude with some summary reflections on the lessons that living wage initiatives may have for minimum-wage policy more broadly.

Living wage: alternative approaches

The Irish (and UK) living wage calculations are based on the methodological approach of minimum incomes standard research and the construction of 'baskets' of goods and services necessary to achieve what societal consensus would consider a 'basic but acceptable'

DOI: 10.4324/9781003054078-8

standard of living. The wage needed to achieve such a standard of living varies across many different parameters beyond the basket and its contents. Whose living standards should such a wage guarantee? (workers' alone or worker and family dependants, working for how many hours? (full= or part-time), based on what level of household work intensity? (dual/single earner), for example. Living standards also vary over time with changes in aggregate material well-being and changing social norms. What counts as a basic but acceptable standard of living is assessed relative to the customs of the country, that is, based on a social consensus about what it is reasonable to expect fellow citizens not to do without in order to live with dignity.

These calculations are both time- and place-specific (including significant within-country regional variation) as well as being data and resource intensive. They also raise the issue of whether state transfers (and deductions via the tax system) should be factored into the calculation. These have been an increasingly important contributor to household income of those on low pay in recent decades, notably in countries with active living wage campaigns. In practice, they have been included in such calculations in the UK and Irish living wages and we reflect on this inclusion.

An alternative way of operationalizing a living wage relates such a wage to a proportion of median (or average) hourly wages in the same country. This has the disadvantage that a living wage can no longer secure its principal objective, that is, guarantee a certain standard of living. It has, however, the advantage of being simpler to calculate and thus more practical, especially if applied across multiple jurisdictions as would be the case in the EU-27. Sixty per cent of national median earnings is the most commonly observed threshold (Fernandez-Macias and Vacas-Soriano, 2016), and is aligned in this respect with at-risk-of-poverty estimations which use the same level (albeit in relation to equivalized household income). While only a small number of EU member states currently have statutory minima at or near this level (France, Portugal, and Slovenia – most are closer to 50 per cent (Eurofound, 2020a)), it is nonetheless explicitly cited as a reference target for progressive minimum-wage developments in some countries[1] as well as by union-affiliated researchers (Schulten and Muller, 2019) as a pragmatic proxy for a cross-national living wage, at least in an initial stage.

Most living wage definitions emphasize paid labour as the principal source of household income intended to guarantee an adequate standard of living. There is often limited reference to other forms of household income, notably state transfers, or to the impact of labour taxation. Whether these non-wage elements should be factored into calculations of a living wage is of course open to question. They can be considered as a form of state subsidy to low-wage employers, removing part of the responsibility for such employers to pay their workers a reasonable wage and effectively allowing them to externalize the negative social costs of underpayment to society at large (Schulten and Muller, 2019).

In the original living wage debates at the turn of the last century, the living wage was envisaged exclusively as the responsibility of the employer. The development of the welfare state, in particular, has increased the importance of social transfers to low-wage earners and low-pay households. In practice, most contemporary living wage calculations tend to take account of all available state transfers (negative and positive). The adequacy of wages is therefore related to the efforts of the state regarding the provision of affordable, good quality public goods and services, as well as supports to low-income working households, including family-related benefits.

In some countries where the living wage movement has been especially prominent, for example the USA and the UK, in-work benefits or tax credits – a form of negative taxation – serve as a strong supplementary income support to low-income working households. Most living wage initiatives assume that workers pay the relevant income taxes and claim all of the benefits to which they are entitled. Take-home pay plus eligible social transfers combined should generate income to afford the living wage living standard.

Access to core public services such as education or health in many EU member states is often subsidized or free at point of use for most low-earning households. This 'social wage' (Gautie and Schmitt, 2010) is an important complement to labour income and contributor to living standards. Those below certain income thresholds may benefit from an array of subsidized provision in relation to public housing, childcare, subsidized heating, transport, and so on. Again, the assumption in most current living wage calculations is that the subsidized cost of such services and provision is what counts for living wage calculations. The living wage is based only on what workers have to pay out of their pocket.

The core assumption is that the state has a role in boosting income for low-wage earners, supplementing labour income with targeted transfers or accessible and subsidized public services in order to ensure that low-paid work does not necessarily leave households below poverty thresholds. Living wage calculations should take these non-labour sources of income into account. The more generous they are, the lower the living wage burden on employers. In this view, a living wage is a shared responsibility of the employer and the state. According to Canadian living wage proponents,

> a key way in which employers can reduce the payroll costs of the living wage is to advocate for progressive policy changes to increase government benefits to low-income earners and enhance public services that improve quality of life for all families.
> (CCPA, 2017)

Policy background

The idea that the income from paid labour should provide for a 'basic but reasonable standard of living' – the core commitment of all living wages – is commonly acknowledged in EU policy instruments and 'soft law' on the one hand, but in a context where EU treaty law ('hard law') is explicit in limiting the EU's competence as regards legislating on pay or wage bargaining on the other hand. These are areas in which member states alone have the right of legislative initiative, as clarified in Article 153 of the Treaty on the Functioning of the European Union (TFEU) (European Union, 2012) dealing with work and employment. There has however been some nuancing of these roles in recent years, as we will see.

There is an affirmation of the right to adequate pay in the Community Charter of the Fundamental Social Rights of Workers (1989): 'workers shall be assured of an equitable wage, i.e., a wage sufficient to enable them to have a decent standard of living'. Similar commitments are made in international treaties or conventions to which the EU and/or member states are signatories (for example, the European Social Charter (1961)) and the International Labour Organisation's (ILO's) conventions on minimum-wage setting). Indeed, as long ago as 1919, the founding ILO Constitution called for 'the payment to the employed of a wage adequate to maintain a reasonable standard of life as this is understood in their time and country'; perhaps the most precise formulation of a living wage policy objective and one that resonates through to those initiatives currently operational.

Any effort to implement such principles in EU legislation, as indicated, has to cross the significant hurdle that pay lies outside the scope of formal EU legislative competences according to the TFEU. In practice, notably in the aftermath of the global financial crisis, the European Commission has discovered new ways of intervening as regards pay policy, including minimum-wage policy. Under the so-called European Semester, a platform of governance was devised to intensify economic policy coordination, in particular across the Eurozone member states, with the twin objectives of helping the Union recover from the financial crisis and to stabilize the single currency. During the initial stages of the crises, one motivation was the perception that the crisis in the Eurozone periphery was largely a problem of competitiveness that could be addressed through wage moderation or reductions (internal devaluation) as well as structural reforms (Eurofound, 2014). Countries receiving EU bailouts signed memoranda that included cuts in minimum-wage levels, cuts in public pay levels, and reforms aimed at decentralizing the collective bargaining system (Grimshaw et al, 2014).

According to Schulten and Müller (2013: 331), this new governance system represented 'a new European interventionism', characterized by an 'increasingly authoritarian top-down approach' and a 'one-sided focus on fiscal austerity and cost competitiveness' which considers wage moderation as the main adjustment tool to correct macroeconomic imbalances. Regarding this assessment, EU policy recommendations for member states ('country-specific recommendations') became more interventionist and the EU gained greater influence on national wage policies in this way.

With economic recovery consolidating in the EU from 2013 onwards, the policy discourse on wage levels moved away from a focus on pay moderation to one more motivated by concerns of social inequality and poverty, including in-work poverty. Trade unions have demanded stronger wage growth (ETUC, 2017) given that wage growth has failed to match productivity growth for many years, as a result of pre-crisis wage moderation (notably in Germany) and post-crisis limitations on pay increases arising for both cyclical reasons and because of official policy levers (including public sector pay freezes). Calls for wage growth are especially relevant in the Central and East European member states against the background of persistent East–West wage disparities and the concern, for example, that Eastern European manufacturing workers are not getting fair compensation compared to Germany-based counterparts in the same companies (Lopatka, 2017). National minimum-wage rates rose especially fast, both in nominal and real terms, in these countries over the last decade. In addition, calls for stronger wage growth have come from EU institutional actors based on a more macroeconomic logic. Inflation has been consistently below the European Central Bank (ECB) target of 2 per cent for many years, leading to calls from the ECB, for example, for wage rises to push inflation towards its target level (Jones, 2017). Wage increases are likely to be more macro-economically effective if targeted at low earners who tend to consume a higher share of any increase in income.

The fact that the Semester process has been used to encourage wage moderation in the years up to 2013 has led to it being invoked – not without a certain irony – as a potential mechanism to introduce an EU minimum-wage policy (Schulten and Muller, 2019: 280) in more recent years – 'in terms of its regulatory setting a pragmatic way to circumvent the legal uncertainties would be to integrate a European minimum-wage policy into the European Semester'. This would be a soft law solution based on something similar to the European Commission-coordinated processes of economic policy monitoring in place for over a decade.

Since 2019, renewed momentum has been given to the cause of a EU-level coordination of minimum wages, notably with the proclamation of the European Pillar of Social Rights (EPSR) (European Commission 2017). This represents a fresh EU-level engagement with the issue of pay adequacy amongst other social policy objectives. The Pillar's 20 commitments are structured in three categories: equal opportunities and access to the labour market, fair working conditions, and social protection/inclusion. Similar to its predecessor, the 1989 Charter, it has a clear strategic policy objective of emphasizing the social dimensions of European integration and underlining that it is not only, or mainly, an economic process. The EPSR makes reference to the need for fair wage levels and provides implicit support to the concept of living wages, especially in the commitments marked in bold below:

- 'Workers have the right to **fair wages that provide for a decent standard of living'** (6a)
- '**Adequate minimum wages** shall be ensured, in a way **that provide for the satisfaction of the needs of the worker and his/her family** in the light of national economic and social conditions, whilst safeguarding access to employment and incentives to seek work. In-work poverty shall be prevented' (6b)
- 'All wages shall be set in a transparent and predictable way according to national practices and respecting the autonomy of the social partners' (6c)

The EPSR is declaratory in character, a soft law initiative that does not directly translate into an expansion of justiciable rights of European citizens. As a result, the relevance of the EPSR ultimately depends on the concrete actions of the different stakeholders involved (EU institutions, the member states, social partners, and civil society). Subsequent developments at the European- and the member state level have however given substance to the hopes of low-pay campaigners that the undertakings in the Pillar are to be enacted and not just remain paper promises.

Then European Commission president-designate Ursula von der Leyen, presenting her political guidelines for the next European Commission (2019–2024) in mid-2019, indicated she would 'propose a legal instrument' within the first 100 days of her mandate 'to ensure that every worker in our Union has a fair minimum wage' by 2024 (von der Leyen, 2019:8). This announcement also reflects policy positions in some of the larger member states, notably from the German chancellor, Angela Merkel, and the French president, Emmanuel Macron, who pronounced positively on a potential European coordination of national minimum wage-setting (cited in Schulten and Muller, 2019).

While somewhat delayed, the European Commission published its proposal for a directive on adequate minimum wages in the EU in October 2020. The aim of the proposed directive is to create a framework for minimum wage-setting in the 27 member states, taking account firstly of the fact that the EU has no formal competences as regards pay-setting (an exclusively national prerogative), and secondly of the different national approaches to wage floor-setting in the EU. If /when enacted, it would provide some EU-level coordination of minimum wage-setting with the stated objective that 'workers across the EU are protected by adequate minimum wages, allowing for a decent living wherever they work in Europe' – that is, similar to living wage commitments (European Commission, 2020). An important element of the proposal is that it explicitly underlines the role of collective bargaining as the main instrument to ensure fair wages and working conditions. The six member states that do not currently have a statutory minimum wage will not be obliged to introduce one, a recognition of the effectiveness and relatively high levels of negotiated wage floors. The measures foreseen in the proposal include annual reporting by member states to the Commission alongside structured dialogue and, for the 21 member states with statutory minima, the development of clear and stable criteria for setting and updating minima, a strengthened role for social partners in minima setting, limitations of deductions or variations, as well as strengthened enforcement and compliance.

Minimum wages in EU member states: converging to a living wage?

Over three-quarters of EU member states (21 of 27) have a statutory minimum-wage policy regulating low-pay employers and sectors. Those that do not have a statutory minimum wage (such as Sweden, Austria, and Denmark) tend to have even stronger protections for the majority of those on low pay via comprehensive systems of collectively bargained wages at sectoral level. These protections are not always sufficient, however. In-work poverty affected nearly one in ten EU-27 workers in 2019 (9 per cent). One reason is that statutory minima are set too low. In the majority of EU member states covered in recent reviews of statutory wage floors (Eurofound, 2020a), the minimum wage is below the level at which an individual earner living alone can ensure an income above the poverty threshold based on his or her wage earnings alone (60 per cent of national median disposable income).

Figure 8.1 shows the evolution of the minimum wage in a selection of EU member states compared to median wage levels in the same country (the Kaitz index). The most generous minimum wages in relative terms in 2018 were in France, Portugal, and

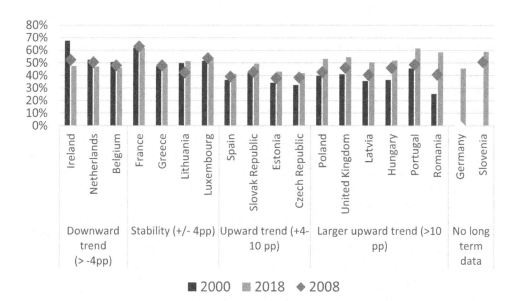

Figure 8.1 Longer term trend of development of statutory minimum wages relative to median wages of full-time employed workers.

Source: Eurofound (2020a), author's elaboration based on OECD data. Statutory minimum wage regime was introduced in Germany in 2015.

Slovenia – each near or over 60 per cent of median wage levels. They are also therefore lower than the 'low pay' threshold as defined by Eurostat (two-thirds or less of national gross hourly median earnings) and, in around half of the countries indicated, below the 'very low pay' threshold (< 50% of median pay). Minimum-wage levels have nevertheless increased relative to median wages in a majority of countries over the period 2000–2018, and the steepest increases were recorded in Eastern European countries, notably Romania.

Minimum-wage thresholds are set with multiple objectives. The UK Low Pay Commission, tasked with monitoring and revising the UK national minimum wage annually, was required to set a minimum wage that would 'support a competitive economy, be set at a prudent level, be simple and straightforward, and make a difference to the low-paid' (Low Pay Commission, 2002). The low-key commitment as regards 'making a difference' to the low-paid is indicative that minimum-wage levels are generally arbitrary from an individual needs perspective. They are often not based on any estimation of minimal worker need and this is, in any case, only one of several contending policy objectives, notable amongst which is the avoidance of disemployment effects predicted by standard economic models.[2] As living wages are set at a level to allow a worker to attain a socially acceptable living standard, they are invariably higher than their statutory counterparts. If existing minimum wages were perceived to be effective in this regard, there would be no need to campaign for living wages.

Which workers in which sectors would most benefit from raising minimum-wage rates to living wage levels? This is not possible to estimate using the 'gold standard' living wage approach based on consensual or reference budget methods (Goedemé et al., 2015). The extensive data processing required has only been done in a small number of living wage countries. It can, though, be estimated if we use the emerging standard, 60 per cent of median gross hourly full-time earnings, as a proxy measure of where a living wage might lie using existing wage data. As Figure 8.2 shows, there is a strong concentration of earners at or below this threshold in service sectors. The highest share is in **accommodation and food** services where nearly half of employees fall into this category (47 per cent). Around a third of employees in '**other services**' – including personal services, hairdressing, repair, activities of clubs/organizations – and '**administrative and support service activities**' – including cleaning, call centres, travel and employment agencies, security and buildings maintenance – were also earning below 60 per cent of median pay in 2014, as were a quarter in the **wholesale and retail** sector. These four sectors together accounted for over half (53 per cent) of all workers earning below the threshold.

Sectors such as manufacturing (10 per cent) and construction (12 per cent) recorded a much lower incidence despite average educational qualifications of job holders being similar or lower to those in the above-mentioned service sectors. Both sectors benefit from effective wage premia based on being predominantly male-employing and/or with relatively high levels of collective representation. In the **utilities** sectors (electricity, water, and waste), **public administration, education,** and **knowledge-intensive service** sectors (financial services, information and communication), only a marginal share of employees (2–8 per cent) earned less than 60 per cent of median earnings.

In the next section, we describe one current living wage campaign in Ireland, inspired by its UK counterpart, but operationally different in a number of important respects. We also review recent initiatives at social partner and state level in other member states, which draw on similar concerns regarding wage adequacy for the low paid.

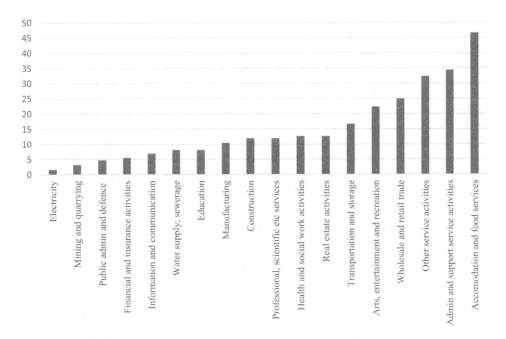

Figure 8.2 Share of European Union employees earning less than 60 per cent of median full time hourly pay, percentage by sector (NACE 1d).

Source: Structure of Earnings Survey (SES), 2014 (author's elaboration). Notes: based on hourly earnings excluding overtime. SES-2014 was a large enterprise sample survey carried out in EU member states. Research microdata file used includes only data from EU-23 (missing countries: AT, DK, IE, EL, HR). No data in SES for the following sectors: agriculture. For public admin and security, data is available for some but not all countries. Sample includes all enterprises with at least 10 employees, while some countries voluntarily add data on micro-enterprises (< 10 people). As the countries where this additional data is included are not identified clearly, and wages are likely to be lower in this category, estimates should be treated as indicative.

A living wage campaign: Ireland

Ireland provides an example of a living wage campaign originating in civic action and religious organizations supported by research centres, instead of in grass-roots campaigns as in the USA and the UK. The Vincentian Partnership for Social Justice (VPSJ), a Catholic charity, has been one of the main proponents of living wages in Ireland following earlier research in calculating 'minimum essential living standards' (MESL).

A principle of the Irish MESL – as with the minimum income standards that underpin the UK living wage – is that it is based on social consensus. The process of devising the living wage basket of goods and services is bottom-up and deliberative. Focus group discussions involve typically eight to twelve people from a mixture of socio-economic backgrounds. Group participants are selected on basis of household type: single working-age adults without children discuss the needs of workers without children, working parents discuss the needs of households with children. In this way, separate budgets are developed for different household formations based on input from citizen representatives. The discussions are moderated by experts/researchers and aim to develop a 'negotiated consensus' among the socially mixed groups, with meetings conducted over many sessions (Living Wage Ireland, 2017). In the focus groups, participants first attend an orientation meeting. A first focus group produces an agreed draft list of items, and a second group reviews the work of the first group and reaches a consensus on a second draft listing of items. This is then rechecked, for each costed item in each category, and a final consensus reached by a third different focus group. The MESL is therefore based on detailed qualitative research, following a consistent method using the same set of steps and checks in each iteration. In this way, changes in the living wage baskets can be considered as reflecting changes in society at large and not just the opinions of one group (see Table 8.1 for the MESL calculations).

Living wage proponents highlight the 'bottom-up' nature of the process to devise the living wage baskets. Though experts are involved in mediating the discussions, the baskets are based 'on what members of the public think' is required for an acceptable living standard (Hirsch and Valadez-Martinez, 2017). This distinguishes them from minimum wage-setting or advisory bodies where there is input from a diversity of social partners, businesses, and civil society as well as state representatives (for example, the UK Low Pay Commission). But these are generally 'expert commissions'; discussions of worker/household needs are absent or of relatively low priority and there is little if any direct citizen or worker input.

The reference for calculation of the living wage in Ireland is a single full-time worker without dependants, unlike the UK where it is a weighted average of different household types. This simplifies the calculations but means that the headline rate may be inadequate to meet the needs of many households, notably those with dependent children (though detailed tabulations are provided for different, more complex household types with estimates of 'family income needs'). Rates are calculated for four different regions (the capital city region of Dublin, 'cities', 'towns', and 'rural/rest of Ireland'). The national rate, which is the official campaign rate, is the employment-weighted average of the figures calculated for each of these regions. The extra cost of living in the capital – almost entirely attributable to higher housing costs – means that the national rate fails to cover

Table 8.1 Breakdown of living costs (%) by expenditure category

Ireland

Minimum essential living standard

Cost category	%
Housing	36.4
Household energy	7.3
Household goods / services and communication	7.9
Clothing	2.5
Personal care	3.4
Transport	6.9
Food	14.4
Social inclusion/participation and Education	11.2
Health and Insurance	4.7
Personal costs	2.1
Savings and contingencies	3.1
Total (€372.73 per week)	**100.0**

Source: VPSJ (2016).

the minimum standard of living required there while being generous for the other regions (at least for single workers without dependants).

The Irish living wage is publicized as an hourly wage rate (to facilitate comparison with the statutory rate) and was first set for Ireland at €11.45 per hour in 2014. It is adjusted annually, and in 2020 was at a rate of €12.30, an increase of 7 per cent over six years. The year-on-year uprating is capped at the percentage increase in private sector average hourly earnings in the calendar year prior to the update. This is done in recognition of employer requirements for a measure of certainty about future labour costs. The living wage was 22 per cent higher than the legal minimum in 2020, and this gap had reduced by 10 percentage points over the six years of the campaign's existence. Both the statutory minimum (from €8.65 to €10.10, + 17%) and average private sector wages increased at a faster rate than the living wage rate during the same six-year period.

There is no accreditation scheme or institution for Living Wage Employers in Ireland, such as exists in the UK (through Citizens UK/the Living Wage Foundation), so the campaign aims mainly to raise public awareness regarding the issue of low pay. The main vehicle for doing so is the announcement of the annual revision of the living wage rate. Some employers, for example, the energy utility SSE and retailers Aldi and Lidl, have nonetheless independently announced that they do or will voluntarily pay their Irish employees the Irish living wage. Other organizations have linked with the VPSJ and are represented on the Irish Living Wage technical group which revises the national living wage rate on an annual basis since 2014. These include unions (Unite), researchers (universities as well as the Nevin Economic Research Institute), and other charities (Social Justice Ireland). The Irish Living Wage is also supported by Ireland's largest union, the Services Industrial Professional and Technical Union, and the Think-tank for Action on Social Change.

Though a single example, the Irish living wage campaign makes clear that any living wage estimate is based on a number of decisions – on reference worker and household type, hours of work, region – which could be constructed differently and are in different national iterations. Moreover, this is before adding the complex process of identifying needs and costing services and products that correspond to a basic but acceptable standard of living. The showpiece hourly rate is necessarily a simplification given so many input variables and will not provide a living wage to those working part-time or with irregular hours or to many workers with dependants.

One measure of the success of living wage campaigns is official emulation, for example, the UK government's decision to rebadge the national minimum wage as a national 'living wage' in 2015. In late 2020, the Irish living wage received a similar endorsement as the governing coalition in its Programme for Government (Government of Ireland, 2020: 74) announced that that it would seek to 'progress to a living wage over the lifetime of the Government', closing at least some of the gap between the minimum wage and the living wage hourly rate, which in 2020 amounted to 22 per cent.

Related initiatives in other EU member states

While, to our knowledge, there are no other national initiatives in the EU currently (in 2020) that claim the 'living wage' brand, there is widespread debate around the issue of wage adequacy and the need in particular to raise minimum-wage levels and secure 'decent' wages. These have resulted in social partner campaigns with living wage rationales and have contributed to a number of member states explicitly taking on a more needs-based approach in their minimum-wage policymaking and using it to justify above-cost-of-living increases when adjusting rates. The following outlines a sample in brief of some of this recent activity on a country-by-country basis.

While there is no statutory minimum wage in **Austria**, organized labour (OGB) has called for a minimum wage of €1,700 a month for full-time work, to be implemented in sectoral collective agreements. Though not articulated as such, the living standard envisaged is akin to that of a living wage (Eurofound, 2018; Eurofound, 2020a).

In **Belgium**, the ABVV-FGTB trade union has organized a campaign demanding a minimum wage of €14 per hour (compared to a current statutory rate of €9.65). The 'Fight for €14' is modelled on the successful US city-based 'Fight for $15' campaigns, the most recent extension of local US living wage campaigning (Flohimont, 2019).

The Confederation of Independent Trade Unions in **Bulgaria** (CITUB) included the living wage concept in its work programme 2017–2022:

> In asserting our principle of decent wages we need to impose an upgrade on the minimum wage mechanism, to encompass a living wage. Although not universal and obligatory, the living wage is a reliable mechanism to overcome the drastic inequalities in pay and an important element in the transition to having a sustainable middle class.

CITUB has recommended that living wage rates be calculated for different regions (Eurofound, 2018).

In **Denmark**, while there is no translation of the term 'living wage', the notion of 'en løn man kan leve af', literally translated as 'a wage you can live off', is discussed. An interesting development has been research on the concept of 'living hours', understood as the number of hours of work required for an acceptable standard of living assuming a normal hourly salary (Ilsoe, 2016), given the sharp rise in low-hours work.

In **Slovenia,** the reform of the Minimum Wage Act in 2018, first implemented in 2019, includes mechanisms from 2021 onwards to bring the statutory minimum wage closer to a living wage. The new mechanism foresees that the level of the statutory minimum wage will be determined based on a minimum basket of basic goods and services, which would be topped up to allow a decent living, though details regarding the top-up have yet to be decided (Eurofound, 2020a).

In 2019, the national parliament in **Romania** discussed a law that explicitly linked the statutory minimum wage to a costed consumer basket along living wage lines (Eurofound, 2020a).

In **Poland**, the concept of decent wages (*godna płaca*) was prominent in policy discussions in the mid-2010s against the background of poor employment conditions among segments of the workforce characterized by a high incidence of fixed-term contracts, civil law contracts, and low wages. The Law and Justice Party, as part of a successful re-election campaign in 2020, announced a substantial gradual rise of the minimum wage up to PLN 4,500 (€1,047.10) by 2024. This is estimated to increase minimum wages to more than 60 per cent of average wages (Eurofound, 2018; Eurofound, 2020a).

In **Spain**, the governing coalition in 2019 announced plans to raise minimum wages to 60 per cent of the average wage by 2024, as recommended in the European Social Charter, in order 'to allow all persons in employment to enjoy a decent standard of living' (PSOE and Podemos, 2019). The Catalan regional government in 2019 recommended a higher minimum wage to reflect higher average wage levels in the region (Eurofound, 2020a).

In the last-mentioned cases in Poland and Spain, some interesting points emerge in relation to minimum-wage policy with strong relevance for living wages. Firstly, both the Polish and the Spanish government decisions are part of a multi-year programme of targeted, real increases in the value of the minimum wage, similar to some other EU member states and the UK (see Eurofound 2020a: 39). Secondly, the targeted increases are ambitious and substantial – significantly above inflation as well as predicted average wage growth – and motivated in part by living wage concerns. The specific targeted level of 60 per cent of **average** wages (the ESC reference rate for 'a fair remuneration sufficient for a decent standard of living') rather than **median** wages is significant as it implies a higher rate. Average wages are invariably higher than median wages given the skewed nature of the wage distribution with high-wage outliers raising average but not median values. The difference between median and average is higher where wage inequality is higher, which adds a further normative logic to basing targets on average wages – they boost incomes by more for the low-paid while reducing wage inequality. Thirdly, they embody political commitments to raising the returns from labour of the low paid but from political groupings of contrasting identities – progressive socialist in Spain and conservative traditionalist in Poland. This underlines that minimum wages and living wages and the basic ideas underpinning them are popular not only among potential beneficiaries but also among the general public (see Fedorets and Schroeder, 2017, for a review of relevant survey data). This popularity is increasingly identified by political parties across the political spectrum, rather than being the preserve of left-of-centre or social democratic parties as was previously more likely to be the case. Fourthly, as the Catalan example suggests, if designed to meet needs, living wages and minimum wages should be adjusted to local cost of living. There are strong within-country, regional variations in such costs which are rarely reflected in legal minimum wages – which usually set one rate for the entire country. Living wage initiatives have tended to take account of these differences (as in the UK), or at least research and document them, even when fixing on a single national living wage rate (as in the Irish example). Finally, again with reference to the Catalan example, an important detail is that the Catalan regional government has no competence to set a mandatory minimum wage; it is the exclusive competence of the national Spanish government to do so. However, regional authorities have other levers to influence such rate-setting, notably through their own role as a public sector employer, through public procurement – by setting reference salary levels in public contracts, to the extent permissible by competition law – and also by encouraging social partners to use the indicated salary level as a baseline for collective agreement negotiations. These are also levers that have been used to significant effect by public authorities when engaged by living wage campaigns (see for example Eurofound, 2018: 21).

Conclusions

Statutory minimum wages have become a popular policy tool. They boost wages amongst the lowest paid in a period of growing income inequality. The evidence from research increasingly suggests that when prudently set, they do so with little or no negative effects on employment outcomes. They have 'made a difference' to those on low pay. Living wage campaigns seek to raise the bar and they do so based on a simple and compelling idea, that work should pay enough for a basic but decent standard of living in the place where workers live. Living wage rates are invariably higher than minimum wages (in a range of 15–30 per cent in the two main European examples, in the UK and Ireland), and one of their core objectives is to influence policymakers and narrow this gap over time.

Their advocacy is heavily rooted in a mix of qualitative and quantitative research. Growing bodies of work in minimum income standards and reference budget setting promise to strengthen the methodological basis of living wage calculations, including possibly for cross-national application. An important lesson from successful living wage campaigns is that the methodological rigour, predictability, and transparency of these calculations has been an important precondition of the credibility and acceptability of the living wage 'brand' and hence of its voluntary take-up by employers.

The momentum behind a coordinated EU minimum-wage policy owes much to the sharpening of policy concern with wage adequacy created and sustained by living wage and decent wage initiatives. This is also evident in the more activist state approach to minimum wage-setting at member state level over the last decade where the relative and absolute level of minimum wages in most countries has risen faster than average wages and inflation.

The appeal to policymakers of minimum wages is not just their popularity. It is also that they are seen to address issues of growing inequality in advanced societies and the persistence of in-work poverty. Paid employment has traditionally been the most effective exit path from poverty but appears less able than before to fulfil this role. The growth of precarious employment related to the increasing flexibilization of work, the develop- ment of compound non-standard forms of employment involving low or non-guaranteed hours of work (Eurofound, 2020b), as well as declining levels of worker representation and union bargaining power, all contribute to the depreciation of worker's wages. These are exacerbated, in some countries, by declining levels of state transfer to those on low pay combined with rising costs, in particular for housing and childcare. Statutory minimum wages can only partially address such broader social policy problems. A minimum wage converging to living wage rates may do a lot more.

Notes

1 It was set as the target to be met in the UK by 2020 when the UK national minimum wage was rebranded as the 'national living wage' in 2015 and set on a course of progressive, incremental annual increases. The target has in 2020 been reset to two-thirds of median earnings by 2024, which would mean that minimum wage earners in the UK would no longer be categorized as 'low-paid'.
2 The concept of worker's needs was more explicit in the early history of minimum wage laws, and many of the justifications of the fledgling minimum wage regimes resemble those of con- temporary living wage definitions. The first national minimum wage law, Australia in 1894, defined the minimum wage as a 'wage that meets the normal needs of the average employee regarded as a human being living in a civilized society'. One of the earlier US state minimum wage laws (Wisconsin, 1913) referred to 'Compensation sufficient [for a worker] to maintain himself or herself under conditions consistent with his or her welfare [...] [in] reasonable com- fort, reasonable physical well-being, decency and moral well-being' (Anker, 2011: 84).

References

Anker, R. (2011). *Estimating a living wage: a methodological review.* ILO Geneva.
Canadian Centre for Policy Alternatives (CCPA) (2017). *Working for a living wage: making paid work meet basic family needs in Metro Vancouver,* 2017 Update. Accessed at www.policyalternatives.ca/ livingwage2017

Eurofound (2014). *Pay in Europe in the 21st century.* Publications Office of the European Union: Luxembourg.

Eurofound (2018). *Concept and practice of a living wage.* Publications Office of the European Union: Luxembourg.

Eurofound (2020a). *Minimum wages in 2020: Annual Review.* Publications Office of the European Union: Luxembourg.

Eurofound (2020b). *Labour market change: Trends and policy approaches towards flexibilisation.* Publications Office of the European Union: Luxembourg.

European Commission (2017). *The European Pillar of Social Rights.* Publications Office of the European Union: Luxembourg.

European Commission (2020). *Advancing the EU social market economy: adequate minimum wages for workers across Member States* (press release, 28 October).

European Trade Union Confederation (2017). *Pay rise campaign: minimum wages should not be poverty wages.* ETUC: Brussels.

European Union (2012). *Consolidated version of the Treaty on the Functioning of the European Union,* Official Journal of the European Union.

Fedorets, A., and Schroeder, C. (2017). 'Economic aspects of subjective attitudes towards the minimum wage reform'. *SOEP paper* No. 949.

Fernandez-Macias, E., and Vacas-Soriano, C. (2016). 'A coordinated European Union minimum wage policy?', *European Journal of Industrial Relations,* 22(2), 97–113.

Flohimont, O. (2019). '"Fight for 14". The campaign for a decent minimum wage of €14 per hour in Belgium', *Transfer,* 25(3), 381–386.

Gautié, J., and Schmitt, J. (Eds.). (2010). *Low-wage work in the wealthy world.* Russell Sage Foundation: New York.

Goedemé, T., Storms, B., Stockman, S., Penne, T., and Van den Bosch, K. (2015). 'Towards cross-country comparable reference budgets in Europe: first results of a concerted effort', *European Journal of Social Security,* 17(1), 3–30.

Government of Ireland (2020). *Programme for government: our shared future.* Dublin.

Grimshaw, D., Bosch, G., and Rubery, J. (2014). 'Minimum wages and collective bargaining: what types of pay bargaining can foster positive pay equity outcomes?', *British Journal of Industrial Relations,* 52(3): 470–498.

Hirsch, D., and Valadez-Martinez, L. (2017). *The Living Wage.* Agenda Publishing: Newcastle.

Ilsoe, A. (2016). 'From living wage to living hours – the Nordic version of the working poor', *Labour & Industry,* 26(1): 40–57.

Jones, C. (2017). 'Why the ECB wants the unions to increase wage demands', *Financial Times* (28 September).

Living Wage Ireland (2017). *Calculating a living wage for the Republic of Ireland.* Living Wage Technical Group: Dublin.

Lopatka, J. (2017). 'No more low cost: East Europe goes up in the world', *Reuters* (25 July).

Low Pay Commission (2002). *National minimum wage, LPC report 2002.* Low Pay Commission: London.

PSOE and Podemos (2019). *Coalición Progresista: Un nuevo acuerdo para España, government programme,* PSOE and Unidas Podemos: Madrid.

Schulten, T., and T. Müller (2013). 'European economic governance and its intervention in national wage development and collective bargaining'. In: *Divisive integration: The triumph of failed ideas in Europe – revisited,* ed. Steffen Lehndorff. ETUI: Brussels, 331–363.

Schulten, T., and Müller, T. (2019). 'What's in a name? From minimum wages to living wages in Europe', *Transfer,* 25(3): 267–284.

Vincentian Partnership for Social Justice (2016). *Submission on European Pillar of Social Rights.* VPSJ: Dublin.

Von der Leyen, U. (2019). A Union that strives for more: my agenda for Europe. Political guidelines for the next European Commission: 2019–24. Publications Office of the European Union: Luxembourg.

9 Wages and working conditions in outsourced services in Europe

Mathew Johnson and Karen Jaehrling

Introduction

The fragmentation of production systems as a result of organizational outsourcing and subcontracting poses significant challenges for the effective regulation of wages and working conditions (Doellgast et al., 2016; Mori, 2017). Thus, workers in certain labour market segments, such as those working for second- and third-tier firms within complex supply chains, face multiple challenges in respect of earning a decent living (Arnholtz and Refslund, 2019; Berntsen and Lillie, 2016; Marchal and Marx, 2018. These challenges arise from aggressive cost competition between contractors (Grimshaw et al., 2019), and the uneven exposure of certain workforce segments to various *protective gaps* such as low minimum standards, limited social protection, a lack of voice, and poor enforcement of labour market regulation (Grimshaw et al., 2016; Rubery et al., 2018). These regulatory and market imbalances threaten to push workers below the widely recognized relative poverty threshold of 60 per cent of median earnings, and increase the risk that workers are not able to maintain a dignified existence (Schulten and Müller, 2019).

There are a number of possible responses to these issues of regulating pay, terms and conditions, and work arrangements, including the extension of collective bargaining agreements to outsourced and subcontracted workers, higher statutory minimum wages, and the use of labour clauses to boost wages for those working under contract to public authorities. Although it has not been badged as a living wage initiative as such, each of these strategies may serve to close gaps between directly employed and outsourced workers, and help improve the relative and absolute position of those at the bottom of the wage distribution. Given the concentration of women in low-paying and often insecure roles, there are also wider potential egalitarian impacts from such initiatives that are worthy of closer analysis.

This chapter presents a contextualized comparison of innovative examples from Germany (DE), Spain (ES), and the UK where social partners have sought to bolster pay, living standards, and working conditions for outsourced and subcontracted workers through different channels. Specifically, in our selected countries, we look at examples in three sectors where there are clear risks of low pay: catering (ES); care work (UK); and steel manufacturing (DE). Although each of these examples was partly successful in its own right, we seek to explore the interactions between different types of intervention and the roles of employers, trade unions, and the state in tackling low pay and precarious work among outsourced workers. We also identify a number of compromises and trade-offs that emerge in practice between basic pay, enhancements, working hours, and career prospects as social partners seek to close protective gaps.

DOI: 10.4324/9781003054078-9

This chapter starts with a brief review of processes of institutional and organizational change and the impact on low pay, living standards, and precarious work in outsourced and subcontracted services, before outlining different options for closing gaps between labour market segments. It then presents the three empirical examples from Spain, the UK, and Germany, where different configurations of trade unions, employers and the state have sought to tackle low pay and precarious work in both public and private supply chains. It concludes with a short discussion around future directions for regulating pay and working conditions in outsourced services.

Low pay and precarious work in outsourced and subcontracted services: common patterns and different trajectories

Patterns of labour market segmentation are recognized as having a strong effect on the decision to outsource services; in particular the decision to outsource public services where greater cost effectiveness is assumed to follow from contracting out low-skilled jobs. However, the recent literature has also drawn our attention to the important interplay between changing institutional and regulatory regimes, the fragmentation of production processes, and the competitive dynamics within sectors in shaping outsourcing decisions and the resulting impact on pay and conditions.

Where gaps between public and private sector wages are high, there are clear incentives to outsource non-core activities, but outsourcing is also increasingly used to lower labour costs and to bypass trade unions even in core industries (Benassi and Dorigatti, 2018; Grimshaw et al., 2015; Mori, 2017). Although collective bargaining coverage has declined in many European countries over the last 40 years, employers may still seek out ways to evade or dilute collectively agreed standards through firm-level flexibility and the use of alternative sources of cheap labour such as posted and migrant workers (Bernsten and Lillie, 2016). Workers may be employed at the end of long supply chains by firms that achieve competitive advantage by not following rules in sectors where labour inspectorates struggle to monitor and enforce regulations (Jaehrling et al., 2016). This potentially creates a two- or three-tier workforce doing related jobs but covered by different collective agreements or not covered by collective agreements at all (Mori, 2017). As pay and conditions are only protected for those workers who transfer directly to a new contractor (under the EU Transfer of Undertakings Protection of Employment (TUPE) directive), this leaves employers free to hire new workers on inferior pay and working conditions, creating a two-tier workforce even within outsourced firms.

Alongside the risk that workers do not earn a living wage, outsourcing can also reduce long-term labour costs by eroding pension schemes, removing health insurance contributions, and weakening internal job ladders which reduce earnings growth (Dube and Kaplan, 2010). The challenge of achieving a decent living is therefore not just a problem of low hourly wages but also of poor terms and conditions, limited working hours, and the instability of contracts. For example, workers may be engaged on contingent contracts such as zero-hours contracts (ZHC), which offer no guarantee of working hours from week to week, and strip out pay for 'unproductive' time such as rest periods and travel between work sites, which can mean hourly pay levels that fall below the statutory minimum wage (Bessa et al., 2013). In addition, such workers face high levels of work intensity and the further erosion of discretionary effort (Rubery et al., 2015). Bidders for public contracts often face intense cost competition and slim profit margins, and in labour-intensive services such as cleaning, catering, and care work this inevitably means downward pressure on pay and working conditions (Grimshaw et al, 2019).

There are also specific challenges arising within national contexts, depending on the industry structure, institutional frameworks, and resulting trajectories of outsourcing. For example in Spain, there is a strong segmentation in terms of pay and working conditions between the public and private sectors, which generally follows the contours of sectoral collective agreements. However the rapid growth of ancillary services and, in particular, multiservice companies that span several industries (such as cleaning, catering, and facilities management) has blurred the boundaries between sectors and occupational groups (Godino and Molina, 2019). The issue is made more complex by the layering of regional and provincial agreements on top of basic sectoral standards, which can mean marked variations across geographical areas in terms of basic pay and conditions, but also in terms of how work is organized and the classification of certain occupations within the wage hierarchy (Recio et al., 2012).

Germany also has relatively high wage gaps both between and within sectors in line with collective agreements. Despite a strong tradition of multi-employer bargaining and industrial unionism (one collective agreement for all occupational groups within a company/industry) even within the private sector, this has not prevented firms evading the collective agreements for part of the workforce by subcontracting to firms that opt out of the voluntarist bargaining system. A significant shift has therefore been the outsourcing of services and jobs within large and formerly highly integrated and institutionally protected sectors such as chemicals and steel manufacturing. Outsourcing and subcontracting started with ancillary services before expanding into core business areas through the use of subsidiaries, posted workers, and temporary agency labour, which the trade unions tacitly allowed as a means to protect pay and conditions among core workers, although they increasingly recognize the need to protect all workers within supply chains (Benassi and Dorigatti, 2018).

In the UK, the main issue has been the large-scale privatization of public services since the 1980s, which has led to the transfer of public sector workers to firms that are not covered by sectoral collective agreements for areas such as health, the civil service, and local government, and are beyond the reach of established trade unions (Mori, 2017). This means that many outsourced workers in both core and non-core services such as cleaning, catering, care, and waste are now employed under contract in parts of the private sector where pay and conditions are set unilaterally by employers using statutory minima as a benchmark, which creates a strong risk of low living standards. The public–private gap has deteriorated in recent years as a result of sustained public sector austerity, but the removal of the short-lived two-tier code that prevented private sector contractors hiring new staff on inferior pay and conditions has created significant scope for the dilution of standards over time (Grimshaw et al., 2015).

Closing protective gaps

In this section we consider a number of alternative strategies that have been proposed as mechanisms by which to tackle segmentation and improve the pay and conditions of outsourced workers: **reintegration and re-municipalization**; the extending of **collective bargaining agreements**; **increased minimum wages**; the use of **labour clauses** in external contracts; and the adoption of **voluntary codes of conduct** by employers. These strategies vary in terms of their 'bite' (that is, the extent to which they substantively raise standards) and their inclusiveness (that is, the extent to which they cover a large share of outsourced workers and any exemptions that are in place). Mechanisms that have a high bite and include a high proportion of workers are potentially the most effective but are likely to come at a higher (economic and political) cost. Conversely, those strategies that have a relatively low bite or coverage may be more feasible and sustainable in challenging institutional and market contexts and therefore should not be discounted.

Insourcing and re-municipalization

Despite the short-term cost savings that can arise from outsourcing, some have questioned the overall value for money of external contracts when lower unit costs are set against considerations of control over service standards. As Giustiniano et al. (2015: 49) argue, 'cost savings may be cancelled out by strategic and organizational rigidity, such as a less effective span of control over the activities and the formal and informal practice of power'. In France and Germany, localized efforts have been made to re-municipalize certain public services that are 'natural monopolies' which generate stable revenues and benefit from strong mechanisms of accountability and control such as energy, water, and waste services (e.g. Grimshaw et al., 2015; Hall, 2012).

In the UK, examples of insourcing have increased, but tend to be more of a localized and emergency response to market or provider failure (Hall, 2012). For example, the collapse of the outsourcing construction and facilities management firm Carillion in early 2018 saw individual local authorities bringing school support, catering and cleaning staff back in-house and onto local government pay and conditions.[1] Similarly a number of London boroughs have taken control of leisure, waste, and cleaning services once external contracts have come to an end as a means to reduce staff turnover and management fees. However, despite optimistic predictions of a 'return of the pendulum', these examples remain the exception, and in many European countries there is still a heavy reliance on the private sector to deliver public services as a result of sustained pressure on public sector finances. Unions generally remain opposed to outsourcing, but strategies have evolved from hostility and denial to concession bargaining on protection of pay and conditions and job security. However, unions may resist such transformations where more favourable pay and conditions are in place among private contractors (Grimshaw et al., 2015).

Extend/strengthen collective bargaining

Collective bargaining is strongly linked with a lower incidence of low pay and in-work poverty, and lower overall levels of wage inequality, and coordinated bargaining in Nordic countries has been credited with helping shore up living standards even in typically low-paying sectors such as cleaning and hospitality (Alsos et al., 2019, and see Chapter 10 in this volume). Where services remain contracted out, an important means to harmonize standards is to extend collectively agreed pay and conditions to subcontracted firms, along with protections around working time, and social security contributions. In some contexts, automatic extension mechanisms mean that all firms and workers are legally covered by the relevant sector- or industry-level agreement, whether or not firms are part of employer associations and whether or not workers are union members (Koukiadaki et al., 2016). In other contexts, non-union firms may be encouraged to voluntarily sign sector-level agreements in order to prevent unfair wage competition and to give them preferred status when bidding for public contracts (Arnholtz and Refslund, 2019). In the UK, a legal test case was brought, but was eventually lost, by the Independent Workers Union of Great Britain (IWGB) to establish joint employer status between the University of London and the private facilities management firm Cordant that would have established collective bargaining rights for outsourced workers.[2]

Minimum wages

Statutory minimum wages have become well established as a legitimate means to protect against extreme low pay and exploitation while also helping to achieve broader egalitarian and redistributive goals to slow the rise of low-wage work, protect living standards, and to narrow wage inequality within the labour market (Belser and Rani, 2015). This reflects the growing recognition that market forces alone do not provide a decent standard of living even for those on full-time contracts.

However, the ability of minimum wages in isolation to address these multiple goals depends on prevailing wage levels and the degree of wage dispersal. There is also a general recognition that poverty is shaped by sufficiency of working hours, the availability and generosity of in-work wage subsidies, and pooled income within the household. Nevertheless, minimum wages have come to be increasingly associated with the notion of a fair wage that allows for more than a simple subsistence lifestyle. Indeed, the fact that in the UK, for example, low wages increase the risk of working poverty by a factor of ten (Lawton and Pennycook, 2013: 36) illustrates the importance of a fair minimum wage as a tool to fight against poverty.

To this end, minimum wages are increasingly used by governments to achieve specific macroeconomic goals. For example, after steady growth in the UK's statutory minimum wage since its introduction in 1998, recent sharp rises, combined with sluggish growth at the median, have pushed minimum rates for workers aged 25 and over (labelled the National Living Wage) to 60 per cent of median earnings, and the UK is on track to achieve a target of two-thirds of median earnings by 2024. Similarly, after a long period of slow growth in the Spanish minimum wage, policymakers have recognized the problem of endemic low pay in sectors with low collective bargaining coverage and have enacted significant rises since 2018. Similar responses can be seen in Germany, where the introduction of the first national statutory national minimum wage in 2015 was a coordinated response by the social partners to the problem of the rising low-wage share, which was also designed to provide an incentive for supplementary negotiations within sectors (Bosch, 2018).

The recognition that in many countries minimum wages 'are nothing more than poverty wages' has proved to be a strong catalyst for widespread calls for minimum wages to move towards becoming functional living wages – that is set at a level that provides a decent minimum standard of living judged by the norms of a particular society (Schulten and Müller, 2019). In countries such as Germany and Spain where collective bargaining has survived, albeit in a somewhat weakened state, the living standards of low-paid workers have become a focal point of trade union negotiation strategies in recent years (Schulten and Müller, 2019). In contrast, in the UK where collective bargaining in low-wage industries is weak and fragmented, the living wage has become more of a campaigning issue driven by a shifting coalition of civil society, business, and labour organizations (Johnson et al., 2019).

Labour clauses in public contracts

In more unfavourable institutional contexts, where the scope to extend collective bargaining is limited and trade unions are not closely involved in setting minimum wages, labour clauses have emerged as important mechanisms to set minimum standards for outsourced workers. These labour clauses may set out rates of pay, terms and conditions, social security contributions, and training and development opportunities for workers. Although wage clauses for outsourced workers and automatic extension mechanisms for collective agreements have been used in the past to prevent 'undercutting', the notion of socially responsible procurement has given fresh impetus to the systematic incorporation of non-commercial considerations such as living wage clauses into external contracts (Jaehrling et al., 2018).

Labour clauses usually require additional investment by client firms to fund higher pay and conditions as well as dedicated resources for enforcement, and there are growing concerns that employers may claw back increased wage costs by reducing hours or increasing work demands (Rubery et al., 2015). Furthermore, public authorities may combine labour clauses with provisions that *indirectly* affect price levels and working conditions offered by contracted companies in a negative way (Jaehrling, 2015). Similarly, the notion of chain liability places responsibility on clients at the head of supply chains to monitor and enforce standards, but where first-tier clients subcontract to several smaller firms that in turn bring in self-employed workers, there are doubts about whether the rules are followed (Arnholtz and Refslund, 2019).

More broadly, recent research has raised concerns about the extent to which such clauses constitute 'binding' rules for subcontractors given sustained competitive pressures in the market for certain services (e.g. cleaning, catering, and older people's care, Rubery et al., 2015), the heavy burden of austerity acting upon public authorities across Europe (Grimshaw et al., 2016), and the ongoing issue of legal uncertainty around the 'enforceability' of non-statutory wage rates across EU borders (Reflsund et al, 2020). There is also the long-standing debate around whether trade unions have the appetite and bargaining power to pursue multiple local-level deals for a largely privatized, fragmented, and highly precarious workforce (Benassi and Dorigatti, 2018).

Voluntary codes of conduct

Alongside these institutional measures to address low pay, a number of voluntary initiatives have emerged in recent years that seek to bind clients and suppliers to improved standards. This closely mirrors the rise of private regulation applied to global value chains through audits and codes of conduct, and reflects growing consumer concerns about issues of ethics and exploitation in garment and electronics supply chains. There are also concerns among employers about the quality, stability, and sustainability of fragmented supply chains, and recent agreements signed with trade unions have committed some global brands to key standards such as 'fair wages', although in most cases these are benchmarked to local market rates of pay rather than a true living wage (Rubery and Johnson, 2019).

More broadly there are concerns that these voluntary and private systems of regulation are a means to contain negative publicity and to forestall more binding regulations (Williams et al., 2011).

Country initiatives

We now turn to a consideration of different initiatives in our selected countries which seek to tackle problems of low pay and poor working conditions in three sectors: catering (ES); care work (UK); and steel manufacturing (DE).

Spain – building a new collective agreement for outsourced catering workers

The case study for Spain focuses on the role of collective bargaining in addressing the twin issues of low pay and insufficient hours for outsourced catering workers (Muñoz de Bustillo Llorente and Pinto Hernández, 2016). Catering falls within the HORECA industry (hotels, restaurants and catering), which is a significant part of the Spanish economy linked with tourism, and contributes close to 15 per cent of national GDP. The catering sector includes services that are provided on-site for company employees and state institutions such as schools, hospitals, and universities ('collectives'). Increasingly these services are provided under contract by outsourced providers (particularly to large employers and state institutions). It is a labour-intensive sector and employs cooks, cleaners, waiters, administrators, and lunchtime monitors in schools (many of whom are female workers), but relies extensively on self-employment and part-time work which, in line with national trends, is increasingly involuntary.

In 2016, the representative trade unions, CCOO and UGT, signed the first national collective agreement for 'catering services supplied to collectives' (I Convenio Estatal de Restauración Colectiva). The new agreement was designed to set binding minimum standards across the sector, but also to provide a framework for supplementary negotiations at firm level through Article 9 of the collective agreement. This article emphasizes that firm-level agreements should not 'play a destabilizing role' nor be used as a 'formula to lower working conditions'. This collective agreement is also important as it was signed after a long period of stalemate in collective bargaining and in a challenging context of unilaterally imposed labour reforms of 2011 and 2012.

For the unions, this was a major breakthrough in that it provided a platform for protecting wages and working time. Crucially, it also provided a framework for monitoring both contracted hours and actual hours worked, which had previously been very weak at local level. For employers, a key advantage was trading off higher wages and a minimum of ten hours per week in return for flexible scheduling from month to month as they could increase hours during one month, which workers then reclaimed as paid leave during the next month. Signing a single national agreement with both major trade unions, with some scope for supplementary regional and local enhancements, also helped contain some of the pressure for significantly higher standards that might be set through localized collective bargaining with strong trade unions.

Although the collective agreement covers all categories of workers, it delivered bottom-weighted increases for the lowest-paid jobs (including monitors) that were in excess of what other collective agreements had delivered in most years since the global financial crisis of 2008–2009. It also included protections against rising inflation in future years to protect real wages. In tandem with increased hourly rates, a key feature of the agreement from the perspective of overall earnings was the increase in minimum weekly hours of workers employed as 'monitors'. In contrast with cooks and cleaners who might work for several hours before and after the lunch service across multiple school sites, monitors were only contracted for the lunch period at a single location to coordinate the serving of meals and to supervise children. This meant that their paid working time could be as little as 45 minutes per day, which created significant challenges in terms of earning a sub-sistence wage, and resulted in significant unpaid overtime. The new agreement set a min-imum of ten hours per week (monitored closely by the trade unions), which represents for many monitors a doubling of their take-home pay. The collective agreement also includes (non-binding) recommendations for firms to use open-ended contracts when hiring, and to convert existing fixed-term contracts to open-ended ones unless there is a clear justification not to do so.

This case study underlines the importance of collective bargaining, not only in terms of delivering hourly wage increases for some of the lowest-paid workers in a challenging economic and legal context, but in guaranteeing minimum working hours for part-time workers, an important factor behind low overall earnings in the sector.

UK – localized labour clauses for outsourced care services

Local government is the lowest-paid part of the UK public sector, and significant budget cuts since 2010 have placed additional pressure on pay, terms, and conditions. The local government sector makes extensive use of outsourced labour, typically to provide low-paid services such as cleaning, catering, and care services; work which is largely performed by women in part-time roles. Strict value for money considerations in the procurement of care services typically means low wages with few enhancements, leading to long hours and a risk that workers do not achieve the legal minimum wage let alone a full living wage. There is, however, evidence that, despite a drastic slowdown in sector-level collective bargaining in recent years, individual local authorities are increasingly willing to use their positions as buyers to improve employment standards among first-tier suppliers in care services. This could be done through the use of spe-cific procurement clauses such as requirements to pay the living wage, or redesigning contracts to enable guaranteed hours contracts and payment for travel time, each of which increases overall earnings.

Against this context, in 2012 the UK's largest public sector trade union, UNISON, launched a voluntary 'charter' for care commissioning. The charter sets out a number of key principles of compassionate care, and a range of underpinning business and employ-ment standards to be embedded locally through dialogue between commissioners, union branches, and providers. So far, 46 out of 206 commissioning authorities in England, Scotland, and Wales have formally adopted the charter, but interviews with union officers, along with local authority commissioning managers and a care provider, show that where there is the political will, local authorities can achieve 'social ends' such as reducing pre-carious and low-paid work through better procurement. This was achieved at one large local authority in the north of England by: increasing the hourly fees paid to external contractors (costing an additional £2.7m per year); stipulating specific conditions of employment for contracted workers (including a 'local' living wage of £8.01 per hour); and consolidating contracts in order to reduce the number of providers and increase the volume of work (thus stabilizing incomes and working patterns for providers).

The findings also suggest that behind the political rhetoric, the commissioners of social care services are very clearly pragmatists: they want the best standards possible within the available budget. However, they recognize that the lower pay and conditions across much of the private and independent sector (compared with directly employed staff) is one of the main drivers for outsourcing in the first place. Commissioners engaged tactically with providers to agree 'sustainable' fees, and as might be expected, providers in turn appeared to respond positively to this 'high-road' form of contracting. At the same time, the provider interviewed still accepted work from 'low road' authorities, and simply allowed differential levels of pay and conditions to emerge between internal workforce segments organized along geographical lines. The local union branch was largely focused on the uprating of pay among contractors (which they saw as an important lever to reduce the incentive for further outsourcing). The local living wage of £8.01 per hour was seen as a 'stepping stone' to achieving a full living wage, which was achieved the following year (and has since been uprated in line with increases in the UK living wage). Higher hourly rates combined with guaranteed hours contracts and payment for travel time were all important to improve the take home pay of care workers. Yet recruitment remains challenging in the local labour market where many supermarkets are also Living Wage Employers. Nevertheless, labour clauses remain a highly localized solution to structural problems in the care sector and in low-wage labour markets in the UK, where pay rates are still largely influenced by increases in the statutory national minimum wage.

Germany – voluntary agreements in the 'shadow of the law'

As in other sectors, the use of subcontracting has become an increasingly contentious issue in the German steel industry. Subcontracts have existed for a long time following the outsourcing of peripheral services such as catering and machinery cleaning. In a more recent development, activities that are part of, or at least closer to, a firm's core business are increasingly being outsourced as well, such as logistics and packaging. This is certainly one reason behind the more critical stance of both worker representatives and public opinion. As Benassi and Dorigatti (2018) argue, the closer an outsourced activity is to the core of the production process, the more trade unions and works councils of lead companies are likely to develop inclusive strategies for the subcontracted workforce in order to protect the interest of their core constituency. This motive is explicitly given in a leaflet produced by the trade union IG Metall: 'When greater job security and fair pay is expected of out-side companies, they raise their prices. That makes the jobs of the core workforce a little bit safer, since outsourcing becomes less attractive'. Yet there are also other factors explaining why trade unions, as well as lead companies themselves, have stepped up efforts to improve working conditions for the subcontracted workforce. New legal regulations (introduced in 2017 with the new law on temporary agency work) sanctioned more strongly the use of bogus subcontracts, and the introduction of the minimum wage legislation in 2015. This, in conjunction with the general contractors' chain liability, helped commissioning firms realize that infringements of the law by subcontractors also harbour considerable economic risks for themselves. Thus, as Wright and Brown (2013: 24) note with regard to firms' strategies for socially sustainable sourcing: 'Although these strategies may deliver business benefits, lead firms will generally not adopt them unless pressured or persuaded by third parties'. In the case of the German steel industry, the legal reforms, as well as the comparatively strong trade unions and works councils, are just such a (semi-)external force capable of driving the development of both strategies from the top down and bottom up.

The 'bottom-up' measures included a trade union campaign aimed at supporting employees and pressurizing employers of contracted companies to conclude collective agreements and enable the election of works councils. This was complemented by 'top-down' strategies of lead firms' management, which in turn were encouraged by trade unions. Most importantly, a collective agreement on the use of subcontracts was concluded between IG Metall and the employer's association in several regions in Germany in 2014. It stipulates that, whenever possible, employers should enter into contracts for services only with firms bound by collective agreements. At the very least, subcontractors should agree in writing to comply with statutory norms such as the national minimum wage. Moreover, companies are obliged to put in place appropriate measures for monitoring contracted firms' compliance with these obligations.

How effectively have these measures helped secure 'living wages' among the subcontracted workforce? As our case study in one large steel company illustrates (see Jaehrling et al., 2016), these complementary approaches have helped narrow the pay and protection gaps between the core workforce and contract workers. On numerous occasions, the local trade union in collaboration with the works council of the lead firm and subcontracted workers has managed to organize works council elections and conclude collective agreements – mostly company agreements restricted to the individual subcontractor. According to our IG Metall interviewee, the wage levels fixed in these agreements are still typically at least 15–20 per cent below the level of the steel industry agreement, but for subcontracted employees this is still an improvement from where no collective agreements were in place. However, IG Metall also recognized the limitations of union mobilization strategies, due to the short-lived nature of the contractual relationships between the lead firms and the subcontractors, which often last only months: 'It's the task of Sisyphus.' (IG Metall union secretary). Corresponding 'top-down' strategies that require all contractors to conclude and apply collective agreements would significantly bolster these bottom-up strategies. In reality the measures adopted by the client firm were more modest, and simply required contracting firms to comply with the national minimum wage and key health and safety provisions. In the view of our IG Metall interviewee, this can partly be explained by a lack of commitment and knowledge by the purchasing department of the client firm. The collective agreement landscape is now so fragmented that extensive knowledge on the part of the purchasing department is required in order to decide which collective agreement should apply (e.g. logistics, cleaning, or catering) and what the rates of pay are: 'now that the minimum wage sets the legal wage floor, so to speak, we only need to ask "Are they paying 8.50 euros or not?" This is very convenient for purchasing managers' (IG Metall union secretary). Perhaps the biggest obstacle to effective monitoring lies in the sheer volume of subcontractors in the steel industry as several thousand labour supply companies operate over the course of a year, accounting for up to 20 per cent of all workers on-site. This is also a key reason why, according to IG Metall, the lead firms' control efforts are often confined to checking first-tier contractors and not second- or third-tier subcontractors.

Discussion and conclusion

Outsourcing and subcontracting clearly have the scope to reinforce segmentation in the labour market, but as this chapter has shown, patterns of segmentation are in a state of flux driven by the complex interactions between a range of institutional and organizational factors. In turn, there are a number of mechanisms by which gaps can be reduced in order to tackle entrenched problems of low pay, falling living standards, and precarious work among outsourced and subcontracted workers and thus reduce the incentives for further outsourcing. Although each of these initiatives delivered tangible improvements for outsourced and subcontracted workers, they were also significant in terms of bringing together trade unions, employers, and state actors to negotiate new frameworks for regulating industrial relations in highly fragmented and cost-sensitive sectors.

The initiatives presented here also have to be seen in the national and sectoral context in which they developed. For example, the sectoral catering agreement in Spain was a remarkable achievement for an increasingly fragmented and cost-sensitive sector, which was made more impressive given the drastic slowdown in collective bargaining activity at national and sectoral level in the immediate aftermath of the global financial crisis. That the agreement has been renewed and uprated several times since 2016 is reflective of a renewed commitment of both employers and trade unions to the principles of social dialogue. At the same time, widening gaps between different regions and provinces are a potential concern in terms of the coordinated upgrading of standards.

Similarly, in a UK context where union membership density and collective bargaining coverage are low for outsourced care workers, the procurement process is an increasingly important mechanism through which working conditions in the private sector are regulated. In this case, the unions have helped agree on living wages that are between 10 and 20 per cent above prevailing minimum wage rates, along with fixed hours contracts and payment for travel time between clients. However, the reliance on the commitment of local politicians, organized union branches, and local rather than national funding means that the take-up of this 'ethical' procurement approach has so far been limited.

The example of the German steel industry illustrates the importance of close intertwining of legal, collective, and company-level approaches to regulation, both with regard to the factors leading up to the development of 'network-oriented employee representation' (Hertwig et al., 2019) and with regard to the content. Many of the top-down measures do not create any new rights, but create new monitoring and sanctioning mechanisms governed by private law, such as the right to unannounced site inspections by lead firms' staff, fines, or the termination of a contract. However, the strong use of subcontractors and the complexity of subcontracting chains means that approaches to the regulation of working conditions come up against the problem of limited resources devoted to controlling them. This extension of the sphere of influence brings with it opportunities to regain the discretionary power that has been lost due to the expansion of the 'second-tier' workforce. Yet it also brings specific difficulties, in particular for the proper implementation of the regulations. Thus from the point of view of ensuring 'fair' employment conditions in such companies, strategies that aim to reduce the excessive use of subcontracts continue to be of importance.

The examples presented here underline the need to consider terms and conditions, working hours, and contract types alongside improvements in hourly rates in order to better protect incomes and living standards among precarious workforce groups. These agreements can provide a platform for further coordinated action to achieve a living wage for low-paid workers. The specific initiatives in Spain, Germany, and the UK have not completely eliminated the gaps between public and private sector employees, or between core and peripheral firms. Thus, there are clearly still incentives to maintain outsourced provision in the short-term. However, where these labour cost differentials decrease, and where the transaction costs of monitoring and enforcement increase, the trade unions may be able to build a stronger case for outsourced services to be fully reintegrated into the organizational structures of client organizations. In order to scale up and sustain improvements, a wide range of mutually reinforcing elements is needed to reduce segmentation and temper the pressures that sustain cost-driven outsourcing.

Acknowledgements

This chapter draws on national reports completed for a European Commission-funded project on precarious work: *DG Employment, Social Affairs and Equal Opportunities VP/ 2014/004, Industrial Relations & Social Dialogue.*

Notes

1 www.localgov.co.uk/Councils-bring-services-in-house-following-Carillion-collapse/44531
2 www.ibblaw.co.uk/insights/blog/union-loses-landmark-outsourcing-appeal

References

Alsos, K., Nergaard, K., and Van Den Heuvel, A. (2019). 'Collective bargaining as a tool to ensure a living wage. Experiences from the Nordic countries'. *Transfer: European Review of Labour and Research, 25*(3), 351–365.

Arnholtz, J., and Refslund, B. (2019). 'Active enactment and virtuous circles of employment relations: How Danish unions organised the transnationalised Copenhagen Metro construction project'. *Work, Employment and Society, 33*(4), 682–699.

Belser, P., and Rani, U. (2015). 'Minimum wages and inequality'. In *Labour markets, institutions and inequality*. Edward Elgar Publishing.

Benassi, C. and Dorigatti, L. (2018) 'The political economy of agency work in Italy and Germany'. In: Doellgast V, Lillie N and Pulignano V (Eds.) *Reconstructing Solidarity*. Oxford: Oxford University Press. 124–143.

Berntsen, L., and Lillie, N. (2016). 'Hyper-mobile migrant workers and Dutch trade union representation strategies at the Eemshaven construction sites'. *Economic and Industrial Democracy, 37*(1), 171–187.

Bessa, I., Forde, C., Moore, S., and Stuart, M. (2013). 'The National Minimum Wage, earnings and hours in the domiciliary care sector'. University of Leeds: *Research Report for the Low Pay Commission*.

Bosch, G. (2018). 'The making of the German minimum wage: a case study of institutional change'. *Industrial Relations Journal, 49*(1), 19–33.

Doellgast, V., Sarmiento-Mirwaldt, K., and Benassi, C. (2016). 'Institutions, cost structures, and the politics of externalization: explaining variation in boundary strategies for call center jobs'. *Industrial and Labor Relations Review, 69*, 551–578.

Dube, A., and Kaplan, E. (2010). 'Does outsourcing reduce wages in the low-wage service occupations? Evidence from janitors and guards'. *Industrial and Labor Relations Review, 63*(2): 287–306.

Giustiniano, L., Marchegiani, L., Peruffo, E., and Pirolo, L. (2015). 'Business outcomes of outsourcing: lessons from management research'. In Drahokoupil, J. (Ed.). *The Outsourcing Challenge: Organizing Workers across Fragmented Production Networks*. Brussels: ETUI. 47–65.

Godino, A., and O. Molina (2019). *Who overcomes collective bargaining? Outsourcing practices, regulatory framework and facility management in Spain*, Country Report –RECOVER project https://ddd. uab.cat/pub/infpro/2019/202073/Country_Report_Spain_EN.pdf

Grimshaw, D., Cartwright, J., Keizer, A., and Rubery, J. (2019). 'Market exposure and the labour process: The contradictory dynamics in managing subcontracted services work'. *Work, Employment and Society, 33*(1), 76–95.

Grimshaw D., Johnson M., Rubery J., and Keizer A. (2016). *Reducing precarious work protective gaps and the role of social dialogue in Europe*. Available at: www.research.mbs.ac.uk/ewerc/Portals/0/Documents/Comparative-Report-Reducing-Precarious-Work-v2.pdf

Grimshaw, D., Rubery, J., Anxo, D., Bacache-Beauvallet, M., Neumann, L., and Weinkopf, C. (2015). 'Outsourcing of public services in Europe and segmentation effects: The influence of labour market factors'. *European Journal of Industrial Relations, 21*(4), 295–313.

Hall, D. (2012). *Re-municipalising Municipal Services in Europe*. (EPSU).

Hertwig, M., Kirsch, J., and Wirth, C. (2019). 'Defence is the best offence: Horizontal disintegration and institutional completion in the German coordinated market economy'. *Work, Employment and Society, 33*(3), 500–517.

Jaehrling, K. (2015). 'The state as a 'socially responsible customer'? Public procurement between market-making and market-embedding'. *European Journal of Industrial Relations, 21*(2), 149–164.

Jaehrling, K., Johnson, M., Larsen, T. P., Refslund, B., and Grimshaw, D. (2018). 'Tackling precarious work in public supply chains: A comparison of local government procurement policies in Denmark, Germany and the UK'. *Work, Employment and Society, 32*(3), 546–563.

Jaehrling, K., Wagner, I., and Weinkopf, C. (2016). *Reducing precarious work in Europe through social dialogue: The case of Germany*. Duisburg: Institute for Work, Skills and Training (IAQ), University of Duisburg-Essen.

Johnson, M., Koukiadaki, A., and Grimshaw, D. (2019). 'The Living Wage in the UK: Testing the limits of soft regulation?' *Transfer: European Review of Labour and Research, 25*(3), 319–333.

Koukiadaki, A., Távora, I., and Lucio, M.M. (2016). 'Continuity and change in joint regulation in Europe: Structural reforms and collective bargaining in manufacturing'. *European Journal of Industrial Relations, 22*(3), 189–203.

Lawton, K., and Pennycook, M. (2013). *Beyond the Bottom Line*. The Challenges and Opportunities of a Living Wage: IPPR and Resolution Foundation.

Marchal, S., and Marx, I. (2018). 'Stemming the tide: What have European Union countries done to support low-wage workers in an era of downward wage pressures?' *Journal of European Social Policy, 28*(1), 18–33.

Mori, A. (2017). 'The impact of public services outsourcing on work and employment conditions in different national regimes'. *European Journal of Industrial Relations, 23*(4), 347–364.

Muñoz de Bustillo Llorente, R., and Pinto Hernández, F. (2016). *Reducing precarious work in Europe through social dialogue: The case of Spain* (Report for the European Commission). University of Salamanca.

Recio, A., Moreno, S., and Godino, A. (2012). *Low-wage jobs, outsourcing and public policies: The cases of cleaning and catering sector in Spain*. www.academia.edu/download/29466997/Low-wage_jobs__outsourcing_and_public_policies_(2012)_-_Recio__Moreno_and_Godino.pdf

Rubery, J., and Johnson, M. (2019). *Closing the gender pay gap: What role for trade unions?* ILO ACTRAV Working Paper. International Labour Organization. Geneva.

Rubery, J., Grimshaw, D., Hebson, G., and Ugarte, S.M. (2015). '"It's all about time": Time as contested terrain in the management and experience of domiciliary care work in England'. *Human Resource Management, 54*(5), 753–772.

Rubery, J., Grimshaw, D., Keizer, A., and Johnson, M. (2018). 'Challenges and contradictions in the "normalizing" of precarious work'. *Work, Employment and Society, 32*(3), 509–527.

Schulten, T., and Müller, T. (2019). 'What's in a name? From minimum wages to living wages in Europe'. *Transfer: European Review of Labour and Research, 25*(3), 267–284.

Williams, S., Heery, E., and Abbott, B. (2011). 'The emerging regime of civil regulation in work and employment relations'. *Human Relations, 64*(7), 951–970.

Wright, C.F., and Brown, W. (2013). 'The effectiveness of socially sustainable sourcing mechanisms: Assessing the prospects of a new form of joint regulation'. *Industrial Relations Journal, 44*(1), 20–37.

10 Are collective bargaining models in the Nordic countries able to secure a living wage?

Experiences from low-wage industries

Kristin Alsos and Kristine Nergaard

Introduction

Discussions on and calls for a living wage have particularly emerged in countries and regions where minimum-wage levels are too low to ensure a decent minimum standard of living (Schulten and Müller, 2019). While the purpose of the minimum wage, as defined by the International Labour Organization (ILO), has been to meet the needs of workers and their families (Alsos et al., 2019), it can be argued that this ambition has been abandoned, triggering calls for a living wage (Schulten and Müller, 2017). In the Nordic countries, there have been no such campaigns, and wage formation is still the domain of the social partners who are in the driving seat when it comes to wage formation (Alsos et al., 2019). Reducing the extent of low wages and ensuring good minimum standards are regarded as tasks for the collective bargaining system, and have been a priority for trade unions. None of the Nordic countries have introduced a statutory minimum wage, and both the employers' organizations and the trade unions have opposed the introduction of a minimum wage at European Union (EU) level (Furåker, 2020).[1] Wages are generally negotiated between the social partners at industry level, were collectively agreed minimum wages are adjusted anually. All countries have a relatively compressed wage structure in an international context, with high minimum-wage rates (Eurostat, 2016).

Strong collective institutions are needed in order for this model to work. A high unionization rate and industry-level agreements that cover large parts of the labour market, together with a coordinated and solidaristic wage policy, have ensured effective wage floors (Dølvik and Marginson, 2018). In some of the Nordic countries, the models have been underpinned by schemes to make collective agreements generally applicable (Alsos and Eldring, 2008).

In this chapter, we look at the factors that have contributed to small wage differences and (relatively) high minimum-wage rates in the Nordic countries. Although all the Nordic countries are very similar in this area, we have chosen to concentrate on the Scandinavian countries of Denmark, Norway, and Sweden, because this is where the greatest similarities in wage formation are found (Andersen et al., 2014). The explanation of why these countries have small wage differences lies both in the national collective bargaining models and in strategies at industry level. We start by giving an overview of wage formation in the Scandinavian countries, and we then use Norway as an example to illustrate how the unions have dealt with the issue of low wages in various industries, and what strategies have been adopted. Norway differs from the other Scandinavian countries with lower union density rates as well as lower bargaining coverage. While low-wage competition due to labour migration has put pressure on the low-wage model in all the Scandinavian

DOI: 10.4324/9781003054078-10

countries, the challenge has been most profound in Norway (Dølvik and Marginson, 2018). This allows us to discuss strengths and weaknesses in the model. Finally, we discuss whether the Nordic model for ensuring decent minimum wages will continue to be effective in the future.

Background

The wage formation models in Denmark, Sweden, and Norway have several similarities (Andersen et al., 2014; Nergaard et al., 2016; Vartiainen, 2011). Pay and other working conditions are negotiated between the social partners at industry level. All three countries have a high unionization rate, and through extensive collective agreement coverage, negotiated terms impact on large parts of the labour force, see Table 10.1. All public sector employees are covered by an agreement, while the share in the private sector varies between 52 per cent in Norway and 83 per cent in Sweden. Bargaining takes place at both industry and company level, and central-level coordination still plays an important role in order to secure sound macroeconomic results.

In discussions about low wages, it is normally industries within the private sector, and particularly the private service sector, that are highlighted. These are industries where the wage level is normally lower than in manufacturing and in the public sector, and which are characterized by atypical forms of employment, young workers, and employees with an immigrant background (Trygstad et al., 2014, 2018a; Jordfald, 2018). The unionization rate, employer organization rate, and collective bargaining coverage are all lower here than in other parts of the private sector, although the level varies between the three countries (Tijdens and van Klaveren, 2007; Nergaard, 2020; Kjellberg, 2019).

In wage formation, it is the traditional unions, as well as the large confederations (Landsorganisasjonen (LO) in Norway and Sweden and Fagbevægelsens Hovedorganisation (FH) in Denmark), that are dominant in the low-wage industries. Thus, it is not common to find other unions undercutting traditional institutional regulations by offering the employers cheaper agreements.[2]

To Ensuring an effective wage floor in these types of models requires collective bargaining to have a wide coverage, since only businesses that are bound by collective agreements are obliged to adhere to wage rates and adjustments. Traditionally, this has been ensured through high unionization rates and employer organization rates. In Sweden and Denmark, this is still the dominant situation; businesses that join the employers' organizations are (with some exceptions) bound by the collective agreements

Table 10.1 Unionization rates, employer organization rates, and collective agreement coverage in Denmark, Norway, and Sweden. Last available year (%)

	Denmark	*Norway*	*Sweden*
Unionization rate	67 (53*)	50	68
Employer organization rate	70	Approx. 80	88
Collective agreement coverage, private sector	74	52	83
Collective agreement coverage, total	83	69	89

Source: Nergaard (2020).

Note: * Union density exclusive alternative unions, i.e. ideological alternatives to the traditional trade unions, see Ibsen (2012) for details.

that the organization has signed (Calmfors et al., 2018). In Norway, the effect of collective agreements has been strengthened through a system of general application (Eldring and Alsos, 2012).

A general application scheme was introduced when Norway joined the European Single Market in 1994, and the Norwegian LO was the driving force behind the establishment. The General Application Act, gives a tripartite committee the authority to decide that all businesses in the relevant industry will be bound by the wage rates in the applicable collective agreement. Both the trade unions and the employers' organizations can call for general application of a collective agreement, but all calls have so far come from the trade unions, although supported by employer organizations in some cases. This can therefore be regarded as a strategy that is mainly used by the unions. General application in a Norwegian context is limited to situations where such regulation is necessary for ensuring that foreign workers' wages and working conditions are equal to those of Norwegian workers, and for preventing distortion of competition to the detriment of the Norwegian labour market (Alsos and Eldring, 2008). The first decision was made in this regard in connection with the EU's eastward enlargement in 2004, and since then several decisions have followed. In 2021, the extension of minimum wages in nine industry-level agreements is in force.

The way that the nationwide industry-level collective agreements regulate wages in the Scandinavian labour markets varies, and there are different agreements and different unions for blue- and white-collar workers. Traditionally, a distinction is made between minimum-wage agreements, normal wage agreements, and so-called figureless agreements (Alsos et al., 2019). The minimum-wage agreements set a minimum level that the parties cannot deviate from, which can be regarded as the absolute wage floor. The agreements further stipulate that increments shall be negotiated in addition to these minimum wages and often on the basis of criteria related to productivity and the financial situation in the individual companies. As a result, the wage level in many of the industries with minimum-wage agreements is significantly higher than the minimum-wage floor, especially in companies with strong unions. Normal-wage agreements reflect the actual wage level. Here, the parties do not have the opportunity to agree on a wage that is higher or lower. In Norway, some of the minimum-wage agreements, particularly in the low-wage sectors, resemble normal-wage agreements because weak local unions or tradition mean there are few negotiations at a local level (Grytli and Stokke, 1998). The figureless agreements have no fixed wage levels, only rules for wage setting through local or individual negotiations. Such agreements are particularly common in well-paid white-collar occupations, and have little significance for the regulation of low wages.

The agreements bind both the companies and the workers who are members of the organizations that are parties to the agreement (Hotvedt et al., 2020). In addition, employers have a duty to treat those with and without union representation equally, and ensure that non-union workers' conditions are no better or worse than others. In companies that practice collective bargaining, therefore, the wage setting will apply to everyone within the relevant occupational groups (Hotvedt et al., 2020).

As collective bargaining coverage is low in some industries, there is potentially a large proportion of workers who are not covered by the minimum-wage rates, including in low-wage industries. Traditionally, this problem has been remedied by the normative effect of the collective agreement. This means that even companies that are not formally bound by collective agreements nevertheless apply the wage rates in the agreements as the going rate in the industry (Hällberg and Kjellström, 2020; Alsos et al., 2021). However, this effect has been put to the test for the last 15 years. Workers who are willing to, or are facing a lack of other alternatives, take work that pays less than the minimum-wage rates in the collective agreement, and companies that do not generally adhere to these rates, have undermined the normative effect in individual industries (Alsos et al., 2021).

The front-runner models and solidaristic wage policy

Wage negotiations are closely coordinated in all of the three countries in order to ensure that wage growth does not exceed the wage growth of the international trading partners, while at the same time seeking to maintain the equilibrium in the labour market (Andersen et al., 2014; Nergaard et al., 2016; Vartiainen, 2011). These front-runner models are based on economic models that were adopted in the Nordic countries in the 1950s and 1960s. Small and open economies, such as those of the Nordic countries, are dependent on wage increases in the exposed sector not rising more than in competing countries, unless this can be justified by productivity gains. Meanwhile, the wage growth in the sheltered sector (industries not exposed to international competition) must not exceed that of the exposed sector, as this can lead to an internal struggle for labour that drives wages up. In practice, this is resolved by the exposed industries bargaining first and setting a norm for how much wage growth the sector can withstand. Prior to this bargaining round, the confederation set an objective that should be followed, thus requiring relatively strong and centralized peak-level organizations (OECD, 2019). Once these front runners have reached agreement, industry parties in other collective bargaining areas enter into negotiations, and under an (informal) obligation of not exceeding the norm already set. To ensure success in this coordination, both the social partners and the governments have established various institutional systems that underpin the models. The systems vary between the countries, but state mediation facilities and common understanding or agreement between the parties are central in all countries (Nergaard et al., 2016).

One of the main goals of the front-runner model is to secure jobs in the domestic labour market. This explains why trade unions support the model – they may not receive the maximum wage increase based on their bargaining power in the short term, but they are setting the framework for companies to be competitive. Furthermore, the model helps restrain wage growth among white-collar workers with extensive bargaining power and to pull groups with low bargaining power up to a higher wage level than they could manage on their own. The latter in particular is crucial to ensuring a decent low wage and is an important reason for such a model also gaining support among low-wage unions. By being the first to the negotiating table and setting the norm, the strong industry unions drag unions that would otherwise not be able to achieve a corresponding wage increase. This can be regarded as a result of the solidaristic wage policy that is particularly found among unions that are members of LO and FH, the main confederations for blue-collar workers.

The solidaristic wage policy can also represent a paradox. High wage growth in industries with low productivity could lead to these jobs disappearing. While this reduces the extent of low wages, it can also represent a barrier to some groups entering the labour market (Calmfors et al., 2019; Konjunturinstitutet, 2014).[3] However, the unions have been willing to take this risk in the knowledge that the transition to new work is supported by good income guarantee schemes and an active labour market policy, dating back to the 1950s and 1960s in Sweden (Elvander, 1988). As part of this, the unions also accepted that wages in industries with low productivity were too high for businesses to be competitive and indirectly accepted the movement of capital and jobs to other, more profitable industries. This illustrates the close relationship between income policy, wage formation, active labour market measures, and the universal welfare state in the Nordic countries (Andersen et al. 2014; Dølvik, 2013).

The manufacturing industry unions, where density rates and collective bargaining coverage are among the highest, have been able to flex their institutional muscles to negotiate wage increments that benefit workers in low-wage industries. This is done through nominal rather than percentage increases, and through agreements without local wage formation or industries with low average wages receiving a higher increase than others. Another component is that the wage bargaining is often based on forecast price growth, and is aimed at securing sustained purchasing power as a minimum. This ensures that the real wage level normally is maintained for all groups whose wages are determined by the bargaining (Alsos and Nergaard, 2018).

The absence of discussions about a living wage in the Scandinavian countries can partly be seen as a consequence of the countries having far lower wage differences than other comparable countries. The differences between the highest paid (D9) and the lowest paid (D1) are below 2.5 in all these countries. This is considerably lower than the Netherlands (3.1), Germany (3.8), and the UK (3.8) (2014 figures[4]). Compared to other countries, the Scandinavian countries have compressed wages, and lowest-paid workers have a relatively high wage level. This is also confirmed in comparisons of the relationship between minimum wages negotiated in collective agreements and average wages, which show that minimum rates in industry agreements in low-wage sectors are at least 60 per cent of the national mean wage (Alsos et al., 2019; Hällberg and Kjellström, 2020). The Swedish National Mediation Office reports that only 1 per cent of Swedish workers' wages are below 60 per cent of the national median wage (2018 figures, Hällberg and Kjellström, 2020). In parallel with this, the unions and the employers' organizations both strongly endorse the view that wage formation is the responsibility of the social partners (NOU 2013: 13; Ahlberg and Bruun, 2017).

Low-wage guarantees through collective bargaining

Among the Nordic countries, Norway has the lowest unionization rate and the poorest coverage of collective agreements. It is therefore reasonable to assume that the use of collective agreements and collective wage bargaining as a regulatory instrument is weaker in Norway than in neighbouring countries. Still (or perhaps therefore), the aim to increase the lowest wages is high on the agenda for the blue-collar-dominated confederation LO as well as for its affiliated unions. This is reflected in its demands and priorities in the collective bargaining negotiations, and its inclusion of income guarantee provisions in the collective agreements (LO Norge, 2021).

Although the desire to increase the lowest wages is a shared goal of LO and the affiliated trade unions, the focus on this is greatest in industries with significant low-wage challenges. In this section, we will show how trade unions in different industries have adopted different strategies to raise the lowest wages and to ensure a minimum wage that will provide an acceptable standard of living.

In order to explain sector differences, we look into two industries (collective agreements) without government intervention in the form of general application, and three industries with government intervention (general application). To illustrate the challenges and measures, we have included industries that have not traditionally been considered low-wage industries (construction) and industries that have had varying degrees of low-wage

Table 10.2 Characteristics of traditional blue-collar workers, office workers, and service personnel (ISCO-08 level 4–9). Norway 2018

	Unionization rate (per cent)	Collective agreement coverage (per cent)	Type of collective agreement	Employees with immigrant background (per cent)	Employees in part-time work (per cent)
Food industry (NACE 10)	50	77	Minimum-wage agreement	37	18
Construction (NACE 41, 43)	27	35	Minimum-wage agreement	24	6
Retail (NACE 47)	23	32	Minimum-wage agreement	15	63
Industrial cleaning (NACE 81.2)	33	54	Normal-wage agreement	74	42
Hospitality sector (NACE 55-56)	18	28	Normal-wage agreement until 2016	44	53

Source: Fafo (for this chapter), based on administrative data.

challenges over a long period, including industries with low union density and many workers with immigrant background (industrial cleaning) and young workers (retail trade and the hospitality sector). The industries cover collective agreements with different types of wage rates (normal-wage agreements and minimum-wage agreements). See Table 10.2 for details.

Norway has no universally accepted definition of low-wage thresholds, or what is seen as an acceptable wage level. In the private sector, agreements with an average wage level below 90 per cent of the manufacturing sector average (blue-collar workers) are described as low-wage sectors.[5] In Table 10.3 below minimum wages in the four sectors in 2018 are listed. For comparison, various measures for low-wage/minimum-wage indicators are included. Figures are given in national currency as well as adjusted for variation in purchasing power across countries.

Food industry – augmented minimum-wage rise

The Norwegian food industry has minimum-wage agreements where it is assumed that additional increments will be negotiated locally. The wage level varies somewhat between the underlying industries (subsectors), but is generally below the national average for the manufacturing sector as a whole. The food industry also includes businesses that are low paid in the traditional sense, that is, companies or subsectors where the wage level is well below the average for the manufacturing sector as a whole. This may be due to the fact that the company-level trade unions have little bargaining power or that other factors make it difficult to get support for raising the wage level in company-level (local) negotiations.

There are two different mechanisms that counteract low wages in the food industry. First, as in other low-paid industries, the workers will benefit from the low-wage profile negotiated through the front-runner model. In cases where bargaining takes place across industries, including in the second year of the agreement period, the parties will agree to

Table 10.3 Minimum wage rates in various industries and individual rates for comparison. Norway 2018

	Currency	National currency	Adjusted for PPP	
Minimum wage, construction (unskilled, with 1 year's experience in the industry)	NOK	183.10	12.6	General application
Minimum wage, food industry	NOK	180.70	12.5	Bargaining
Minimum wage, retail (pay grade 1)	NOK	157.53	10.9	Bargaining
Minimum wage, retail (pay grade 6)	NOK	199.97	13.8	Bargaining
Minimum wage, cleaning	NOK	181.43	12.5	General application
Minimum wage, hotels and resturants, nationwide agreements (20 years or 18 years with at least 4 months experience in the industry)	NOK	167.90	11.6	General application
Comparison basis				
German minimum wage per 1 January 2019	EURO	9.19	8.6	Statutory
UK minimum wage (25 years) 2018	GBP	7.83	7.4	Statutory
UK London Living Wage 2018	GBP	10.55	9.9	Recommended
90% of blue-collar wage in manufacturing (Norway) 2018	NOK	245		Bargaining
60% of median wages (Norway) 2018	NOK	152.12	10.49	(EU recommendation)
50% of mean wage (Norway) 2018	NOK	140.34	9.68	(EU recommendation)

Source: Statistics Norway – Statbank: Purchasing power parities, price level indices and real expenditures.

Note: Purchasing power parities per 2018 (EU27 = 1). Based on household consumption.

a low-wage increment for workers in collective agreements with an average wage level of less than 90 per cent of the average industrial worker's wage (see Table 10.3).

Second, the agreements include guarantee schemes that are intended to ensure that the average wage of individual companies or the industry keeps pace with the wage development of the metal industry. Following an agreement on a new minimum-wage guarantee in 2010, the minimum wages in the food and beverage industry as a whole will be at least 85 per cent of the average wage in the food industry as a whole. The minimum wage will be adjusted annually in line with this principle. The industry has thus (in practice) replaced the traditional low-wage increments with an individual minimum-wage guarantee. The trade union for food industry workers considers this a more effective and appropriate measure to counteract low-wage schemes because it raises the wage level of individuals.[6] Experience has also shown that the lowest-paid workers have received significant pay rises through this model. However, in some cases it is more difficult to achieve additional increases locally because the automatic annual adjustments eat up some of the budget that could have been available for local wage bargaining. In businesses and/or subsectors with high numbers of low-wage earners, the scheme has thus affected the equilibrium between local- and central-level bargaining.

Retail – prioritizing those with a stable connection to the industry

As in many other countries, shop workers are considered a low-wage group in Norway. The industry has a high proportion of part-time workers as well as young workers, including students and pupils in higher secondary education (Jensen and Nergaard, 2017). However, the low-wage challenges also apply to most workers in the sector. As mentioned, living wage campaigns are almost unheard of in the Nordic countries, but the retail trade is one of the industries that has bucked the trend. The Norwegian term for a living wage, *ei lønn å leve av*, was coined by the first female leader of the Norwegian Union of Commerce and Office Employees (HK) in the early 1990s, and was used as a rallying cry for gender equality (Fjellvik, 2008).

The collective agreement for shop workers is a minimum-wage agreement that allows for local bargaining, but these play a far less important role than in manufacturing. The industry has a low unionization rate and low collective agreement coverage, which means that local union representation is often thin on the ground (see Table 10.2). The wage rates and other types of increments agreed in the nationwide collective agreement are therefore important for the wage level in the industry, which is reinforced by the fact that many businesses without a collective agreement adhere to these rates Alsos et al., 2021).

Since 1990, the collective agreement for the retail trade has included a guarantee scheme to ensure that the minimum-wage rates in the agreement do not lag behind. This is done by calculating a guarantee increment based on an assumption that the highest rate (pay grade 6) should be at least 92 per cent of the mean wage in the sector.[7] Based on these calculations, a sum (wage pot) is available for distribution by the parties at central level. Unless the parties agree otherwise, the available funds should be applied to the highest minimum-wage rate, and this is what normally happens.

The negotiations in the retail trade reflect some of the strategic choices that the social partners must make in an industry characterized by part-time workers and a high turnover. The parties must agree on whether increases are applied to the lowest rates, thereby benefiting the youngest workers, who are often working part-time in addition to studying, or whether they should prioritize raising the minimum wage for those who have a firmer connection to the industry and who are more likely to be union members. In retail, it seems as if HK has chosen to prioritize the latter group, and especially those at the top of the ladder (75 per cent of shop workers are paid in this grade 6 or higher). This rate has not only increased the most in absolute terms but also as a percentage. From the employer's side, however, there is some dissatisfaction with this because the wage differences between more experienced workers and managers are too small (Olberg and Oldervoll, 2018). The employers also point out that the guarantee scheme, where the minimum wages are adjusted upwards annually, means that there is little scope for local negotiation.[8]

Construction – emergence of low wages in an industry with no tradition of low-wage challenges

The construction industry has not traditionally been considered a low-wage industry in Norway. The industry is male dominated, with full-time positions, and the average wage level is above average for industrial workers.[9] Although the unionization rate and collective agreement coverage historically have been lower than in manufacturing, the wage rates in the collective agreements have also had an effect on the non-unionized part of the industry. This changed in 2004 when the EU expansion led to significant labour immigration from the new EU countries in Eastern Europe. Many of these workers secured jobs in construction, either directly in Norwegian construction firms, through temporary work agencies, or with subcontractors who only, or mainly, employed immigrants (Arnholtz et al., 2018). It quickly became clear that the wages of these migrant workers were not only below the industry standard, but also in some cases far below the minimum-wage rates in the collective agreement. This mainly applied to firms without a collective agreement (Eldring et al., 2011).

In 2004, LO demanded general application of the wage rates in the collective agreement for construction, and the agreement became one of the first with generally applied minimum-wage rates in the Norwegian labour market. Government intervention in the form of general application is now a permanent feature in the construction sector and has affected the bargaining strategies in the industry. In recent years, the trade unions have placed greater emphasis on raising the minimum-wage rates through bargaining. This led to a strike in 2010, where the main demand was a significant increase in the minimum wage. Paradoxically, increasing minimum wages has a direct effect only on a minority of the union's members, as most earn well above the minimum wage. However, it indirectly improves the competitiveness of businesses with collective agreements, in that they are not outcompeted by businesses that only pay the minimum wage.

Cleaning and hospitality – industries with little regulatory capacity through collective institutions

The general application approach has also been adopted in order to establish a wage floor in parts of the service sector, including the cleaning industry (from 2011) and the hospitality sector (from 2018). Many of the workers in these industries have an immigrant background, and the hospitality sector also has a high proportion of young workers. In both industries, wage levels have mainly been set centrally, without any local bargaining. Large parts of the workforce work in businesses without a collective agreement (see Table 10.2).

In contrast to the construction industry, cleaning and hospitality are traditional low-wage industries where guarantee schemes and special low-wage allowances have been used for a number of years by the unions as a way of supplementing members' wages. The allowances have been more or less evenly distributed. That is, the goal has been for all groups to benefit, and these schemes have helped ensure that average wages in the industries do not lag further behind the average for manufacturing. Nevertheless, it has proved difficult to strengthen these low-wage occupations relative to, for example, manufacturing sector averages.[10]

However, it was the situation in the non-unionized part of the industries that led to the general application of collective agreements. In both industries, reports of low wages in businesses with a high proportion of migrant workers led to calls for general application of wage rates. In the cleaning industry, the main Employers' organization also supported this. Studies show that general application has pushed up wages both in cleaning (Trygstad et al., 2012; Bjørnstad, 2015; Jordfald and Svarstad, 2020) and in hotels and restaurants (Ødegård et al., 2020). Migrant workers are overrepresented among those whose wages have increased following general application (the hospitality sector and cleaning). Still, there are reports of some negative effects for the workers, for example, that cleaners have less time on each assignment and therefore need to work at a faster pace (Trygstad et al., 2012, 2018b).

Discussion

Wages and the problem of low wages are the responsibility of the social partners

The voluntarist principle that wages are the responsibility of the social partners is strong in the Nordic countries, and the question of a government-determined minimum wage has never been seriously discussed. In essence, there is agreement between the trade unions and the employers' organizations that the government will keep an arm's length approach to wage setting (Andersen et al., 2014). This means that the social partners, particularly the trade unions, have assumed a responsibility to ensure an acceptable wage floor. The assessment of what constitutes an acceptable wage floor is not primarily related to what is needed to cover necessary expenses or ensure a certain standard of living; there are other underlying principles. The wage level should facilitate a fair distribution of profits between the employees and employers (fairness), the wage differences should help minimize inequality in society (equality), and through their collective bargaining power, the unions want to raise the wages of the lowest paid (solidarity). Although the unions' wage policy is also based on other principles, these are the ones that mainly facilitate the establishment of a minimum-wage floor that ensures a living wage. A wage policy of this nature also has a bearing on businesses' scope for manoeuvrability; strong trade unions in combination with a low-wage policy mean that employers have little opportunity to increase their competitiveness through reducing wage costs. Consequently, industries and companies that are unable to support the wage level set through bargaining between the social partners will be phased out.

The unions' approach to ensuring a low-wage profile is closely linked to the collective bargaining model where industries that are exposed to international competition establish a financial framework for wage settlements, which is then followed by other industries. While this approach maintains the level for the highest paid and pulls the lowest paid up, it also makes it difficult to change relative differences between industries and occupations: wages in low-wage industries are increased to the same degree as others, but large increases beyond this can be difficult to achieve. This has particularly been regarded as a barrier to public-sector unions whose members are predominantly women (who are not necessarily low paid in the traditional sense), in their efforts to reduce the pay gap between educational groups in both the private and public sector.[11]

Although all of the countries have moved towards a more decentralized wage formation in the last 20–30 years, parts of the wage formation is still centralized in all three countries. A key principle for many collective agreements is that the local social partners must bargain for local increments based on the principle that prosperous businesses should have higher local wage growth than businesses that are not faring so well. Meanwhile, signals from the central organizations ensure that local wage formation does not undermine the macroeconomic principles of wage formation.

Instruments need to be developed in a changing labour market

In the Nordic countries, the wage floor has been set and raised through the profile of wage settlements; nominal increases or other methods that give a higher percentage increase for the lowest paid; extra increments for those who do not bargain at the local level or who have a particularly low average wage; and various types of guarantee provisions stipulated in the nationwide collective agreements, including minimum-wage rates (Alsos and Nergaard, 2018). In addition, the industry-level collective agreements often have provisions that influence pay level, including supplements for overtime and unsociable working hours.

In Norway and Sweden, unions with a high proportion of low-paid members have recently questioned how effective these measures are, including in relation to raising the lowest wages to reduce the relative wage differences. In Sweden, several unions have voiced concern with the model where the export industry sets an upper limit for wage increases, and have proposed an alternative model based on a wider set of indicators (Thonäng, 2019). In Norway, LO has been asked by affiliated unions to evaluate the effectiveness of the present low-wage increments as well as to consider alternatives. The report, which was presented in January 2021, stresses the importance of specific low-wage increments to prevent low-wage groups lagging behind (LO Norge, 2021). Several alternative models for distribution of wage increments are discussed, including distributing increments to companies or individuals with low wage levels.

Some unions, particularly in Sweden, have completely decentralized wage formation in an attempt to secure better wages locally than they achieve through coordinated wage formation. However, this strategy is not suitable for all unions, as it requires a certain amount of local bargaining power. The strategy can also be seen as a reaction to the fact that the rather rigid model for wage formation is not able to even out structural imbalances in wage levels between different groups.

The challenges – can the social partners also ensure an acceptable wage floor in the future?

So far, the models have been relatively successful in upholding the principles of fairness, equality, and solidarity, but some developments may represent a threat to this. First, the inequality between groups in the Scandinavian countries is growing, especially in relation to differences between capital owners and labour (Aaberge et al., 2020 with calculations for Norway). One area of discussion is how, in times of prosperity, a fair distribution can be ensured between capital and labour whilst simultaneously ensuring that wage growth does not exceed that of trading partners. This issue was particularly the subject of discussion in Norway in connection with the international financial crisis in 2008 and 2009, which affected Norway to a lesser extent. The result was that Norwegian businesses in some industries made a profit, while wage growth among trading partners remained low. In Sweden, Lars Calmfors and colleagues have raised the same issue, and question the basis of the Swedish model for wage formation where exposed industries set the framework based on wage growth among trading partners (Calmfors, 2018; Calmfors et al., 2019).

Furthermore, the gap between wage earners at the extreme ends of the wage distribution is increasing, especially in Denmark and Norway (Nergaard et al., 2016). Although inequality is still low in an international context, the trend is for greater differences. The exception here is Sweden, where the difference between the highest and the lowest paid remains stable. This may be related to the strength of the institutional instruments. Collective agreement coverage, particularly in parts of the private sector, is lower in Denmark and Norway than in Sweden. Furthermore, the differences are particularly increasing at the bottom of the wage distribution, which is an indication that the absence of comprehensive minimum-wage regulation makes it impossible to protect all workers (for Norway, see Jordfald and Nymoen, 2016).

However, the fact that some firms are not members of employers' organizations is not a new phenomenon in any of the countries. Kjellberg (2019) observes, for example, that only between 50 and 65 per cent of Swedish manufacturing companies are members of an employers' organization, and thereby automatically bound by a collective agreement. When the collective agreement coverage is much higher, measured by number of workers, this is mainly because the non-members are often small companies. In addition, there is extensive use of direct agreements (so-called 'carbon copy agreements'), where the companies sign a collective agreement with the trade union that is identical to the one the dominant employers' organization has entered into. Denmark and Norway also use the carbon-copy agreements system, but to a much lesser extent, especially in Norway. This is due to the fact that Norwegian trade unions lack the same strong instruments that Swedish (and to a certain degree Danish) trade unions can use to force a non-member company to enter into such an agreement (Lindberg et al., 2015).

In Norway, attempts have been made to counteract the shift towards a more fragmented minimum-wage floor, through the general application of minimum-wage rates in the collective agreements. This includes industries with low collective agreement coverage, such as cleaning and hotels and restaurants. This was considered a radical strategy in the beginning, but trade unions did not seem to find any other measures that could secure an effective wage floor. No similar instrument has been adopted in Denmark or Sweden, where there is even greater scepticism towards government intervention than in Norway. The traditional approach of binding the companies through collective agreements is still the rule in Denmark and Sweden, and while this is a successful strategy in Sweden, Denmark seems to find it more difficult to secure a decent minimum wage for all workers. Further growth in alternative unions without collective agreements could exacerbate these problems (see Ibsen, 2012 for this type of unions). The same applies to a situation where union strength and presence at the workplace declines in sectors or occupational groups where the low-wage challenges are prevalent (Andersen et al., 2014), or if we see the emergence of new types of businesses without a tradition for collective agreements or unionization.

A further decline in union membership rates and collective agreement coverage may lead to more low-paid workers. In such a scenario, it could be questioned why the Nordic trade unions are so sceptical about using a statutory minimum wage as a tool to combat low wages.

Are we going to see living wage campaigns in Scandinavia as well?

The minimum-wage floors in the Scandinavian countries are at a level that seems to be sufficient to qualify as a living wage. The challenge is primarily related to the ability to apply the wage floor to all workers. Although both Denmark and Norway have challenges in establishing such floors in some industries, there are no signs so far of the campaigns we have seen in other countries to introduce a living wage. This may partly be related to the belief that this issue will be resolved between the unions and employers' organizations or in the tripartite cooperation. As all of the countries have strong social partners on both sides, with ambitions to retain their regulatory competence, there is little scope for such movements to emerge within this system. It is therefore difficult to imagine that a campaign would have much momentum unless the parties' ability or willingness to function as described is weakened. Although all of the countries have experienced a negative development in membership numbers, this now seems to have stabilized. It therefore seems unlikely that the living wage will become an area of contention outside the collective bargaining system in the near future.

Notes

1   www.vg.no/nyheter/innenriks/i/yRR79A/tar-kampen-mot-minsteloenn-i-eu
2   One exception is certain cases in Denmark where one of the alternative trade unions has entered into agreements that the traditional unions consider to be below the industry standard (Caraker, 2013)
3   See, for example, the criticism of the Swedish pay structure RÅDETS REKOMMENDATION om Sveriges nationella reformprogram för 2012 och om avgivande av rådets yttrande om Sveriges konvergensprogram för 2012–2015, Bryssel, Europeiska Kommissionen, 2012.
4   https://ec.europa.eu/eurostat/documents/2995521/7766821/3-12122016-AP-EN.pdf/910ee81b-3d8f-43a5-aa14-745dc76bc670
5   The employer organizations will dispute this definition, but usually these collective agreements are given an extra low-wage increment.
6   Interviews with representatives for the union (central-level union officals).
7   I.e. wage statistics from retail sector members of the employer organization Virke.
8   https://frifagbevegelse.no/nyheter/virke-gar-til-angrep-pa-lonnsgarantien-for-butikkansatte-6.158.724827.c7d1c66547
9   Wage statistics for companies that are member of NHO.
10 According to a recent report from a working group in LO Norway, the main effect of these increments is to make sure that wage differentials between low-wage sectors and other sectors do not increase (LO 2021). The report stresses that this type of measure is an increasingly more important instrument in the wage negotiations.
11 This argument is in particular fronted by female-dominated unions among others for nurses, teachers, social workers, and so on. The tendency for the wage bargaining models to uphold or freeze relative wage levels is also discussed by researchers; see Nilsen and Schøne (2007) for Norway, and Jørgensen (2010) for Denmark. This issue is also discussed in the gender equality pay commissions that were set down in Norway (reported in 2008) and Denmark (reported in 2010).

References

Aaberge, R., Modalsli, J.H., and Vestad, O.L. (2020). *Ulikheten – betydelig større enn statistikken viser.* Oslo: SSB analyse 2020.

Ahlberg, K., and Bruun, N. (2017). 'Har det bästa blivit det godas fiende? Om försvaret av den svenska modellen', in Rönnmar, M. and Julén Votinius, J. (eds), *Festskrift till Ann Numhauser-Henning.* Lund: Juristförlaget i Lund.

Alsos, K., and Eldring, L. (2008). 'Labour mobility and wage dumping: The case of Norway.' *European Journal of Industrial Relations,* 14(4): 441–459.

Alsos, K., and Nergaard, K. (2018). *Lönebildningen i de skandinaviska länderna. Lönebildning för jämlikhet – nr 3.* Ett projekt av 6F – fackförbund i samverkan. Katalys No:64. Stockholm: Katalys/6F.

Alsos, K., Nergaard, K., and Svarstad, E. (2021). *Arbeidsgiverorganisering og tariffavtaler.* Fafo-rapport 2021:07.

Alsos, K., Nergaard, K., and Van Den Heuvel, A. (2019). 'Collective bargaining as a tool to ensure a living wage. Experiences from the Nordic countries.' *Transfer: European Review of Labour and Research,* 25(3): 351–366.

Andersen, S.K., Dølvik, J.E., and Ibsen, C.L. (2014). *Nordic labour market models in open markets,* Report 132. Brussels: ETUI.

Arnholtz J, Meardi G, and Oldervoll J. (2018). 'Collective wage bargaining under strain in northern European construction: Resisting institutional drift?' *European Journal of Industrial Relations,* 24(4): 341–356.

Bjørnstad, R. (ed.) (2015). *Virkninger av allmenngjøring av tariffavtaler.* Rapport nr. 2-2015. Senter for lønnsdannelse.

Calmfors, L. (2018). *Industrins lönenormering kan och bör reformeras. Lönebildning för jämlikhet – nr 4.* Ett projekt av 6F – fackförbund i samverkan. Katalys No:65. Stockholm: Katalys/6F.

Calmfors, L., Ek, S., Kolm, A.S., and Skedinger, P. (2019). *Kollektivavtal och lönebildning i en ny tid.* Stockholm: Dialogos.

Caraker, E. (2013). 'Kristelig Fagforening og aftalesystemet'. *Økonomi og Politik,* 86(1): 31–44.

Dølvik, J.E. (2013). *Grunnpilarene i de nodiske modellene. Et tilbakeblikk på arbeidslivs- og velferdsregimenes utvikling.* NorMod 2030. Delrapport 1. Fafo-Rapport 2013: 13.

Dølvik, J.E., and Marginson P. (2018). 'Cross-sectoral coordination and regulation of wage determination in northern Europe: Divergent responses to multiple external pressures'. *European Journal of Industrial Relations,* 24(4): 409–425.

Eldring, L., and Alsos, K. (2012). *European minimum wage: A Nordic outlook.* Fafo-report 2012:16.

Eldring, L., Ødegård, A.M., Andersen, R.A., Bråten, M., Nergaard, K., and Alsos, K. (2011). *Evaluering av tiltak mot sosial dumping.* Fafo-rapport 2011:09.

Elvander, N. (1988). *Den svenska modellen löneförhandlingar och inkomstpolitik: 1982–1986.* Stockholm: Allmänna förlaget.

Eurostat (2016). *Structure of earnings survey: How are earnings distributed in the EU. Differences across Member States and economic activities.* Newssrelease 248/2016. https://ec.europa.eu/eurostat/documents/2995521/7766821/3-12122016-AP-EN.pdf/910ee81b-3d8f-43a5-aa14-745dc76bc670

Fjellvik, E. (2008). *HK 100 år.* Oslo: Handel og Kontor i Norge.

Furåker, B. (2020). 'The issue of statutory minimum wages: Views among Nordic trade unions.' *Economic and Industrial Democracy,* 41(2): 419–435.

Grytli, T., and Stokke, T.Aa. (1998). *Norges største tariffavtaler: Omfang, lønnsdannelse og arbeidstidsordninger.* Fafo-notat 1998:03.

Hällberg, P., and Kjellström. C. (2020). *Collective agreements and minimum wages A report from the Swedish National Mediation Office.* Stockholm: Swedish National Mediation Office.

Hotvedt, M.J., Munkholm, N.V., Pind, D.A., Westregård, A. Ylhäinen, M., and Alsos, K. (2020). *The future of Nordic labour law. Facing the challenges of changing labour relations.* Report from: The future of work: Opportunities and challenges for the Nordic models. TemaNord 2020:534.

Ibsen, C.L. (2012). *Trade Unions in Denmark.* Berlin: Friedrich-Ebert-Stiftung.

Jensen, R.S., and Nergaard, K., (2017). *Varehandelen som inkluderingsarena. Rekruttering, opplæring og arbeidstrening.* Fafo-rapport 2017:25.

Jordfald, B. (2018). *Lønnsfordeling i privat sektor. Bygg og HORECA.* Fafo-rapport 2018:19.

Jordfald, B. and Nymoen, R., (2016). *Hva skjer nederst i lønnsfordelingen i privat sektor?* Rapport nr 8-2016. Senter for lønnsdannelse.

Jordfald, B., and Svarstad, E. (2020). *Renholderes lønnsbetingelser før og etter allmenngjøring. Privat og offentlig sektor.* Fafo-rapport 2020:13.

Jørgensen, H. (2010). *Forhandlingssystemet i det offentlige og ligelønnen.* CARMA-Center for Arbejdsmarkedsforskning, Aalborg Universitet.

Kjellberg, A. (2019). *Kollektivavtalens täckningsgrad samt organisationsgraden hos arbetsgivarförbund och fackförbund.* Studies in Social Policy, Industrial Relations, Working Life and Mobility 2019. Lund: Department of Sociology, Lund University.

Konjunkturinstitutet (2014). *Lönebildningsrapporten 2014.* Stockholm: Konjunkturinstitutet.

Landsorganisasjonen i Norge (LO) (2021). *Lavlønnsmodeller.* Oslo: LO.

Lindberg, H.M., Karlson, N., and Grönbäck, J. (2015). *Ultima ratio: svenska konfliktregler i ett internationellt perspektiv.* Stockholm: Iustus.

Nergaard, K. (2020). *Organisasjonsgrader, tariffavtaledekning og arbeidskonflikter 2018/2019.* Fafo-notat 2020:12.

Nergaard, K., Alsos, K., and Seip, A.A. (2016). *Koordinering av lønnsdannelsen innen de nordiske frontfagsmodellene.* Fafo-notat 2016:25.

Nilsen, K.M., and Schøne, P. (2007). *Den norske forhandlingsmodellen i et likelønnsperspektiv.* Rapport 2007:5, Oslo: Institutt for Samfunnsforskning.

NOU (2013). *Lønnsdannelsen og utfordringer for norsk økonomi.* Oslo: Finansdepartementet.

Ødegård, A.M., Andersen, R.K., Jordfald, B., Nergaard, K., and Trygstad, S.C. (2020). *Utelivsbransjen – utvikling i arbeidsforhold etter 2014.* Fafo-rapport 2020:26.

OECD (2019). *Negotiating Our Way Up: Collective Bargaining in a Changing World of Work.* OECD Publishing, Paris.

Olberg, D., and Oldervoll, J. (2018). *Landsoverenskomsten HK-Virke – bestemmelser og bruk.* Fafo-notat 2018:07.

Schulten T., and Müller T. (2019). 'What's in a name? From minimum wages to living wages in Europe'. *Transfer: European Review of Labour and Research*, 25(3): 267–284.

Schulten, T., and Müller, T. (2017). 'Living wages – normative und ökonomische Gründe für einen angemessenen Mindestlohn'. *WSI Mitteilungen*, (7): 507–514.

Thonäng, K.A. (2019). *6Fs förslag på ny lönebildningsmodell. Lönebildning för en ny tid Lönebildning för jämlikhet – nr 8* Ett projekt av 6F – fackförbund i samverkan. Katalys No:73. Stockholm: Katalys/ 6F.

Tijdens, K., and van Klaveren, M. (2007). *Collective bargaining coverage*, WIBAR Report No. 5. Collective bargaining coverage 12/06/2007 Post-conference Update https://wageindicator. org/documents/publicationslist/WIBARCBC/@@download/file/WIBAR-CBC-final.pdf

Trygstad, S.C., Andersen, R., Jordfald, B., and Nergaard, K. (2018b). *Renholdsbransjen sett nedenfra.* Fafo-rapport 2018:26.

Trygstad, S.C., Andersen, R., Hagen, I.M., Nergaard, K., Nicolaisen, H., and Steen, J.R. (2014). *Arbeidsforhold i utelivsbransjen* Fafo-rapport 2014:02.

Trygstad, S.C., Bråten, M., Nergaard, K., and Ødegård, A.M. (2012). *Vil tiltakene virke? Status i renholdsbransjen 2012.* Fafo-rapport 2012:59.

Trygstad, S.C., Larsen, T.P., and Nergaard, K. (2018a). 'Dealing with austerity and migration in the northern European cleaning sector: Social partner strategies to strengthen wage floors'. *European Journal of Industrial Relations*, 24(4): 373–389.

Vartiainen, J. (2011). 'Nordic collective agreements: a continuous institution in a changing economic environment'. In Mjøset, L. (ed), *The Nordic varieties of capitalism. Comparative social research*; v. 28. Bingley: Emerald Group Publishing Ltd., 331–363.

11 The living wage, Fight for $15, and low-wage worker campaigns in the US

Stephanie Luce

Introduction

The term 'living wage' has been around for more than a hundred years and has regained popularity and importance in countries around the world as inequality and working poverty have risen. A 'living wage' in the broad sense is a wage high enough for a worker to support themselves and a family to have a decent life.

Yet in practice, there are many variations in how the term is used and applied by country and campaign. In the US, some use the term 'living wage' in connection to hourly wages set through a formula based on assumptions about geography and family size and type (Luce 2017). In many parts of the country the 'living wage' for a worker with a family is far above the statutory minimum wage. For that reason, 'living wage' has also been used in campaigns to suggest a target wage higher than the minimum. For example, municipal 'living wage' campaigns in the past few decades fought for hourly wages of $10, $12, and then $15 per hour. These were higher than the statutory minimum wage but mostly lower than a true 'living wage'. Unlike other living wage amounts, these are not set by a formula.

'Living wage' campaigns in the US differ from most in the UK and Canada as they aim to set compulsory wage standards for employers. They are city, county, or state laws that mandate a wage floor. This is different from the voluntary living wages that allow employers to opt in or out.

Living wage campaigns

The US federal minimum wage was established as part of the Fair Labor Standards Act in 1938. Before then, a handful of states had passed state-wide minimum-wage laws, starting with Massachusetts in 1912, but many of those applied only to women and children, and some were struck down by courts.

The 1938 federal bill set a wage standard of 25 cents per hour and covered most, but not all, workers. The amount was selected through political negotiation rather than set by a formula. There is no methodology behind it, and it takes an Act of Congress to raise it. This happened somewhat regularly for several decades, but the minimum wage peaked in real value in 1966, then fell steadily in the 1970s and 1980s.

By the early 1990s, the real value of the federal minimum wage was far below what was needed for a worker with a family to support themselves. Pastors and union leaders in Baltimore, Maryland, launched a municipal 'living wage campaign' demanding the city raise its minimum wage to an amount high enough for a worker to meet the federal

DOI: 10.4324/9781003054078-11

poverty guidelines for a family of three. The Mayor argued that the city had no authority to set a citywide wage but agreed to an ordinance that would mandate any business working for the city to pay its employees the living wage.

This idea spread quickly around the country, and over 140 cities and counties passed versions of living wage ordinances by the time the economic crisis hit in 2008 (Luce 2017). The movement slowed considerably but not completely, laying some of the groundwork for the upsurge in wage campaigns to come, starting in 2012.

Higher wages today?

The US federal government last raised the national minimum wage in 2007, under President George W. Bush, just before the economic crisis. That increased the rate in phases, from $5.85 per hour in 2007 to $7.25 by July 2009. The federal rate has remained at $7.25 since that time. However, the federal rate sets a lower rate for employees known as 'tipped workers'. That hourly rate minima is $2.13 per hour, with an assumption that tips will make up the difference to raise their wage to $7.35. These include occupations such as food servers, bartenders, parking lot attendants, and some barbershop, beauty salon, and hotel employees. Employers are required by law to make up the difference if tips are not enough to reach the minimum.

Advocates now hope to raise the federal minimum wage to $15 per hour. In January 2021, president-elect Joe Biden announced a federal pandemic stimulus package that included a $15 per hour minimum wage, as well as the elimination of the lower rate for tipped workers. The Senate Parliamentarian ruled that Biden could not raise the federal minimum wage via a stimulus package so the proposal was dropped, and re-introduced as legislation in the House and Senate, as the Raise the Wage Act of 2021, which would raise the wage to $15 over six years. The Democrats control the House of Representatives and have a slim majority in the Senate, but two Democratic Senators oppose the $15 an hour measure at this time. Even if all 50 Democratic Senators were in favour of the legislation, they do not have enough votes to override a Republican filibuster.

Biden's bold proposal on the higher wage stands in contrast to the Obama administration. In his campaign for the presidency, Barack Obama promised to raise the minimum wage. But when he assumed office in 2009, with Democrats in control of the House and Senate, they failed to pass a minimum-wage increase, citing the global recession and weak economy as a need to hold off.

States can set their own minimum wage rates and regulations. Nineteen states have minimum wage rates higher than the federal, reaching up to $13.50 in Washington State. On November 3, 2020, Florida voters approved a constitutional amendment that will raise their state minimum wage from $8.56 an hour to $15 an hour by 2026. The measure passed with 60.8 per cent of the vote. A number of these states have indexed their state rates to include inflation, so the rate will increase annually with the cost of living. A handful of states also include 'tipped workers' in their state law, so that they are entitled to the same minimum wage as other workers.

Some states allow cities and counties to set their own minimum wage; others do not. As of 2020, more than 40 cities and counties had their own minimum wage laws. Most set a wage of $15.00 per hour, and most indexed to inflation, allowing some cities' minimum wages to rise to over $16.00 per hour. In 2020, at least two cities delayed scheduled wage increases due to the economic slowdown (University of California Berkeley Labor Center 2020).

The Fight for $15 campaign

In 2012, fast-food workers in New York City joined with community allies to picket outside fast-food chains demanding $15.00 an hour and union recognition for collective bargaining. At the time, the minimum wage in New York was still only $7.25 per hour. Consequently, The Fight for $15 campaign was born.

At the same time, on the other side of the country in Washington State, unions and supporters had been campaigning for a $15 minimum wage in the small city of SeaTac outside of Seattle. The measure was put on the ballot and voters approved it in November 2013. In June 2014, the city of Seattle approved a $15 per hour wage for all workers in the city (phased in over six years). The $15 per hour wage was close to a living wage for a single worker with no children in many locations at the time the campaign was launched, but the cost of living has been increasing while the demand has remained the same. Now, $15 is below the living wage for a single worker with no children in many large cities. For example, according to the MIT Living Wage Calculator, in 2020 a living wage rate for a single worker with no children in Seattle was $16.09, in Boston $16.74, in New York City $17.99, and in San Francisco $20.82 (Glasmeier 2020).

The Fight for $15 campaign was launched primarily by the Service Employees International Union, working in partnership with community groups in various locales. The campaign spread quickly across the country, and spread from fast-food workers to airport workers, home health aides, retail workers, adjunct professors, childcare workers, and more. Fight for $15 held several National Days of Action with strikes and rallies in the U.S. joined by fast-food workers from Brazil, Japan, and the UK in a global protest on May 15, 2014 (Franco 2017). The campaign spread internationally, and currently there are campaigns in over 300 cities in 60 countries (Pasquier et al. 2020).

The US campaign has called for '$15 and a union': a $15 per hour minimum wage and for workers to have the right to union recognition (Fight for $15 n.d.). To date, the campaign has not led to successful unionization of fast-food restaurants, primarily because the franchising system means that unionizing McDonald's or Burger King, for example, would have to happen one store at a time. A more likely approach is for the union to win a global framework agreement with a company, a practice more common in Europe. In 2017, labour organizers got New York City to pass the Fast Food Deductions Law that creates an infrastructure for fast-food employees to 'opt in' to a dues deduction programme to fund non-profit organizations fighting on their behalf (New York City n.d.). Under the new law, a new organization, Fast Food Justice, was formed and signed up over 1,200 fast-food workers who were willing to join the group and pledge $13.50 a month. In return, Fast Food Justice would advocate for higher minimum wages and issues such as 'affordable housing, immigration reform, better police-community relations and improvements to New York's subway system' (Greenhouse 2018). An employer's association filed legal challenges, arguing that the law violates restaurant owners' freedom of speech under the First Amendment, by requiring them to send a portion of worker wages to a worker's rights group. The law was eventually delayed in court and the organization is now moving forward to organize fast-food workers. They are working to pass new legislation in New York City that would protect fast-food workers from unfair firings, and that would require the restaurants to use seniority when laying off workers, such as in a recession.

Beyond $15 and union recognition, Fight for $15 has been working with Black Lives Matter and other racial justice groups to challenge structural racism and to show how economic and racial justice are interlinked (Tapia et al. 2017). Black workers make up a disproportionate share of low-wage workers, and many point out that fighting for higher wages is incomplete if we do not also address police brutality so that workers and their families are safe. 'What good is $15 an hour and a union if my daughter is murdered?' said Douglas Hall of Fight for $15. 'That money would have been nothing. There's a direct relation between these issues' (Moberg 2015). The groups have protested together over the past several years. After the police murder of George Floyd sparked uprisings in 2020, Fight for $15 groups participated in protests and supported the national Strike for Black Lives Matter.

Voluntary living wage increases

The UK voluntary living wage model has spread to the US. In 2018, United for a Fair Economy, a national non-profit based in Boston, helped launch the national Living Wage Network. Network partners set a living wage level and a process by which employers can apply to be certified as a living wage partner (Living Wage Network n.d.).

For example, the Tompkins County Worker Center in Ithaca, New York, uses a transparent methodology to set a living wage rate. As of 2019, it was $15.37 per hour. Over 129 employers in Boston are now accredited and committed to paying their employees this wage as a minimum. The employers include childcare centres, bookstores, churches, law firms, social services, and more (Tompkins County Worker Center 2020). The network includes seven partners, which are primarily geographic-based worker organizations. These include three living wage coalitions in North Carolina, and one each in Colorado, Massachusetts, New York State, and Virginia. Most of these organizations are in semi-rural areas or small towns.

The partners have certified over 2,500 small and medium-sized businesses as Living Wage Employers. Many of these have long paid higher wages because they say it is a better way to run their business. A manager at an assisted living facility in Bayfield, Colorado, explained why they pay a living wage: 'We have a low turnover of staff, which ensures our residents receive the best consistent care'. Other employers emphasize ethical reasons. Kathleen Tonnessen from the Manna Soup Kitchen said, 'We see firsthand what those less fortunate struggle with. It is for this reason we believe everyone deserves a living wage – so they can become self-sufficient' (Southern Ute Drum 2018).

Since the network was launched in 2018, it has not had much opportunity to grow, given the Covid-19 pandemic and the recession that hit in early 2020. However, a number of the partner groups had been certifying Living Wage Employers for several years before. For example, Durham Living Wage had certified 29 companies and 13 non-profits as Living Wage Employers by 2015. These companies employed almost 1,000 people. Durham Living Wage requires certified employers to pay 70 per cent above the state minimum wage to workers if no health insurance is provided, or 50 per cent above minimum wage if health insurance is provided. Employers must pay independent contractors almost double the minimum wage (Bridges 2015).

There are other companies that have voluntarily raised their floor wage in recent years, particularly due to pressure from protests and public campaigns. This includes Walmart, Target, Amazon, the Gap, and Starbucks. However, these companies do not participate in the certification programmes and are adopting higher wages on their own accord, not connected to a larger project. These wage floors have been set at rates ranging from $10 to $15 per hour.

Walmart first announced a voluntary wage increase in 2015, from the federal minimum wage of $7.25 to $9 per hour, amidst a wave of Fight for $15 protests that included Walmart as a target. In response, investors began selling Walmart stock. The price of Walmart shares dropped by 3.2 per cent. Share prices dropped further later that year when the company announced that higher wages would impact on profits. However, the company continued with the higher wage of $9 per hour and eventually raised it again, and expanded benefits. Doug McMillion, Walmart CEO, explained that the strategy of higher hourly rates paid off by reducing the retailer's high, and costly, turnover. That in turn seemed to help the company do a better job cleaning, stocking shelves, and improving check-out line speed. Customer ratings improved and sales rose. In 2018, Walmart raised entry pay to $11 per hour in response to public outcry after President Donald Trump pushed through a controversial tax law granting large cuts to major corporations (Debter 2018, Bowman 2018). In 2020, it announced raises to $15 for bakery and deli workers, two occupations more likely to be unionized in other stores and targeted by union organizers for years. The company said this was to test out a new organizational structure (Halkias 2020).

Also, in 2018, Amazon raised its minimum wage for all US employees (including temporary, part-time, and seasonal) to $15 per hour, impacting an estimated 350,000 workers. (At the same time, they raised their minimum wage in the UK to £9.50 per hour ($12.60), with higher rates in London). The move came amidst growing protests against the company for labour and environmental abuses, and after Senator Bernie Sanders introduced a bill in Congress called the Stop BEZOS Act, which would tax large employers whose employees relied on public benefits. Some analysts suspected Amazon's move was to dampen unionization efforts. Others noted the company increased wages just before the holiday season when it would need to hire over 100,000 seasonal workers in a tight labour market (Matsakis 2018). In either case, Amazon urged other companies to join them and noted they would begin lobbying Congress to support the $15 wage.

Impacts of living wage and minimum-wage organizing

Given this variety and diversity of campaigning, it is difficult to generalize the impact of each campaign to increase living wages. As highlighted, some employers have paid higher wages for years and claim it helps them retain skilled workers, provide better customer service, and maintain higher morale (Partnership for Working Families n.d.).

There have been a number of studies attempting to analyse the impact of the mandated wage increases in cities and states. There are myriad technical and data challenges to doing so, as no government data source is designed in a way that makes this easy. For example, the Current Population Survey has small sample sizes in most cities (Brenner et al. 2003). The American Community Survey also has limitations: it reports annual income rather than hourly wage, the data is released a year after it is collected, and wages are top-coded (US Census Bureau no date; Kinney and Karr 2017). Another challenge is that the larger wage minimum increases, such as in Seattle, were implemented while the local economies were growing. While the wage increases are significant to those impacted, they are small relative to the larger macroeconomic trends.

A few studies have explored the large wage increases in Seattle, Washington (which raised the wage from $9 per hour in 2014 to $15 in 2021). Researchers at the University of Washington concluded in 2017 that the Seattle law raised wages, but employers responded by cutting hours, resulting in a net loss for workers (Jardim et al. 2017). Critics argued that the methodology was flawed because it compared workers in the Seattle labour market to those in the rest of the state that had very different conditions (e.g. Dube 2017). The following year, the same University of Washington researchers released a new study with greater nuance, finding that the majority of workers covered benefited from the law, and only a small group (new labour market entrants) were worse off due to fewer hours (Jardim et al. 2018). Critics once again raised methodological concerns, including the flawed comparison group, and failure to include new labour market entrants and those employed by chains or multi-site businesses (Zipperer and Schmitt 2017; Zipperer 2018).

Studies by University of California, Berkeley researchers found that the Seattle law led to higher overall wages, without job losses (Reich et al. 2017; Allegretto et al. 2018). A team of economists analysed minimum-wage laws passed since 1979 and concluded that minimum-wage laws have resulted in reductions in the total numbers of low-wage jobs but an increase in jobs that pay above minimum wage, for no real net change in the number of jobs (Cengiz et al. 2018).

The wage increases can explain how some of these workers are now earning higher salaries and make them ineligible for public subsidies and tax credits (Pollin et al. 2008; Brenner and Luce 2005). Research evidence shows that most workers are still better off with the higher wage and have more control over how to spend their income rather than receiving some in the form of public programmes, such as food stamps. The raises in pay allow workers to pay off debt, perhaps quit a second job, and even develop some savings (Pollin et al. 2008).

It is difficult to estimate the total number of workers who have benefited from living wage movements, particularly as this depends on whether or not to include 'minimum wage' laws as well as higher living wages. In 2018, the National Employment Law Project estimated that 22 million low-wage workers had won annual wage increases since the Fight for $15 movement began in 2012 through to 2018 (National Employment Law Project 2018). The estimations for US pay rises amounted to $68 billion. Those figures do not include new legislation and raises that took place in 2019 and 2020. The Economic Policy Institute estimated that phasing in a federal minimum-wage increase to $15 by 2024 would impact over a quarter of the US workforce and provide $120 billion in wages to low-wage workers (Economic Policy Institute 2019).

The minimum-wage increases also appear to have impacted the low-wage labour market in a significant way. Though wage inequality continues to rise, average wages finally began to rise for workers in 2013 to 2019, particularly in states that had passed minimum-wage increases. Wages at the lowest tenth percentile grew by 17.6 per cent in that period for the 26 states and Washington, DC, that had experienced at least one minimum-wage increase. Even states without a minimum-wage increase saw a growth in pay of 9.3 per cent, suggesting the effects of a tighter labour market and perhaps spillover effects from the minimum-wage gains (Gould 2020). In the early years of recovery after the 2008 recession, wage growth was concentrated on higher-wage workers, but with the passage of state minimum-wage increases, low-wage workers began to experience the fastest growth (Casselman 2019).

Employment versus local and state labour laws

The increase in local and state wage laws is happening alongside an increase in other employment laws. Many of the organizations that have advocated living wage and minimum-wage laws have also campaigned for, and achieved in many places, other forms of employment laws, such as paid sick day ordinances, family and medical leave laws, and regulations that give more protections for workers regarding scheduling. These laws are part of a longer-term trend strategy to eradicate low pay. Galvin (2019) found that states began passing more state employment laws in the 1960s. Counties and cities followed. In his analysis of state laws from 1960 to 2014, he found the number of state employment laws quintupled.

The pace has continued since 2014. According to XPert HR, a human resource consulting firm, increasingly, employers must learn about local laws as well as federal and state (Webb-Ayer 2019). Some speculate that because worker advocates have been unable to win much at the federal level, their focus has turned to the local and state level and this will likely continue for a while (Deschenaux 2019). While local and state employment laws can provide gains to millions of low-wage workers in the US, at the same time, Galvin (2019) reminds us that many employment laws still fail to address the underlying problem of a power imbalance between employers and workers.

Employment laws seem to have arisen to try to patch the gaps left by labour law. Yet the way federal labour law is written, it pre-empts cities and states from doing more regarding local laws. It seems that increasingly employment laws are being designed to do exactly the kinds of things collective bargaining should have covered. In this way, employment law is just a stopgap, or work-around failed labour law. Galvin raises concerns about, 'the emergence of new employment laws at the subnational level designed to address the very same problems labour law no longer effectively addressed, but in different forms and through different mechanisms' (Galvin 2019: 81). In the end, the fundamental problem remains, that workers have unequal power and the laws cannot resolve such imbalances or inequalities of power.

Workers may be winning higher wages, but when the wage increase is voluntary, the employer can always rescind their promise or make other cuts that affect direct pay. For example, after pressure, Target Stores raised its entry wage to $15 an hour plus additional benefits (Target 2020). Some workers reported that Target reduced their workweek to below 30 contractual hours, making them ineligible for benefits (Boehm 2019). There is no systematic research on Target or the other similar sized large companies that voluntarily raised entry wages, but what is clear is that employers still have power to adjust wages and working conditions with little input from employees.

With stronger labour laws, workers might be able to form unions and engage in collective bargaining. This would be a strategy to secure better wages, along with securing minimum hours and benefits, through a contract. A union provides a grievance procedure so that workers are better able to enforce wage laws. Indeed, labour unions will push President Biden to pass labour law reform in the form of the Protecting the Right to Organize Act (also known as the PRO Act).

Another concern about the nature of city and state wage laws is that the outcome is a complex patchwork of pay regulation for minimum wage and living wage ordinances. Crafting local ordinances allows for some experimentation and adaptation to local context. But, at the same time, the vast patchwork of city and state laws can be confusing. In fact, some human resource agencies say they support stronger federal laws but object to the local laws because this requires companies to maintain more staff and devote more resources just to maintain local regulations that can change year to year and vary city by city. Conversely, workers may have a hard time keeping up with these change themselves, and if they happen to have multiple jobs, one in one city and one in another (or one private sector and one public), the laws will vary. The patchwork complexity of state and local ordinances is also harder to enforce.

Many living wage advocates understand the limitations of focusing only on single wage standards. This is why the Fight for $15 movement pushed for union recognition as well as the higher wage. So far, the campaign has not led to any success in unionization in any national chain fast-food restaurants. 'Restaurants and other food services' have a union density of only 1.9 per cent (Hirsch and Macpherson, 2003). In May 2017, the campaign achieved progress in New York City. The City Council passed a law requiring fast-food chains to develop payroll deduction programmes, where employees can opt to have a share of their wages go toward non-profit organizations that advocate on their behalf. These organizations must register with the city. The National Restaurant Association immediately filed a legal challenge, claiming the law violated the first amendment rights of employers. After several years in court, the most recent ruling has allowed the law to stand. There have been some union victories in association with Fight for $15 campaigns, though these are primarily smaller-scale, on-off, and not in fast-food chains. For example, some gig workers have joined the Fight for $15 movement, and in early 2020 a group of Instacart workers in Illinois voted to unionize with the United Food and Commercial Workers (Gurley 2020).

Living wages, federal jobs, and a basic income

We know that living wages benefit low-wage workers, but what about those without jobs, or those without regular hours of work? Recent presidential candidates Bernie Sanders and Elizabeth Warren, and current members of Congress Alexandria Ocasio-Cortez and Ed Markey, are among those who advocate for a $15 minimum wage, but also support other programmes that could benefit low-wage workers. For example, Ocasio-Cortez and Markey are co-authors of the Green New Deal Resolution, which states that it is the duty of the federal government to create a Green New Deal to 'create millions of good, high-wage jobs' (Ocasio-Cortez 2019). The jobs would be in infrastructure repair and development, clean public transit, and development of high-speed rail and electricity from renewable and zero-emissions power (Snaith 2020). Sanders proposed a federal jobs programme, even before the pandemic recession hit. His proposal was for the federal government to hire 25 million people so that everyone who wanted a job could get one that paid a living wage. This included 20 million people working on the Green New Deal, and 5 million in healthcare and early childhood education. A living wage was defined as $15 per hour plus health insurance.

Another presidential primary candidate, Andrew Yang, proposed a universal basic income grant, which he called a 'Freedom Grant'. Yang argued that technology changes would put one out of three people out of work in the coming 12 years and therefore a universal basic income of $1,000 per month for every adult was a better solution to a job market crisis. The mayor of Stockton, California, launched a small pilot basic income programme in 2018 that has shown promising results but is quite limited (125 recipients receive $500 per month) (Holder 2020). The living wage is completely compatible with a federal jobs programme. Many advocates tend to counterpose a jobs programme and living wage campaigns with a basic income proposal, but there is no reason they cannot be compatible as well. However, given the limited resources and budgets of both advocacy organizations and public budgets, it is difficult in practice to push for all three.

Conclusion

One reason living wage campaigns have been particularly popular compared to the other two alternatives of full employment policies and a basic income grant is that it is possible to win living wages at various levels: city, county, and state governments, as well as with individual employers. With Trump in the White House and Republicans controlling the Senate, it was impossible to win any gains for workers at the federal level. Many advocates have high hopes that the Biden administration will pass a $15 minimum wage. Polls show strong support for a higher minimum wage, with 70 per cent of all voters in favour of raising the minimum wage to an amount that would keep workers above the poverty line, and while only 48 per cent of Republican voters approved of a minimum-wage increase before the pandemic, recent polls show that support has soared to 62 per cent (Dunn 2021). Organizing campaigns will likely continue at both the local and state level. Advocates know that implementing a living wage can make a significant difference for low-wage workers who get the pay awards. At the same time, with tens of millions of people out of work, underemployed, and in precarious work, living wage campaigns will only succeed in the long term if they are able to win deeper structural changes that allow workers to win more power *vis-à-vis* employers.

References

Allegretto, S., Godoey, A., Nadler C., and Reich M. (2018). *The New Wave of Local Minimum Wage Policies: Evidence from Six Cities*. September 6. Berkeley, CA: Center on Wage and Employment Dynamics, University of California, Berkeley.

Boehm, E. (2019). 'Target Employees Won the 'Fight For $15' But Weren't Ready for the Trade-Offs'. *Reason*, October 21. https://reason.com/2019/10/21/target-15-bucks-per-hour-didnt-work-out/ Downloaded October 20, 2019.

Bowman, J. (2018). 'With Another Wage Hike, Walmart Doubles Down on an Effective Strategy'. *Motley Fool*, January 12. https://www.fool.com/investing/2018/01/12/walmart-raises-wages-again.aspx Downloaded June 2, 2021.

Brenner, M.D., and Luce, S. (2005). 'Living Wage Laws in Practice: The Boston, New Haven and Hartford Experiences'. Amherst, MA: Political Economy Research Institute.

Brenner, M.D., Wicks-Lim, J., and Pollin, R. (2003). 'Measuring the Impact of Living Wage Laws: A Critical Appraisal of David Neumark's How Living Wage Laws Affect Low-Wage Workers and Low-Income Families'. University of Massachusetts-Amherst: PERI Working Paper No. 43.

Bridges, V. (2015). 'Durham Living Wage Project Encourages, Promotes Employers That Pay More'. *The News and Observer*. March 26. www.newsobserver.com/news/local/counties/durham-county/article16377152.html Downloaded March 26, 2020.

Casselman, B. (2019). 'Why Wages Are Finally Rising, 10 Years after the Recession'. *New York Times*, May 2. www.nytimes.com/2019/05/02/business/economy/wage-growth-economy.html Downloaded February 5, 2020.

Cengiz, D., Dube, A., Lindner, A., and Zipperer, B. (2018). *The Effect of Minimum Wages on Low-Wage Jobs: Evidence from the United States Using a Bunching Estimator*. CEP Discussion Paper No 1531. London: Centre for Economic Performance.

Debter, L. (2018). 'Walmart Raises Minimum Wage after Tax Reform'. *Forbes*, January 11. www.forbes.com/sites/laurengensler/2018/01/11/walmart-raises-minimum-wage-after-tax-reform/?sh=7e06d74973c9, Downloaded June 1, 2021.

Deschenaux, J. (2019). 'How to Comply with New State and Local Laws'. *SHRM*, May 31. www.shrm.org/hr-today/news/hr-magazine/summer2019/pages/how-to-comply-with-new-state-and-local-laws.aspx Downloaded November 22, 2020.

Dube, A. (2017). 'Minimum Wage and Job Loss: One Alarming Seattle Study Is Not the Last Word'. *New York Times*, July 20. www.nytimes.com/2017/07/20/upshot/minimum-wage-and-job-loss-one-alarming-seattle-study-is-not-the-last-word.html Downloaded November 22, 2020.

Dunn, A. (2021). 'Most Americans Support a $15 Federal Minimum Wage'. Pew Research Center, April 22. https://www.pewresearch.org/fact-tank/2021/04/22/most-americans-support-a-15-federal-minimum-wage/ Downloaded June 2, 2021.

Economic Policy Institute. (2019). 'Raising the Federal Minimum Wage to $15 by 2024 Would Lift Pay for Nearly 40 Million Workers'. https://files.epi.org/pdf/160909.pdf Downloaded May 5, 2020.

Fight for $15. (no date). Website. https://fightfor15.org/about-us/ Downloaded November 21, 2020.

Franco, L.A. (2017). 'Organizing the Precariat: The Fight to Build and Sustain Fast Food Worker Power'. *Critical Sociology*, 45(4–5): 517–31.

Galvin, D.J. (2019). 'From Labor Law to Employment Law: The Changing Politics of Workers' Rights'. *Studies in American Political Development*, 33(1): 50–86.

Glasmeier, A.K. (2020). *Living Wage Calculator.* Massachusetts Institute of Technology. livingwage. mit.edu.

Gould, E. (2020). *State of Working America Wages 2019.* Washington, DC: Economic Policy Institute.

Greenhouse, S. (2018). 'Fast-Food Workers Claim Victory in a New York Labor Effort'. *New York Times*, January 9. www.nytimes.com/2018/01/09/business/economy/fast-food-labor.html. Downloaded September 23, 2020.

Gurley, L.K. (2020). 'Instacart Workers Win Historic Union Election'. VICE. www.vice.com/en/article/qjdvgm/instacart-workers-win-historic-union-election downloaded February 1, 2020.

Halkias, M. (2020). 'Walmart to Change Store Jobs and Raise Wages, Including a $15 Minimum in Bakery and Deli'. *Gazette Xtra*. September. www.gazettextra.com/work_wheels/walmart-to-change-store-jobs-and-raise-wages-including-a-15-minimum-in-bakery-and/article_a7480cc9-9fba-5f0a-8df0-e617e0665e94.html Downloaded November 21, 2020.

Hirsch, B.T., and Macpherson, D.A. (2003). 'Union Membership and Coverage Database from the Current Population Survey: Note', *Industrial and Labor Relations Review*, 56(2): 349–354 (updated annually at unionstats.com). Downloaded November 22, 2020.

Holder, S. (2020). 'Stockton Extends Its Universal Basic Income Pilot'. *Bloomberg CityLab*. June 20. www.bloomberg.com/news/articles/2020-06-02/stockton-extends-its-universal-basic-income-pilot Downloaded November 21, 2020.

Jardim, E., Long, M.C., Plotnick, R., van Inwegen, E., Vigdor, J., and Wething, H. (2017). *Minimum Wage Increases, Wages, and Low-Wage Employment: Evidence from Seattle*. Cambridge, MA: NBER Working Paper 23532.

Jardim, E., Long, M.C., Plotnick, R., van Inwegen, E., Vigdor, J., and Wething, H. (2018). *Minimum Wage Increases and Individual Employment Trajectories*. Cambridge, MA: NBER Working Paper 25182.

Kinney, S.K., and Karr, A.F., (2017). 'Public-Use vs. Restricted-Use: An Analysis Using the American Community Survey'. CES 17-12. Washington, DC: Center for Economic Studies.

Living Wage Network. (n.d.). Website. www.livingwagenetwork.org/partners

Luce, S. (2017). 'Living Wages: A US Perspective'. *Employee Relations*, 39(6): 863–874.

Matsakis, L. (2018). 'Why Amazon Really Raised Its Minimum Wage to $15'. *Wired*, October 2. www.wired.com/story/why-amazon-really-raised-minimum-wage/ Downloaded October 2, 2018.

Moberg, D. (2015). 'In Latest Round of Fast-Food Strikes, Fight for $15 Tells Politicians: "Come Get My Vote"'. *Working in These Times*, November 11. https://inthesetimes.com/article/fight-for-15-fast-food-strikes-politicians-black-lives-matter Downloaded June 2, 2021.

National Employment Law Project. (2018). *Data Brief: Impact of the Fight for $15: $68 Billion in Raises, 22 Million Workers."* https://s27147.pcdn.co/wp-content/uploads/Data-Brief-Impact-Fight-for-15-2018.pdf Downloaded November 21, 2020.

New York City. (n.d.) Website. 'Fast Food Deductions Law'. https://portal.311.nyc.gov/article/?kanumber=KA-02724 Downloaded November 21, 2020.

Ocasio-Cortez, A. (2019). *116th Congress, First Session. Resolution.* February 7. https://ocasio-cortez.house.gov/sites/ocasio-cortez.house.gov/files/Resolution%20on%20a%20Green%20New%20Deal.pdf Downloaded November 21st, 2020.

Partnership for Working Families (n.d.). Website. 'Policy and Tools: Living Wage'. www.forworkingfamilies.org/resources/policy-tools-living-wage#:~:text=A%20living%20wage%20policy%20requires,above%20the%20federal%20poverty%20line. Downloaded November 22, 2020.

Pasquier, V., Daudigeos, T., and Barros, M. (2020). 'Towards a New Flash Mob Unionism: The Case of the Fight for 15 Movement'. *British Journal of Industrial Relations*, 58(2): 336–363.

Pollin, R., Brenner, M.D., Wicks-Lim, J., and Luce, S. (2008). *A Measure of Fairness: The Economics of Living Wages and Minimum Wages in the United States.* Ithaca, NY: Cornell University Press.

Reich, M., Allegretto, S., and Godoey, A. (2017). *Seattle's Minimum Wage Experience 2015–16.* Berkeley, CA: Center on Wage and Employment Dynamics, University of California, Berkeley.

Snaith, E. (2020). 'What Is the Green New Deal and How Does Biden's Climate Plan Compare?' *The Independent.* November 3. www.independent.co.uk/environment/green-new-deal-biden-what-is-cost-b1503522.html. Downloaded November 21, 2020.

Southern Ute Drum. (2018). 'The Living Wage Network: A Coalition of Living Wage Certifiers'. www.sudrum.com/news/2018/03/02/the-living-wage-network-a-coalition-of-living-wage-certifiers/ Downloaded March 2, 2018.

Tapia M., Lee, T.L., and Filipovitch, M. (2017). 'Supra-union and intersectional organizing: An examination of two prominent cases in the low-wage US restaurant industry'. *Journal of Industrial Relations*, 59(4): 487–509.

Target (2020). *Factsheet $15 Starting Wage and Frontline Bonus.* https://corporate.target.com/press/releases/2020/06/fact-sheet-15-starting-wage-and-frontline-bonus. Downloaded November 17, 2020.

Tompkins County Worker Center (2020). www.tcworkerscenter.org/living-wage/ Downloaded November 17, 2010.

University of California Berkeley Labor Center. (2020). *Inventory of US City and County Minimum Wage Ordinances.* June. https://laborcenter.berkeley.edu/inventory-of-us-city-and-county-minimum-wage-ordinances/ Downloaded November 21, 2020.

US Census Bureau. (n.d.). 'About the American Community Survey'. www.census.gov/programs-surveys/acs/about.html. Downloaded November 22, 2020.

Webb-Ayer, J. (2019). 'Five Municipal Trends Keeping HR on Their Toes'. XPert HR. New York: Reed Information Services.

Zipperer, B. (2018). 'Six Reasons Not to Put Too Much Weight on the New Study of Seattle's Minimum Wage'. Washington, DC: Economic Policy Institute. October 18. www.epi.org/blog/six-reasons-not-to-put-too-much-weight-on-the-new-study-of-seattles-minimum-wage/ Downloaded November 22, 2020.

Zipperer, B., and Schmitt, J. (2017). 'The "High Road" Seattle Labor Market and the Effects of the Minimum Wage Increase'. Washington, DC: Economic Policy Institute. www.epi.org/publication/the-high-road-seattle-labor-market-and-the-effects-of-the-minimum-wage-increase-data-limitations-and-methodological-problems-bias-new-analysis-of-seattles-minimum-wage-incr/ Downloaded November 22, 2020.

12 The living wage movement in Canada

Danielle van Jaarsveld, Samantha Coronel, and Reed Eaglesham

Introduction

In Canada, unions, anti-poverty advocates and politicians have turned to the living wage to address concern about growing income inequality despite the presence of a national healthcare system, and stronger labour and employment regulations than the US. The prevailing living wage definition in Canada refers to the 'hourly rate of pay at which a household can meet its expenses once government transfers have been added and government deductions from wages and government taxes have been subtracted' (Richards et al., 2008: 24). From 2001 to 2020, the living wage movement spread from British Columbia (BC) and Ontario, where the living wage movement initially took root, to the Northern territories (Evans and Fanelli, 2016; Evans, Fanelli and McDowell, 2021). In contrast to living wage movements in other developed countries, Canada's experience with the living wage shows evidence of regionalism, with the living wage gaining more traction in some parts of the country relative to others (Rose et al., 2003). Thus, we trace the evolution of the living wage movement against the backdrop of Canadian regionalism.

We organize this chapter in the following manner. First, we describe the characteristics and economic realities of the low-wage workforce. Second, we examine the evolution of the living wage movement in Canada by province and territory. Third, we share first-hand perspectives about the living wage from public hearings, interviews, and focus groups with employers, living wage advocates, and the low-wage workforce in BC. Fourth, we highlight three cases involving the implementation of the living wage. Finally, we conclude by acknowledging that while some policymakers and advocates consider the living wage as a way to draw attention to the limitations of the minimum wage to support a decent living, the Covid-19 pandemic has ignited discussion around the universal basic income (UBI) and other policy alternatives.

Characteristics of the low-wage workforce in Canada

Living wage campaigns in Canada emerged to address growing income inequality. Relative to other industrialized nations, Canada ranks seventeenth in income inequality and twentieth in overall poverty rate compared to 36 OECD countries (OECD, 2021a; OECD, 2021b). Domestically, the income of top earners in Canada is increasing more rapidly compared with their lower income counterparts, leading to growing income inequality over time (Fortin and Lemieux, 2015; Fang and Gunderson, 2016; see Green et al., 2016). From 1998 through 2018, the proportion of employees in Canada earning the minimum

DOI: 10.4324/9781003054078-12

wage doubled from 5.2 per cent to 10.4 per cent (Dionne-Simard and Miller, 2019). One of three low-income measures Statistics Canada uses, the Market Basket Measure (MBM), refers to the income necessary to cover a basket of essential goods and services 'for a reference family of two adults and two children for each size of area of residence in each province' (Michaud et al., 2004: 7; Heisz, 2019; Djidel et al., 2020). Using the MBM, in 2018, 3.2 million Canadians, or 8.7 per cent of the population, lived below the official poverty line (Statistics Canada, 2018).

Consistent with other developed economies, low-wage work is concentrated in specific occupations and industries including retail trade, and accommodation and food services (Evans and Fanelli, 2016). For example, in 2018, 32.7 per cent of all minimum wage workers were employed in retail trade, whereas 26.0 per cent worked in accommodation and food services (Dionne-Simard and Miller, 2019). Declining unionization in the private sector (15.8 per cent) and increasing reliance on non-standard work arrangements are further eroding the quality of these jobs (Galarneau, 2017; Jeon et al., 2019; Statistics Canada, 2020).

Increasing the minimum wage is one approach for improving low wages. Each province and territory in Canada has jurisdiction over the minimum wage, resulting in some variation in minimum wages across the country as Table 12.1 shows. For example, in 2020, Saskatchewan had the lowest minimum wage ($11.45/hour), whereas Nunavut had the highest minimum wage ($16.00/hour). While minimum wage regulations exist to establish a wage floor, some occupational groups are excluded from coverage, including farm workers in BC (Morissette and Dionne-Simard, 2018).

Before 2017, the minimum wage remained unchanged for many years in some provinces and territories. For example, in 2010, BC's minimum wage was the lowest in the country by real value, having remained unchanged at $8 for almost a decade (Fortin and Lemieux, 2015). In 2018, the BC provincial government led by the BC New Democratic Party (BC NDP) in a minority government with the BC Green Party followed the advice of the provincial independent Fair Wage Commission (FWC) and committed to raising the minimum wage annually until it reaches $15.20 in June 2021 (Cohen et al., 2018). Politically, the Green Party of BC, and the Green Party of Canada, are advocates for the living wage and the universal basic income. The BC Greens included the formation of the FWC as part of their agreement to work with the BC NDP, and included as part of the FWC's work addressing 'the discrepancy between minimum wages and livable wages' (*2017 Confidence and Supply Agreement between the BC Green Caucus and the BC New Democrat Caucus*, 2017). Between 2017 and 2018, other provinces also increased the minimum wage, including Alberta and Ontario (Bennett, 2016; Ministry of Labour, 2019; Mahboubi, 2018).

Regionalism and the living wage movement in Canada

The living wage movement in Canada started in BC in the early 2000s (Ludgate, 2021). The ingredients that contributed to the living wage movement emerging in BC included a conservative political party in power, the BC provincial Liberal party, which stalled increases in the minimum wage during its 16 years in power and, notably, passed Bill 29, the Health and Social Service Delivery Improvement Act in 2002, eliminating many jobs predominantly held by women; thus, transforming them from family-supporting jobs into low-wage and precarious jobs (Zuberi, 2011; *FWC Living Wage Public Hearing*, 2019).

Table 12.1 Minimum wage rates by province and territory

Province/Territory	Minimum wage per hour
Alberta (October 1, 2018)	$15.00
British Columbia (June 1, 2021)	$15.20
Manitoba (October 1, 2021)	$11.95
New Brunswick (April 1, 2021)	$11.75
Newfoundland and Labrador (April 1, 2021)	$12.50
Northwest Territories (September 1, 2021)	$15.20
Nova Scotia (April 1, 2021)	$12.95
Nunavut (April 1, 2020)	$16.00
Ontario (October 1, 2021)	$14.35
Prince Edward Island (April 1, 2021)	$13.00
Quebec (May 1, 2021)	$13.50
Saskatchewan (October 1, 2020)	$11.45
Yukon (April 1, 2021)	$13.85

Source: Statistics Canada (2017).

The Hospital Employees' Union (HEU), the union representing healthcare and community social service workers in BC, expressed serious concern about these policy changes. HEU leaders began witnessing first-hand the negative effects that privatization in the healthcare sector had on their members. Alongside several stakeholders, including First Call: BC Child and Youth Advocacy Coalition, they started strategizing about how to address these concerns (Ludgate, 2021). The idea of a living wage emerged from these discussions in part influenced by the UK living wage movement. In 2007, First Call, in partnership with the BC Office of the Canadian Centre for Policy Alternatives (CCPA-BC), conducted focus groups with low-wage workers to help develop a living wage calculation. A non-partisan Canadian think tank, the Canadian Center for Policy Alternatives (CCPA) produces research reports on environmental, social, and economic issues and, hence, was a natural partner for this work.

Simultaneously, round-table discussions were held, building support for a living wage campaign in BC with multiple stakeholders including ACORN Canada, Vancity (a province wide credit union), the CCPA-BC, the United Way, unions including the HEU, and the United Food and Commercial Workers (UFCW), and other community groups (Ludgate, 2021; Keddy, 2015). Drawing support from within their communities, these round-table discussions highlight the grass-roots beginnings of the living wage movement in Canada.

A year later, in 2008, CCPA-BC published a living wage calculation for Vancouver and Victoria (Richards et al., 2008). This living wage calculation estimates what a family of four with two parents working full-time (35 hours per week), and two children – a four-year-old who is in full-time day care, and a seven-year-old who is in before- and after-school care need to earn in order to 'achieve a decent standard of life' (Richards et al., 2008: 10). The CCPA-BC's living wage calculation is conservative, consisting of items necessary to provide 'a basic level of economic security' (Richards et al., 2008: 7), lift families above the poverty line, and 'based on the actual costs of living in a specific community' (Richards et al., 2008:17).

This initial living wage calculation became the foundation for the living wage calculation that is in widespread use in Canada, with many municipalities and businesses relying on this calculation to understand the cost of living in their local community (Carlaw et al. 2016). This living wage calculation is fairly flexible, taking into consideration, for example, transportation differences between urban and rural locations or the higher cost of food in the Northern territories. The ability to locally tailor the calculation has made the movement appealing especially to rural communities (A. Montani and H. Seiferling, personal communication, April 15, 2019). Yet, the living wage movement in Canada remains voluntary.

In 2011, the City of New Westminster in BC became the first city in Canada to become a certified Living Wage Employer (Wells, 2016; Ludgate, 2021). Since then, eleven BC municipalities have followed New Westminster's lead by becoming certified Living Wage Employers including Metro Vancouver, the City of New Westminster, Central Saanich, Victoria, and Burnaby. Vancity Credit Union promotes the benefits of the living wage in communities through their involvement with their local branches in many locations around BC (Carlaw et al., 2016; Wells, 2016). These efforts evolved into the BC Living Wage for Families Campaign which certifies Living Wage Employers and actively supports building the movement. While the Living Wage for Families Campaign handles the certification process for employers in BC, the CCPA-BC branch develops the living wage calculation annually. To date, over 150 BC employers, including private sector companies, non-profits, cooperatives, and unions, are certified Living Wage Employers. While the movement has grown considerably in BC with some communities incorporating a living wage policy into their social procurement strategy, some living wage campaigns have failed, such as efforts to introduce a living wage policy in Esquimalt, BC, and Surrey, BC.

In recent years, living wage levels in some Canadian jurisdictions have declined, with the introduction of new federal and provincial tax benefits. For example, in 2019, living wage calculations for BC communities such as Metro Vancouver, Greater Victoria, and North Central BC declined by 6.7 per cent, 5.4 per cent, and 15 per cent respectively, as shown in Table 12.2.

In BC, this decline occurred due to the elimination of provincial health insurance premiums, increases to the provincial minimum wage, and the introduction of a new childcare benefit (Ivanova and Saugstad, 2019). Declining living wage levels across BC in 2019 raised an implementation question for Living Wage Employers on how to respond. Interestingly, the Living Wage Employers we interviewed or who attended the public hearings held in 2019 in BC, did not reduce their wage levels in response to the decline.

BC's neighbouring province, Alberta, has a fairly robust living wage movement relative to Manitoba and Saskatchewan (Evans, 2017). In 2019, the City of Edmonton, Alberta's second-largest city, officially became a Living Wage Employer. Similar to Vancouver and

Table 12.2 A comparison of living wage levels in British Columbia (2018–2019)

Location	2018 Living Wage per hour	2019 Living Wage per hour	Dollar Difference per hour	% Change per hour
Metro Vancouver	$20.91	$19.50	$1.41	-6.7%
Greater Victoria	$20.50	$19.39	$1.11	-5.4%
Revelstoke	$19.37	$18.90	$0.47	-2.4%
Fraser Valley	$17.40	$15.54	$1.86	-10.7%
Kamloops	$17.31	$15.93	$1.38	-8.0%
Parksville/Qualicum	$17.02	$15.81	$1.21	-7.1%
Comox Valley	$16.59	$15.97	$0.62	-3.7%
North Central BC	$16.51	$14.03	$2.48	-15.0%

Note: All values are expressed in Canadian dollars; See Ivanova et al. (2018); Ivanova and Saugstad (2019).

other locations in BC that experienced a decline in the living wage, Edmonton also witnessed a decrease in its living wage from 2015 through 2018. The largest city in Alberta, Calgary, initially considered becoming a Living Wage Employer in 2007 related to the adoption of a Sustainable Environment and Ethical Purchasing Policy (Cook, 2008), but the initiative failed to pass (Hudson, 2021). Several smaller communities in Alberta have commissioned reports on the living wage in partnership with the Central Alberta Poverty Reduction Alliance (Haener, 2013).

Ontario, home to approximately half of Canada's population, and a centre for job creation, has its own living wage movement but is less developed than its BC counterpart. In 2001, the living wage movement took root in connection with efforts to increase Ontario's minimum wage. A report prepared by the Centre for Social Justice's Foundation for Research and Education and the Ontario Federation of Labour examined strategies for moving towards a minimum wage that reflected a living wage (Schenk, 2001). The Ontario Federation of Labour advocated for a minimum wage set at 70 per cent of the average wage, indexed to the cost of living (Schenk, 2001). In 2002, the coalition 'Justice for Workers' started to campaign to increase the provincial minimum wage (Eaton and Dagg, 2004). These efforts helped focus attention on wages, and more specifically, on the concept of the living wage. By 2008, the CCPA calculated a living wage for Toronto (Mackenzie and Stanford, 2008). At present, 332 employers in Ontario are Living Wage Employers ('Living Wage Employers', n.d.; Luxton and McDermott, 2021).

Living wage campaigns exist beyond Toronto in other communities in Ontario. In 2013, in Hamilton, Ontario, the public school board of Hamilton became the first public institution and the first publicly elected body in Ontario to adopt the living wage (Johnstone and Cooper, 2013; Wells, 2016). In 2015, the Hamilton Chamber of Commerce became the first Chamber of Commerce in Canada to officially become a Living Wage Employer (Wells, 2016; Gouter, 2021). A few recent attempts to have the City of Hamilton become a Living Wage Employer occurred in 2019 and 2020 –however, only crossing guards are paid a living wage by the City of Hamilton (Gouter, 2021).

In 2015, Cambridge, Ontario, became the first municipality in the province to be a Living Wage Employer. Cambridge is part of the Waterloo Region that also includes Waterloo, and Kingston, Ontario. Recently, three Ontario communities, the Municipality of North Perth (2019), Huron County (2019), and Kingston (2020) became certified Living Wage Employers (Pickthorne, 2020; Simmons, 2019). Other Ontario communities including Waterloo, and Ottawa, have considered implementing a living wage and voted on it, but the initiative has failed to pass (Keddy, 2015).

Further east, the living wage movement in the Maritimes (Prince Edward Island, Nova Scotia, Newfoundland and Labrador, and New Brunswick) is much less developed. Interest in the living wage has emerged in connection to efforts to increase the minimum wage in Newfoundland and Labrador, Nova Scotia, and New Brunswick. In October 1, 2020, the Halifax Regional Council in Nova Scotia (NS) adopted a Supplier Code of Conduct that includes a living wage requirement for Halifax Regional Municipality's contractors and sub-contractors (Munro, 2020). Meanwhile, in Prince Edward Island (PEI), the Canadian Union of Public Employees (CUPE) PEI, and the PEI Federation of Labour, are advocating for the implementation of a basic income guarantee, and on July 11, 2019, the province formed a special committee on poverty tasked with calculating the cost of implementing a basic income guarantee pilot for the province (Special Committee on Poverty in PEI, 2019).

Relative to the other provinces, Québec has generous and comprehensive family care policies that help support low-income families. Specifically, Québec charges a flat fee for day care that helps increase women's labour force participation and helps reduce a key cost for families. Since 2015, the Institute de Recherche et d'Informations Socioéconomiques (IRIS; Institute of Socioeconomic Research and Information) has calculated the living wage in Québec; a calculation separate, but influenced by the CCPA calculation (Leduc, 2017). In their first report, they calculated the annual living salaries rather than living wages needed for Montréal and Québec City. In their 2020 report, IRIS included calculations for Saguenay, Trois-Rivières, Sept-Îles, Gatineau, and Sherbrooke in addition to Montréal and Québec City (Couturier et al., 2020).

Interest in the living wage movement is also emerging in Canada's Territorial North (Yukon, Northwest Territories, and Nunavut), stemming from concern over the high cost of living in these areas (Daley et al., 2015; Evans and Fanelli, 2016; Haener, 2015, 2019; Hammond, 2021). Daley et al. (2015) measured poverty and inequality in Canada's North using the Statistics Canada Survey of Household Spending. They found that the cost of living in Canada's North is 1.46 times higher than in Canada's ten provinces, and that 27.1 per cent of Northern households experience poverty, helping generate support for the living wage movement and increasing minimum wage levels in Canada's Territorial North (Daley et al., 2015).

In 2012, the topic of a living wage arose in discussions between the Yukon Anti-Poverty Coalition, with the Territorial government, and the Whitehorse Chamber of Commerce as a means to address poverty (Hammond, 2021). In 2016, the first living wage calculation based on the Canadian Living Wage Framework in Canada's Territorial North was released for Whitehorse, with the capital of the Yukon becoming one of the highest living wage rates in Canada at $19.12 per hour. Living wage rates in Yellowknife are even higher at $20.96 in 2017, and are estimated to be $23.95 as of 2019 (Hammond, 2019). In 2019, 11 employers were certified as Living Wage Employers in the Northwest Territories. In Nunavut, support for the living wage has emerged as part of the union Public Service Alliance of Canada North (PSAC North) campaign to increase the minimum wage. In 2017, the Living Wage North campaign was developed by the union to persuade the Nunavut government to adopt a living wage of $26.00 per hour in response to increases to the Consumer Price Index (LeTourneau, 2018). In November 2019, ten Nunavut MLAs expressed their support for the living wage, presenting a petition on behalf of their constituents (Anselmi, 2019). In March 2020, Nunavut passed a minimum wage of $16.00 per hour, currently the highest minimum wage in Canada (Nunavut News, 2020).

Regionalism is a distinguishing feature of the living wage movement in Canada, as the uneven progress on the living wage across provinces and territories reveals. The move to unify and nationalize the movement continues. Across Canada, living wage movements follow similar patterns as they evolve and grow. They are often initiated by a grass-roots group of community organizations to address poverty. Over time, they gradually converge on a living wage calculation based on the Canadian Living Wage Framework and develop a process for voluntary accreditation as a Living Wage Employer. In contrast to the UK and the US, where the highest living wages are found in urban locations such as London and San Francisco, the highest living wages in Canada exist in less populated, remote locations in the Territorial North including Nunavut, the Northwest Territories, and the Yukon.

Perspectives from the workforce and employers on the living wage

Compared with other provinces and territories, the living wage movement in BC is the most developed in Canada. In 2017, the decision by the BC provincial government to have the FWC examine the gap between the minimum wage and living wage demonstrated progress on the living wage in BC. As part of this work with the FWC, in 2019, we held eight public hearings and conducted focus groups and key informant interviews to understand how to reduce the difference between the minimum wage and the living wage. We collected input from multiple stakeholders involved in the living wage movement in BC including unions (for example, HEU, BC Federation of Labour), CCPA-BC, the Living Wage for Families Campaign, poverty advocates, Chambers of Commerce, employers and Living Wage Employers. A complete list of interviews is available from the authors. In collaboration with the BC Poverty Reduction Coalition and the Living Wage for Families Campaign, we also held focus groups with participants who were either unemployed or working in low-wage jobs. These insights helped shed light on the lived experience of the low-wage workforce in BC; the motivation behind why organizations, businesses, and municipalities across the province are implementing living wage policies; and the associated benefits and consequences of implementing a living wage.

Our focus group participants identified housing, transit and transportation costs, and the cost of food as their largest expenditures. These key expenditures were consistent with insights from our public hearings and interviews, where housing, childcare, and transit and transportation costs emerged as the top three factors contributing to high living costs in BC. Across both urban and rural areas, however, the lack of affordable and quality housing emerged as the primary concern. The president of the Canadian Union of Public Employees Local 1858, cited a recent survey of her local's members where 'something like 30 per cent [of their members] were spending more than half of their household income on rent or mortgage'. While this exorbitant housing cost by itself is a serious issue, the actual supply of available, decent housing is also limited. Numerous focus group participants shared common experiences such as living with rat infestations, black mould, and smoke because it was all they could afford. Despite settling for poorer quality housing, many still had to forgo items such as internet in their homes, healthy food, owning a telephone, or medical prescriptions. As one public hearing participant eloquently expressed:

> Low-wage workers in British Columbia are being squeezed between two arms of the pincers on inequality: wages are too low and living costs are too high.

Another common theme emerging from our focus groups was the need to work multiple jobs to support themselves (Ivanova et al., 2018; Ivanova and Strauss, 2020). Respondents reported working a combination of multiple part-time jobs to two full-time jobs *and* one part-time job, leaving very little time to spend with family or friends. Additionally, trying to manage these challenging work schedules with a childcare or school schedule creates considerable stress. This necessity to work multiple jobs also surfaced at our public hearings. One woman at a hearing in downtown Vancouver who was a minimum wage worker commented:

> [You] basically [have] no social life if you look at it because there is no way you can show up in your kids' life or be able to pay your rent, provide food, provide packed lunches for them, give them pocket money. It's almost impossible.

A Hospital Employees Union (HEU) leader, characterized this experience as 'profound social isolation':

> (hearing) stories of members who would get up in the morning before their kids were up, leave for work, work all day; and for some members what they do is they simply change their, uh, uniform at the end of the shift [for their next shift with a different contractor] … They then get on the bus and go back home after their kids have gone to bed.

The HEU union leader described this experience for her members as not being able to have a family life because: 'they almost never see their children'.

Long commutes to work also appeared to be shrinking low-wage workers' already small amount of free time; long work commutes emerged as a key theme and one of the second most frequently cited insights from our focus groups, public hearings, and interviews. Long commute times ranged anywhere between 1.5 hours to 3 hours due to low-wage workers being unable to afford to live near work. One focus group participant described a regular day as waking up early at 5:00 a.m., taking public transit at 6:00 a.m., working until 3:00 p.m., taking public transit for about 1.5 hours to a second job, working until 12:30 a.m., and finally, sleeping at about 1:30 a.m. All this before having to wake up and repeat this schedule 3.5 hours later.

Implementing the living wage among employers in British Columbia

In the previous section, we shared the key concerns the low-wage workforce identified to explain the challenges they encounter trying to earn a decent living. Considering the multiple benefits of a living wage for both employers and employees, in this section, we examine the employer motivations for implementing a living wage and/or going through the accreditation process to become a Living Wage Employer. While the leading justification for those we interviewed was that they were already paying a living wage, the second, most commonly cited reason was that employers wanted to a) ensure that they support their community and staff, and b) ensure that if the employer was a municipality, city councillors supported the policy. The three most commonly cited consequences of implementing the living wage were that it improved employee recruitment, increased employee morale and engagement, and had no financial impact for the employer. We conducted case studies of three employers in BC: (1) the City of Vancouver (public sector, unionized), (2) the S̲k̲wx̲wú7mesh Úxwumixw, (the Squamish Nation), and (3) Buckerfield's (private sector small business, unionized). What emerges from these case studies is the heterogeneity in motivation for adopting a living wage policy, and the variation in its implementation.

In 2016, the City of Vancouver's Council initially passed a motion to adopt a 'Healthy City Strategy'. They consulted with their counterparts in New Westminster, the first municipality in BC to be certified as a Living Wage Employer, and Vancity Credit Union, a Living Wage Employer and active supporter of the movement, for advice on implementation and the certification process. This interaction between multiple proponents of the policy who advise and support others, helps further the living wage movement in Canada. These key stakeholders, along with the CCPA-BC, the Living Wage for Families Campaign, UFCW, and HEU, continue to support employers who are considering adopting the living wage in BC. In 2017, the motion to pass the policy succeeded and fairly soon after, the City of Vancouver became certified by the Living Wage for Families Campaign on April 4, 2017, with the policy going into effect in June 2017.

Employees of the City of Vancouver's contractors as opposed to the City of Vancouver's direct staff experienced a greater improvement to their wages as a result of the living wage policy because, at the time, the City of Vancouver's direct staff were already paid above the living wage. Instead of creating a blanket living wage policy for all contracts, the City of Vancouver established a contract threshold of $250,000/year to determine whether a contract would fall under their living wage policy. Only contracts valued at $250,000/year or more would be required to pay a living wage. If the contractors are found to be non-compliant, there is also a termination clause included as another mechanism for enforcement. Overall, through these contractors, approximately 300 employees were directly impacted by the living wage policy, and the effect and response have been positive. At our public hearing in downtown Vancouver, the chief procurement officer and director of supply chain for the City of Vancouver, said that:

[They've] received letters from, for example, … our graffiti removal services about employees saying just that it changed my life. [So] It's very rewarding.

The impact of the City's policy even had a trickle-down effect, persuading the security services contractor to adopt a living wage for all their staff. If one contract for a vendor is a Living Wage Employer, they need to create a separate process to differentiate between contracts. Furthermore, all of the vendor's staff want to work on a living wage contract because they would get paid more than if they were staffed on a different contract. Thus, the City of Vancouver's implementation of a living wage policy created positive, unintended consequences.

While municipalities have shown a significant interest in the living wage, Indigenous communities in BC are also implementing the living wage. For example, on August 2, 2020, the Squamish Nation, S̲k̲wx̲wú7mesh Úxwumixw, became the third Indigenous community in BC to become a Living Wage Employer behind Huu-ay-aht First Nations in 2014 and the Yuułuʔiłʔatḥ Government, Ucluelet First Nation, in 2017 (Thomson, 2014). The Squamish Nation is located in the geographic area ranging from North Vancouver to Howe Sound ('The Nation Today', n.d.).

Approval for their living wage policy came from their Council in 2019 following a long approval process. The policy finally came into effect on August 2, 2020, with the support of the 16 members on the Squamish Nation's Council who were the main drivers behind the policy's adoption. This motivation arose primarily from Council's recent focus on the issue of wages. They sought to raise wages to stay competitive in the labour market, but Council also wanted to ensure that they were taking care of the people within their community. The Squamish Nation Living Wage policy applies to contractors, full-time employees, and temporary and casual employees. This living wage policy covers 400 employees, with 91 experiencing an increase in their wages resulting from the new living wage policy. The policy, and the Squamish Nation's certification as a Living Wage Employer through the Living Wage for Families Campaign, is still fairly new, so some concerns about wage compression issues and the possibility of revising the total compensation structure will still need to be resolved.

While the previous two examples involved employers that completed the formal living wage certification process with the Living Wage for Families Campaign, the third example involves an employer that bypassed the formal living wage certification process. Buckerfield's is a chain of agricultural stores in operation for the past 100 years with nine locations across BC that employ approximately 100 employees. They adopted a living wage to standardize a differentiated pay scale. The CEO, Kelvin McCulloch, explains:

> We have employees who have worked 40 years for the company ... they've worked for the company for 40 years and we see them every day and realize well whatever money those people have they got from working in this company and whatever retirement they have, they got working in this company ... Because they put their working careers into this company ... So, if they didn't get a living wage from the company and even get a pension, I mean, they wasted their entire working careers and I can't face them, right!? [This] would just be wrong.

Because Buckerfield's chose not to certify with the Living Wage for Families Campaign, their employees begin earning a living wage after one year of full-time employment, and the living wage policy excludes part-time employees. The policy was first implemented in Buckerfield's only unionized store in Duncan, BC, located in the Cowichan Valley. Once the union approved the pay scale, the rest of the locations in BC were updated based on the Cowichan Valley calculation (Social Planning Cowichan, 2016).

The motivation for Buckerfield's to adopt a living wage included addressing uneven pay scales, and as a benchmark to pay staff fairly. While the payroll costs increased more than 10 per cent in the first year, McCulloch reports that the impact of the policy 'continues to pay dividends' and describes it as the 'the best marketing program [they've] ever had'.

Employers implemented a living wage policy across these three cases, for various reasons. However, the living wage policy language itself differed with respect to whether it affected direct employees or non-standard staff. While the first two cases, the City of Vancouver and Sḵwx̱wú7mesh Úxwumixw (the Squamish Nation), pursued formal living wage certification through the Living Wage for Families campaign, adopting the CCPA-BC's living wage calculation, Buckerfield's decided not to become a certified Living Wage Employer with the Living Wage for Families campaign. In all three cases, the decision to implement a living wage policy offers potential tangible benefits for employers and the workforce, and these benefits are viewed as outweighing the costs of implementation. The employers across these three cases share a common goal of treating their workforce fairly.

Discussion and conclusion

In some respects, the ingredients for Canada's living wage movement are similar to those of other developed economies. As this chapter shows, it is difficult to generalize about the living wage movement in Canada given the regional variation in progress on the living wage by province and territory with more developed Living Wage campaigns in BC and Ontario featuring a voluntary Living Wage Employer certification process. Indeed, the living wage movement in Canada offers some benefits for the low-wage workforce by creating support to increase the minimum wage, and higher wages when employers voluntarily implement a living wage policy.

Similar to the US, leadership on the living wage is coming from municipalities as employers, and involves coalition building among multiple stakeholders ('2019 Living Wage Employers Announced', 2019). In some cases, municipalities are implementing a living wage as part of their commitment to the social procurement movement or other larger strategies/initiatives.

At the same time, the living wage movement in Canada features some distinct characteristics. First, the living wage movement focuses on cities, but is also gaining support in smaller communities recognizing that poverty exists in both urban and rural locations. For example, living expenses in Canada's Northern territories are higher than in Canada's largest cities. Moreover, smaller communities are recognizing the potential social benefits a living wage could offer (Harris et al., 2018). In a similar vein, Indigenous communities in Canada, specifically in BC, are implementing the living wage (Thomson, 2014).

Second, in contrast to the United States, Canada has a stronger social safety net to help support the low-wage workforce. Yet, the low-wage workforce still finds it difficult at the present minimum wage levels to sustain a decent living. In some jurisdictions such as Vancouver, BC (2018–2019), and Edmonton, Alberta (2017–2019), the living wage declined in recent years due to the introduction of new benefits at the federal, provincial, or municipal level. Emergency government support provided during the pandemic could further reduce living wage calculations at a time when unemployment will be increasing (Department of Finance Canada, 2020; Statistics Canada, 2021). How living wage advocates will address this challenge is an open question.

Third, involvement by a national advocacy organization, the CCPA, connects living wage advocates and supports living wage calculations for communities across Canada. A primary reason why the living wage campaign has gained some traction across the country is the availability of a consistent method for calculating the living wage. When the living wage is implemented in a community, although the CCPA has a specific living wage definition, a fair amount of flexibility exists in how the living wage is implemented—as some of the case studies reflect. In contrast to the UK, which has two living wages, one for London and one for outside London (Heery et al., 2017), a living wage calculation based on the Canadian National Living Wage Framework is available for approximately 89 communities across Canada. In our focus groups and interviews, the low-wage workforce expressed concern that living wages were too low to live on. The time lag in the availability of Statistics Canada data that influences the living wage calculation could jeopardize the timeliness of the cost-of-living information. This data may not reflect dramatic increases and decreases in food prices or in rents that we are experiencing in the Covid-19 pandemic. Moreover, respondents also questioned whether basing the calculation on two parents working full-time is realistic given the lack of available childcare.

The living wage represents one potential policy to address inequality. As awareness about social, economic, and environmental impact increase, some municipalities are incorporating living wage policies into a broader social procurement policy exemplified by the Village of Cumberland (BC), and the Halifax Regional Municipality (NS). Governments through policymaking and the development and enforcement of labour and employment legislation, along with Employers, bear a great responsibility for creating jobs that can support individuals, and families to have a decent quality of life. One of the most important factors for helping prevent greater income inequality in Canada is the creation of better quality jobs. Moreover, other potential solutions such as improving existing labour and employment regulations, and the UBI, are being considered, especially against the backdrop of recovering from the pandemic (Johnson and Roberto, 2020; Koebel and Pohler, 2019; Green et al., 2021).

References

2017 Confidence and Supply Agreement between the BC Green Caucus and the BC New Democrat Caucus (pp. 1–10). (2017, May 29). Retrieved from https://bcndpcaucus.ca/wp-content/uploads/sites/5/2017/05/BC-Green-BC-NDP-Agreement_vf-May-29th-2017.pdf.

2019 Living Wage Employers Announced. (2019, October 24). Retrieved June 15, 2020, from Alternatives North website: https://alternativesnorth.ca/2019/10/24/2019-living-wage-employers-announced/.

Anselmi, E. (2019, November 12). 'Nunavut MLAs make the case for a living wage'. *Nunatsiaq News*. Retrieved from https://nunatsiaq.com/stories/article/members-make-case-for-living-wage-in-nunavut/#:~:text="This petition recognizes our territory,to speak on the matter.

Bennett, D. (2016, September 13). 'It's official: Alberta's minimum wage will be $15 an hour by 2018'. *Global News*. Retrieved from https://globalnews.ca/news/2936591/its-official-albertas-minimum-wage-will-be-15-an-hour-by-2018/.

Carlaw, K., Evans, M., Harris, L., and Janmaat, J. (2016). *A Living Wage for Revelstoke, BC: Economic Impact Assessment Report*. Retrieved from https://icer.ok.ubc.ca/wp-content/uploads/sites/88/2018/11/Analysis-of-a-Living-Wage-for-Revelstoke-Nov-12-2016.pdf.

Cohen, M. G., Limpright, I., and Peacock, K. (2018). Minimum Wages for Those with Alternate Rates in British Columbia: Farm Workers Paid by Piece Rate, Liquor Servers, Live-in Home Support Workers, Resident Caretakers, Live-in Camp Leaders. *British Columbia Fair Wages Commission*, 1-90. Retrieved from www.sfu.ca/content/dam/sfu/labour/fairwagescommission/FWC_Second_Report_March_2018_FINAL.pdf.

Cook, D. (2008). *The Impact of a Living Wage Policy for The City of Calgary: Review of Literature*. Ruff Institute of Global Homelessness. Retrieved from https://ighhub.org/sites/default/files/lwp_literature_review.pdf.

Couturier, E.-L., Labrie, V., and Nguyen, M. (2020). *Le revenu viable 2020 dans l'échelle des revenus*. Institut de recherche et d'informations socio-économiques. Retrieved from https://cdn.iris-recherche.qc.ca/uploads/publication/file/Revenu_viable_2020_WEB.pdf.

Daley, A., Burton, P., and Phipps, S. (2015). 'Measuring poverty and inequality in northern Canada'. *Journal of Children and Poverty*, 21(2): 89–110. https://doi.org/10.1080/10796126.2015.1089147.

Department of Finance Canada. (2020, March). *Government Introduces Canada Emergency Response Benefit to Help Workers and Businesses*. Government of Canada. Retrieved from https://www.canada.ca/en/department-finance/news/2020/03/introduces-canada-emergency-response-benefit-to-help-workers-and-businesses.html.

Dionne-Simard, D., and Miller, J. (2019). *Maximum Insights on Minimum Wage Workers: 20 Years of Data*. Statistics Canada.

Djidel, S., Gustajtis, B., Heisz, A., Lam, K., Marchand, I., and McDermott, S. (2020). *Report on the Second Comprehensive Review of the Market Basket Measure* (Ottawa: Statistics Canada). Retrieved from www150.statcan.gc.ca/ n1/pub/75f0002m/75f0002m2020002-eng.htm.

Eaton, J., and Dagg, A. (2004). 'Organizing homeworkers in Toronto's garment industry'. In D.M. Figart (Ed.), *Living Wage Movements: Global Perspectives* (pp. 85–100).

Evans, B. (2017). 'Alternatives to the low waged economy: Living wage movements in Canada and the United States'. *Alternative Routes: A Journal of Critical Social Research*, 28: 80–113. Retrieved from www.alternateroutes.ca/index.php/ar/issue/view/1597.

Evans, B., and Fanelli, C. (2016). 'A survey of the living wage movement in Canada: prospects and challenges'. *Interface*, 8(1): 77–96.

Evans, B., Fanelli, C., and McDowell, T. (Eds.). (2021). Rising Up: The Fight for Living Wage Work in Canada. Vancouver: UBC Press.

Fang, T., and Gunderson, M. (2016). 'Poverty dynamics among vulnerable groups in Canada'. In D.A. Green, C.W. Riddell, and F. St-Hilaire (Eds.), *Income Inequality: The Canadian Story* (pp. 103–127). Institute for Research on Public Policy. Retrieved from http://irpp.org/research/income-inequality-the-canadian-story/.

Fortin, N.M., and Lemieux, T. (2015). 'Changes in wage inequality in Canada: An interprovincial perspective'. *Canadian Journal of Economics*, 48(2): 682–713. https://doi.org/10.1111/caje.12140.

FWC Living Wage Public Hearing. (2019). Vancouver.

Galarneau, D. (2017). *Unionization Rates Falling*. Statistics Canada. www150.statcan.gc.ca/n1/pub/11-630-x/11-630-x2015005-eng.htm.

Gouter, D. (2021). 'The Living Wage Campaign in Hamilton: Assessing the voluntary approach.' In B. Evans, C. Fanelli, and T. McDowell. (Eds.), Rising Up: The Fight for Living Wage Work in Canada (pp. 211–229). UBC Press.

Green, D.A., Riddell, W.C., and St-Hilaire, F. (2016). Income inequality: The Canadian story. Ottawa: Institute for Research on Public Policy. Retrieved from http://irpp.org/research/income-inequality-the-canadian-story/

Green, D.A., Kesselman, J.R., and Tedds, L.M. (2021). *Covering All the Basics: Reforms for a More Just Society*. Vancouver, BC. Available at SSRN: https://ssrn.com/abstract=3781825.

Haener, M. (2013). *A Living Wage for Grande Prairie: Background Report*. Retrieved from www.cityofgp.com/sites/default/files/uploads/reports/2013_gp_living_wage_background_report.pdf.

Haener, M. (2015). *Yellowknife 2015 Living Wage*. Retrieved from http://livingwagecanada.ca/files/9714/4190/6174/Yk_Living_Wage_2015_final.pdf.

Haener, M. (2019). *Northwest Territories 2019 Living Wage: Yellowknife, Hay River, Inuvik.* Retrieved from https://anotheralt.files.wordpress.com/2019/03/nwt-2019-living-wage-report-final.pdf.

Hammond, K. (2021) 'The emergence of the Living Wage Movement in Canada's Northern Territories.' In B. Evans, C. Fanelli, and T. McDowell. (Eds.), *Rising Up: The Fight for Living Wage Work in Canada* (pp. 97–114). Vancouver: UBC Press.

Harris, L., J. Janmaat, M. Evans, and K.I. Carlaw (2018) 'Negotiating the frame for a living wage in Revelstoke, BC: An econ-anthropological approach', *Human Organization*, 77(3): 202–213.

Heery, E., Hann, D., and Nash, D. (2017). 'The Living Wage campaign in the UK'. *Employee Relations*, 39(6): 800–814. https://doi.org/10.1108/ER-04-2017-0083.

Heisz, A. (2019). *An update on the Market Basket Measure comprehensive review.* (Ottawa: Statistics Canada). Retrieved from https://www150.statcan.gc.ca/n1/pub/75f0002m/75f0002m2019009-eng.htm.

Hudson, C. (2021). 'Why business-led Living Wage campaigns fail: The case of Calgary, Alberta, 1999-2009.' In B. Evans, C. Fanelli, and T. McDowell. (Eds.), Rising Up: The Fight for Living Wage Work in Canada (pp. 230–250). Vancouver: UBC Press.

'Huron County becomes third municipality to pay living wage'. (2019, December 20). *CBC News*. Retrieved from www.cbc.ca/news/canada/london/living-wage-jobs-employees-huron-municipality-ontario-1.5405072.

Ivanova, I., Klein, S., and Raithby, T. (2018). *Working for a Living Wage: Making Paid Work Meet Basic Family Needs in Metro Vancouver 2018 Update*. Canadian Centre for Policy Alternatives. Retrieved from www.policyalternatives.ca/sites/default/files/uploads/publications/BC Office/2018/04/BC_LivingWage2018_final.pdf.

Ivanova, I., and Saugstad, L. (2019). *Working for a Living Wage: Making Paid Work Meet Basic Family Needs in Metro Vancouver 2019 Update*. Ottawa: Canadian Centre for Policy Alternatives.

Ivanova, I., and Strauss, K. (2020, May 27). 'Paid sick leave finally on the agenda: Here's why it matters'. *Policynote*. Retrieved from www.policynote.ca/paid-sick-leave/.

Jeon, S.-H., Liu, H., and Ostrovsky, Y. (2019). 'Measuring the gig economy in Canada using administrative data'. *Analytical Studies Branch Research Paper Series* (No. 437; Vol. 11F0019M). Retrieved from www.statcan.gc.ca.

Johnson, A.F., and Roberto, K.J. (2020). 'The COVID-19 pandemic: Time for a universal basic income?' *Public Administration and Development*, 40(4): 232–235. https://doi.org/10.1002/pad.1891.

Johnstone, A., and Cooper, T. (2013, May 29). 'Living wage: The best way to fight child poverty in Hamilton'. *The Hamilton Spectator*. Retrieved from www.thespec.com/opinion/columnists/2013/05/29/living-wage-the-best-way-to-fight-child-poverty-in-hamilton.html.

Keddy, S. (2015). *Evaluating Living Wage Campaigns: An analysis of the Factors That Influence Local Political Decision-Making* (Master's thesis, University of Waterloo).

Koebel, K., and Pohler, D. (2019). 'Expanding the Canada workers benefit to design a guaranteed basic income'. *Canadian Public Policy*, 45(3): 283–309. https://doi.org/10.3138/cpp.2019-016.

Leduc, G. (2017, March 1). 'Salaire minimum à 11,25 $ l'heure : insuffisant pour vivre dignement, selon l'IRIS'. *LeSoleil*. Retrieved from www.lesoleil.com/affaires/salaire-minimum-a-1125--lheure-insuffisant-pour-vivre-dignement-selon-liris-5873a8af9b90f31a53a509a47539fb17.

LeTourneau, M. (2018, December 7). 'PSAC calls for minimum wage increase, plan for living wage'. *Nunavut News*. Retrieved from https://nunavutnews.com/nunavut-news/psac-calls-for-minimum-wage-increase-plan-for-living-wage/.

Living Wage Employers (n.d.). Retrieved October 30, 2020, from Ontario Living Wage Network website: https://www.ontariolivingwage.ca/living_wage_Employers_directory?page=7.

Ludgate, C. (2021). 'The BC Living Wage for Families Campaign: A decade of building.' In B. Evans, C. Fanelli, and T. McDowell. (Eds.), Rising Up: The Fight for Living Wage Work in Canada (pp. 171–186). UBC Press.

Luxton, M. and McDermott, P. (2021). 'Getting by but dreaming of normal.' In B. Evans, C. Fanelli, and T. McDowell. (Eds.), Rising Up: The Fight for Living Wage Work in Canada (pp. 115–133). UBC Press.

Mackenzie, H., and Stanford, J. (2008). *A living wage for London? Canadian Centre for Policy Alternatives*. Retrieved from www.policyalternatives.ca/sites/default/files/uploads/publications/Ontario_Office_Pubs/2008/A_Living_Wage_for_Toronto.pdf.

Mahboubi, P. (2018, February 18). 'The ripple effect of Ontario's minimum-wage increase'. *The Globe and Mail*.

Michaud, S., Cotton, C., and Bishop, K. (2004). 'Exploration of methodological issues in the development of the market basket measure of low income for Human Resources Development Canada'. *Statistics Canada*. Retrieved from https://www150.statcan.gc.ca/n1/en/catalogue/75F0002M2004001

Ministry of Labour. (2019, May 30). 'Minimum wage increases June 1'. *BC Gov News*. Retrieved from https://news.gov.bc.ca/releases/2019LBR0018-001078#:~:text=Effective June 1%3A, increase of %241.30 per hour.

Morissette, R., and Dionne-Simard, D. (2018). *Recent Changes in the Composition of Minimum Wage Workers*. Statistics Canada.

Munro, N. (2020, October 1). 'Halifax to require its contractors to pay workers a living wage'. *The Chronicle Herald*. Retrieved from www.saltwire.com/halifax/news/local/halifax-to-require-its-contractors-to-pay-workers-a-living-wage-504519/

Nunavut News. (2020, March 12). 'Nunavut government hikes minimum wage to $16 an hour'. Retrieved from https://nunatsiaq.com/stories/article/nunavut-government-hikes-minimum-wage-to-16-an-hour/#:~:text=The Minister of Justice just,increase from %2413 to %2416!.

OECD (Organization for Economic Cooperation and Development) (2021a). *Income Inequality*. Retrieved February 5, 2021. https://doi.org/OECD (2021), Income inequality (indicator). doi: 10.1787/459aa7f1-en .

OECD (Organization for Economic Cooperation and Development) (2021b). *Poverty Rate*. https://doi.org/10.1787/0fe1315d-en.

Pickthorne, C. (2020). *City of Kingston: Certified Living Wage Employer*. Retrieved July 7, 2020, from Ontario Living Wage Network website: www.ontariolivingwage.ca/city_of_kingston_certified_living_wage_employer.

Richards, T., Cohen, M., Klein, S., and Littman, D. (2008). 'Working for a living wage: 2008 making paid work meet basic family needs in Vancouver and Victoria'. In *Canadian Centre for Policy Alternatives*. Retrieved from www.policyalternatives.ca/sites/default/files/uploads/publications/BC_Office_Pubs/bc_2008/ccpa_bc_living_wage_2008.pdf.

Rose, J.B., Thompson, M., and Smith, A.E. (Eds.). (2003). *Beyond the National Divide: Regional Dimensions of Industrial Relations* (vol. 78). Published for the Canadian Industrial Relations Association/Association canadienne des relations industrielles and the School of Policy Studies, Queen's University by McGill-Queen's University Press.

Schenk, C. (2001). *From Poverty Wages to a Living Wage*. Retrieved from www.socialjustice.org/uploads/pubs/FromPovertyWagestoaLivingWage.pdf.

Simmons, G. (2019, May 8). 'North Perth certified as second municipal living wage employer in Ontario'. *The Beacon Herald*. Retrieved from www.stratfordbeaconherald.com/news/local-news/north-perth-certified-as-second-municipal-living-wage-employer-in-ontario#:~:text=Calculated annually by the United,working 35 hours a week.

Social Planning Cowichan. (2017). *Cowichan Valley Living Wage 2016*. Retrieved from www.sfu.ca/content/dam/sfu/labour/fairwagescommission/Cowichan%20Valley%20Living%20Wage%202016.pdf.

Special Committee on Poverty in PEI. (2019). Retrieved October 30, 2020, from the Legislative Assembly of Prince Edward Island website: www.assembly.pe.ca/committees/current-committees/special-committee-on-poverty-in-pei.

Statistics Canada. (2017). *Current and Forthcoming Minimum Hourly Wage Rates for Experienced Adult Workers in Canada*. Retrieved February 5, 2021, from Government of Canada website: http://srv116.services.gc.ca/dimt-wid/sm-mw/rpt1.aspx

Statistics Canada. (2018). Table 11-10-0135-01 Low income statistics by age, sex and economic family type [Data table]. https://doi.org/10.25318/1110013501-eng

Statistics Canada. (2020). Table 14-10-0132-01 Union status by industry [Data table]. https://doi.org/10.25318/1410013201-eng.

Statistics Canada. (2021). Table 14-10-0287-02 Labour force characteristics by age group, monthly, seasonally adjusted [Data table]. https://doi.org/10.25318/1410028701-eng

The Nation Today. (n.d.). Retrieved October 30, 2020, from Squamish Nation website: www.squamish.net/about-us/the-nation-today/.

Thomson, H. (2014, October 27). 'Huu-ay-aht leads the way by adopting living wage policy'. Huu-ay-aht First Nations. Retrieved from https://huuayaht.org/2014/10/27/huu-ay-aht-leads-the-way-by-adopting-living-wage-policy/.

Wells, D. (2016). 'Living wage campaigns and building communities'. *Alternative Routes: A Journal of Critical Social Research*, 27: 235–246. Retrieved from www.alternateroutes.ca/index.php/ar/article/view/22400/18182.

Zuberi, D. (2011). 'Contracting out hospital support jobs: The effects of poverty wages, excessive workload, and job insecurity on work and family life'. *American Behavioral Scientist*, 55(7): 920–940. https://doi.org/10.1177/0002764211407835.

13 The belated return of an Australian living wage

Reworking 'a fair go' for the 21st century

Joshua Healy, Andreas Pekarek, and Ray Fells

Introduction

Australia was a forerunner in instituting a living wage. In 1907, it established a basic wage that was to enable a working man and his family to live in 'frugal comfort'. This basic wage underpinned Australia's distinctive system of compulsory arbitration, which served the country well for much of the twentieth century, delivering broadly based real wage growth and coordinated responses to economic downturns. In the 1980s, however, as pressure mounted to liberalize Australia's protected economy and 'free up' its labour market, support for arbitration waned. With encouragement from unions and employers, government policy shifted to prioritize decentralised wage setting ('enterprise bargaining') over the older national and industry-level processes. Australia retains a vestigial 'safety net' of minimum wages, but much of its original arbitration system has been dismantled. Consequently, enforcement mechanisms that protected workers' living standards have been weakened and problems of 'wage theft' have proliferated.

In this challenging environment, the living wage has recently found renewed support from Australia's peak union federation. We explore the reasons for this rekindling of interest, in the country where the living wage originated. We discuss the appeal of, and some of the limits to, reviving a needs-based conception of the living wage in the contemporary Australian system. We also consider why Australia has not been a breeding ground for the kinds of vibrant, community-led living wage movements that have garnered support in other countries (Prowse et al. 2017). A major contributing factor, we suggest, is that, even in its presently narrower role as a safety net, Australia's long-standing formal system has bequeathed a mechanism for setting and regularly updating an extensive, linked structure of minimum pay rates for most workers.

We argue in this chapter that defending and maintaining Australia's evolved minimum wage architecture offers the clearest route to the achievement of a contemporary living wage. Directing resources particularly at stronger enforcement efforts would materially benefit many of Australia's low-paid workers. The current national wage-setting authority, the Fair Work Commission, remains severely constrained in its ability to formally promulgate a living wage, however, by legislated criteria that omit reference to any such concept or requirement. In the context of declining union power and the Commission's much-reduced ability to control aggregate wages growth, opportunities exist for new alliances and community movements to coalesce around the pursuit of a living wage.

DOI: 10.4324/9781003054078-13

The evolution of wage setting and the return of a living wage

The task of fixing minimum wage rates is complex. There are two, broadly competing criteria upon which to base a decision – workers' needs and employers' capacity to pay – and various mechanisms have been used in Australia to weigh and balance these concerns at different times. (Bray, 2013 offers a detailed analysis of these developments.)

Just after the Federation of its former colonies, Australia opted for an arbitral system with the establishment of the Court of Conciliation and Arbitration in 1904. 'Parties' to disputes (typically employers and unions) would argue their case, as in a court of law, and binding decisions ('awards') were made. Through this process, wages and other conditions were gradually established for entire industries and occupations, as other workplaces were brought into the scope of existing awards. Awards became comprehensive documents that prescribed employment rules and entitlements in detail. Today, awards are supplemented by agreements reached between employees and employers at the workplace level, with or without union involvement (Behrens et al. 2020). The Commission certifies agreements to ensure they do not undercut relevant award provisions. Awards thus formally provide both a starting point for bargaining and a 'safety net' of minimum standards (Gahan and Pekarek 2012).

Workers' needs are the first of two criteria on which a minimum wage may be based. In Australia, a needs principle for wage determination was established very early, in the 1907 Harvester judgment, one of the first decisions of its kind in the world. The presiding judge in that case, Justice Higgins, sought evidence on what wage was needed for a labourer to provide for his family (assumed to be a wife and 'about three' children) to live in 'frugal comfort'. This became the foundational or 'basic' wage (FWA 2011). So, from its inception, Australia's system incorporated provision for workers' needs in the regulation of minimum pay rates.

Differentials – in Australia, called margins – were then added to reflect additional skills and in this way a wage structure was built up, and became an award. Referring to that part of wages that was for needs, Justice Higgins said: 'it is necessary to keep this living wage as a thing sacrosanct, beyond the reach of bargaining' (Plowman 1995: 258). His investigation was a pragmatic review of living costs, but one that also took account of prevailing wages, particularly in the public sector.

Initially, the needs-based approach was operationalized by linking wages to inflation. As award coverage expanded, however, the economic impacts of the Court's decisions grew. This elevated a second wage-setting criterion to prominence: employers' 'capacity to pay'. As with assessing needs, inferring capacity is complicated and has been hampered by data limitations. In seeking to balance needs against capacity to pay, the tribunal's role evolved from dispute arbiter to de facto economic manager. Explicit consideration of workers' needs – a living wage – was thus rolled into a wider assessment of what the economy could afford (Hancock 1998). Since the early 1990s, a more decentralized pay-setting environment has seen the tribunal's role reduced to making 'safety net adjustments' to minimum pay rates. Determinations during this later period have been partly guided by evidence about needs but supplemented (and often offset) by additional considerations, including the desirability of maintaining high levels of employment and business competitiveness (Healy 2011a).

Today, the Commission takes an investigative approach when deciding the minimum wage. It is required to weigh up 'relative living standards and the needs of the low paid' against other economic, social, and labour market criteria (see Table 13.1). Comprised by

Table 13.1 Determining minimum wage rates in Australia

Decision-making criteria	Decision-making process
Fair Work Act 2009, section 284	
The minimum wages objective	**Fair Work Commission procedure**
The FWC must establish and maintain a safety net of fair minimum wages, taking into account:	The process involves:
(a) the performance and competitiveness of the national economy, including productivity, business competitiveness and viability, inflation, and employment growth; and	i) written submissions from interested organizations and individuals ii) consultations before the Expert Panel iii) research commissioned by the Expert Panel.
(b) promoting social inclusion through increased workforce participation; and	The Expert Panel is made up of the president of the Commission, three other full-time members of the Commission, and three part-time members. The part-time members' sole function is to work on the annual wage review. Such members must have knowledge of, or experience in, one or more of the following fields:
(c) relative living standards and the needs of the low paid; and	
(d) the principle of equal remuneration for work of equal or comparable value; and	
(e) providing a comprehensive range of fair minimum wages to junior employees, employees to whom training arrangements apply, and employees with a disability.	• workplace relations • economics • social policy • business, industry, or commerce

an Expert Panel, the Commission conducts a formal inquiry in which submissions are made (by unions, social welfare advocacy groups, employers, and governments), independent research is sought, and decisions reflect the weight of evidence and the panel's judgement, rather than being an adjudicated settlement between disputants. Today's approach is forensic and data driven; decisions run to hundreds of pages. Yet, the challenge of balancing competing criteria and divergent interests to define an appropriate minimum wage remains, despite the better evidence available.

Remaking the case for a living wage

The inquiry into workers' needs in the 1907 Harvester case has been a touchstone for much subsequent Australian minimum wage fixing. In today's system, however, claims for higher minimum wages tend to anticipate the 'balancing act' that the Commission must perform, by seeking to prove that the economy *does* have underutilized capacity to pay, rather than by formulating claims primarily around needs-based considerations. The Australian Council of Trade Unions (ACTU, the peak union federation) did present so-called Living Wage claims based on principles of adequacy reminiscent of the Harvester case, in 1997 (Harcourt 1997), and again in 2002 (Healy 2011a). Though these submissions invoked the living wage concept, the amounts sought were largely based on what was thought to be economically affordable, and the Commission's decisions consistently fell short of what the ACTU said was required to re-establish a living wage (Buchanan et al. 2004).

Recently, the pursuit of a living wage has again gained favour among Australian unions, with the ACTU formally adopting a living wage policy objective (Gahan et al. 2018). Contending that the minimum wage had not maintained its value over time, the ACTU proposed 60 per cent of median earnings as a new living wage target (ACTU 2017; McKenzie 2018). An approach based on the median has the benefit of giving a clear aspirational target, and to some extent mutes the contrary incapacity-to-pay argument – if the economy can afford for median earnings to rise, then it can obviously afford for the lowest wages to rise, by an equivalent amount. The goal of a living wage, to be set at 60 per cent of median earnings, was affirmed at the 2018 ACTU Congress, and the Australian Labor Party subsequently contested the 2019 federal election promising to establish a living wage (but was defeated at the poll).

In conducting annual wage reviews, the Commission operates within its legislated terms of reference. These call for a range of economic and social indicators to be taken into account (Table 13.1). The ACTU's (2017) policy paper is critical of these criteria and calls for living costs to be re-evaluated. The peak union federation sees the Commission's current wage-setting parameters as giving excessive attention to economic factors (growth, employment, and competitiveness) at the expense of considerations about whether the minimum rate is sufficient:

> What is usually missing from [the] process is any attempt to define and measure what income the worker needs to have a reasonable standard of living. In other words, there is no serious attempt to check that the base figure on which the minimum wage increase is calculated is adequate to provide a normal family with a civilized existence.
>
> (ACTU 2017: 8)

In calling for the Commission to re-examine living costs, the ACTU recognizes that there is no authoritative living wage calculation in Australia to which its wage claims can be linked. The closest approximations are the budget standards devised by the Social Policy Research Centre (SPRC) at the University of New South Wales. A 'budget standard' is a detailed calculation of the expenditures required for a household to have a predetermined standard of living, given its composition (mix of family members) and location (Saunders 2006: 156). The SPRC initially defined a 'modest but adequate' budget as one enabling a living standard close to the median for the whole Australian community (Healy 2011a). More recently, its method has evolved towards defining a 'healthy' living standard as one that provides for the essentials, while also enabling active participation in social life. The newest budgets, which specify a minimum income for healthy living (MIHL), aim to approximate *two-thirds of the median* income – similar to the Organization for Economic Cooperation and Development's (OECD) low-pay threshold (Saunders and Bedford 2017: 34). Budget standards have been used in submissions to the Commission at different times by unions and social welfare groups, such as the Australian Council of Social Services (ACOSS) (Healy 2011a). The ACTU (2004: 111) used the first budget standards to argue that award wage increases 'substantially reduce the shortfall' between what low-paid workers need to buy and what they can actually afford.

According to the latest budget standards (Saunders and Bedford 2017), an employed single adult needed an income of $597 per week in 2017 (before tax and including housing costs) to live healthily. A working couple with two young children needed nearly twice that much: $1,173. At the time, the full-time National Minimum Wage (NMW) in Australia was $695. Thus, by the measure of these standards, Australian NMW recipients already earned enough for a healthy life, if living alone, but not nearly enough, if they had a family to support. This differentiation in workers' living circumstances powerfully illustrates the difficulty of determining a single wage that can universally prevent poverty – a point that others have also reflected on (Buchanan et al. 2004).

We know from several earlier studies that the low-paid workforce in Australia is diverse in its make-up, including some workers who are young and living at home, along with others who are parents with their own dependent children (Leigh 2007; Richardson and Harding 1999). For those with families, a single wage near the NMW would not buy a healthy living standard. Arguably for that reason, many of Australia's low paid are in households with more than one source of income from which to meet shared needs (McGuinness and Freebairn 2007).

In a decentralized and increasingly fragmented system, there have been renewed calls for the tribunal to give greater attention to the needs of the low paid. Whether the FWC finds itself able to take a more living-cost approach in its determination of minimum wages will, however, largely depend on whether Parliament decides to change the Commission's remit by redefining the 'minimum wage objective' as currently enshrined in the Fair Work Act 2009 (Table 13.1).

Adequacy and capacity: does Australia get the balance right?

We now examine how Australia's system of minimum wage regulation has performed in recent years. Does the system provide a living wage, and, if not, how far away is that goal? We take a comparative approach, presenting data for Australia and four other developed, English-speaking, liberal market democracies: New Zealand, Canada, the United Kingdom (UK), and the United States (US). Our sources are the statistical collections of the OECD and the Australian Bureau of Statistics (ABS). Both are reputable and widely used. All our data come from freely available sources.

The real minimum wage

We begin by comparing real minimum wages, in Figure 13.1. The minimum wage expressed in 'real' terms – relative to prices – is a key measure of its purchasing power, and thus of the living standard it affords. To reflect price differences between countries, Figure 13.1 uses data that are adjusted for purchasing power parity by the OECD. This provides us with consistent evidence on the value of goods and services that each country's minimum wage can buy.

Australia's National Minimum Wage (NMW) has tracked a path of remarkably steady growth. This is a commendable result of an established, annual wage-setting process. Over the past 20 years, the real NMW in Australia rose by 15 per cent, without obvious periods of stagnation or decline. The only visible 'blip' coincides with the global recession in 2008. In comparative terms, Australia's NMW is high. This has been true for some time, although decreasingly so. In 2019, Australia's NMW was worth 18 per cent more than the next highest (New Zealand), whereas, in 2000, Australia was much further ahead. Australia remains a bastion of progressive minimum wage provision, but its once-unassailable position of global leadership is slipping.

Other countries' minimum wage curves in Figure 13.1 are more erratic than Australia's, with good and bad counterexamples. The performance of the US Federal Minimum Wage (FMW) is a negative outlier: in 2019, it was worth *less* in real terms (-5 per cent) than it had been in 2000 (see Luce 2021 in Chapter 11). As we argue below, this was not because the US economy lacked 'capacity to pay'; rather, it is a problem of distribution – and political will. The manifest shortcomings of the US FMW suggest why community-based living wage movements, led by 'Fight for $15', have prospered (Pasquier et al. 2020).

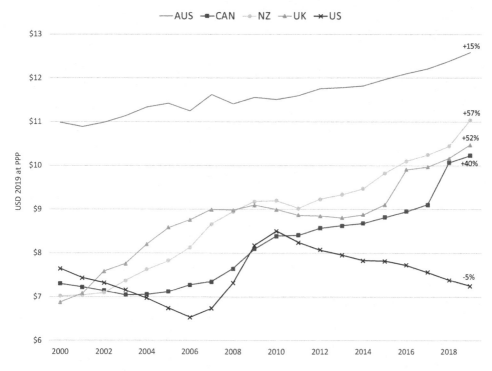

Figure 13.1 Evolution of the real minimum wage in selected OECD countries ($US 2019 PPP). Source: OECD (2020a).

They also help explain why efforts to reform minimum wage laws in the US have lately focused on eliciting action from progressive administrators at state and municipal levels, rather than at federal level.

Though the US wins no plaudits for its dismal minimum wage track record, the three other countries in Figure 13.1 (Canada, New Zealand, and the UK) have made genuine gains. All three saw their real minimum wages appreciate by at least 40 per cent over the past 20 years, with New Zealand leading the pack (a 57 per cent gain).

The minimum-to-median relativity

Another way of evaluating the minimum wage is through a comparison with median earnings. The median is the midpoint of the earnings distribution: half of workers earn more than it, and the other half earn less. The ratio of the minimum to the median is often known as its 'bite' – that is, how far the minimum wage 'protrudes into' the earnings distribution (Hamilton 2018). Unlike the measures of real purchasing power in Figure 13.1, the minimum-to-median is a relative indicator. It indicates whether the minimum wage kept up with or lagged behind the growth of median earnings. In Figure 13.2, we again look at the past 20 years of data for five selected OECD countries, including Australia. And, because the ACTU proposed '60 per cent of the median' as its new living wage target, we also show this level (as a horizontal dotted line) in Figure 13.2.

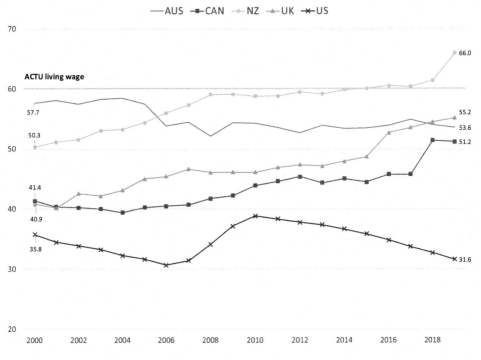

Figure 13.2 The relationship between minimum wages and median earnings by country.
Note: Figures are for full-time workers.
Source: OECD (2020b).

Our first observation on Figure 13.2 is that Australia's NMW declined relative to median earnings over the past 20 years. Most of this decline occurred in the second half of the 2000s, coinciding with the introduction of the Liberal-led coalition (conservative) government's WorkChoices legislation in 2005, and the establishment of a short-lived new minimum wage authority known as the Australian Fair Pay Commission. Since the change of federal government in 2007 and the introduction of Labor's Fair Work Act 2009, the minimum wage has stabilized. In the past ten years, it has settled in the range of 53–54 per cent of Australian full-time median earnings.

Australia fares less well on this indicator of minimum wage performance when compared to other countries, again with the exception of the US. While the minimum fell behind the median in Australia, the opposite occurred in New Zealand, Canada, and the UK. This is consistent with the real gains in Figure 13.1. Australia started the period of comparison, in 2000, with its NMW worth nearly 58 per cent of median earnings; comfortably the highest ratio of the five countries shown in Figure 13.2. Twenty years on, it had fallen not one but two places, behind both New Zealand (at 66 per cent) and the UK (at 55 per cent). Notably, New Zealand is the only country to have reached the ACTU's living wage target. In the early 2000s, this target seemed within reach for Australia, too, but by 2019 it was receding. Other advanced countries have demonstrated that progress towards such a target is possible and that it need not be the end point for improvements.

The decline in the relative value of Australia's NMW in Figure 13.2 cannot be attributed to economic underperformance. Indeed, Australia has enjoyed quite strong increases in its per capita gross domestic product (GDP), a measure of average productivity and the growth in living standards. In Australia, this rose by 28 per cent from 2000 to 2019, more than in the US (25 per cent), UK (23 per cent), and Canada (18 per cent) – but less than in New Zealand (35 per cent) (OECD 2020c). These data imply that Australia had the necessary economic capacity to further boost the NMW and to ensure that its low-paid recipients shared equitably in rising community living standards.

Low pay prevalence

An important feature of contemporary Australian wage determination is that the Commission adjusts a whole structure of award-based minimum pay rates in addition to the NMW. After recent and extensive rationalization, there are now 121 so-called Modern Awards that prescribe minimum wages and other employment conditions for particular industries and occupations.

An upshot of this distinctive institutional feature is that the outcomes of annual wage review cases automatically 'flow on' through all awards, although the Commission has, on occasion, provided increases of different amounts for NMW recipients and workers on higher award rates (Healy 2011b; Healy 2015). International readers may be surprised that the full 'award-reliant' workforce (that is, those on the NMW plus those on higher award rates) accounts for nearly one-quarter (23 per cent, or around 2.2 million) of all Australian non-managerial employees (ABS 2019a). While still sizeable, this proportion is unquestionably lower than in the past, due to legislative reforms, noted earlier, that have given preference to bargained wage settlements and sought to curtail the overall reach of the award system.

An immediately obvious question, then, is whether, with the benefit of a comprehensive structure of minimum pay rates (the NMW plus awards), Australia has done better than other countries at stemming the growth of low-paid employment. We return to the OECD data for an answer. Figure 13.3 shows the average low pay incidence, by decade, for our five comparator countries. Low pay is defined here as *less than two-thirds* of full-time median earnings – a higher threshold than that nominated recently by the ACTU (i.e., 60 per cent of the median), but nonetheless one that provides useful comparative evidence on the proportion of workers that is likely to be 'within scope' of its recommended living wage target.

The short answer is that Australia's unique system did *not* stop low-paid employment from becoming more prevalent in recent decades. Figure 13.3 shows that 14 per cent of Australian full-time workers met the definition of low paid in the 1990s, rising to 16 per cent by the 2010s. While the change is relatively small in magnitude, it is moving in the wrong direction. Other countries' experiences are closely related to their minimum wage trajectories in Figure 13.1. New Zealand (Chapter 15), Canada (Chapter 12), and the UK (Chapter 2) increased the bite of their respective minimum wages, and each saw corresponding declines in low pay prevalence. In the US, in contrast, a falling FMW led to rising low pay prevalence. The differences in low pay prevalence *between* countries are generally much greater than the changes that occurred *within* any of them, and

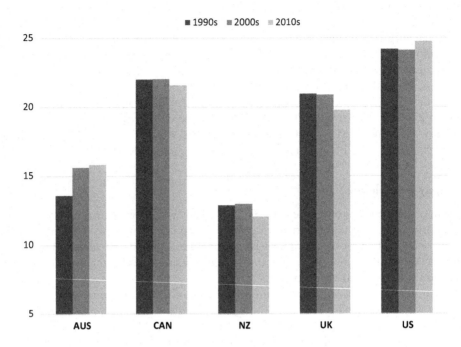

Figure 13.3 Incidence of low pay (less than two-thirds of median earnings), by country and decade.
Note: Figures are for full-time workers.
Source: OECD (2020d).

these cross-country differences are themselves likely to reflect prevailing (and often long-standing) idiosyncrasies in minimum wages and other institutions (Freeman 1998).

Australia's experience warrants further comment, in light of the differing patterns of results in Figures 13.1 and 13.3. While the real Australian NMW has increased since the 1990s, so has low pay prevalence. For some observers, this may be seen as evidence that the Commission should have 'gone further', by granting higher minimum wage increases. As we suggested above, there was sufficient capacity in the economy – judged by rising per capita GDP – to justify such actions. Yet, as we also noted, the whole award pay structure, and not only the NMW, affects Australian low pay prevalence. Here, the NMW is merely the 'leading edge' of changes that will work their way through the entire minimum pay structure, by virtue of flow-on award adjustments. If the NMW lags behind median earnings growth, as Figure 13.2 suggests, that shortfall will flow through to award rates, effectively 'dragging down' the whole minimum pay structure. The result will be an exacerbation of low pay, since many award-reliant workers earn more than the NMW but still less than two-thirds of median earnings (Healy 2011b).

Industry comparisons

The prevalence of low pay is not uniform across the economy. One of its main determinants in Australia is industry, which we look at more closely in Figure 13.4. We locate the centre (median) of the wage structure within each industry. Lower median earnings indicate that

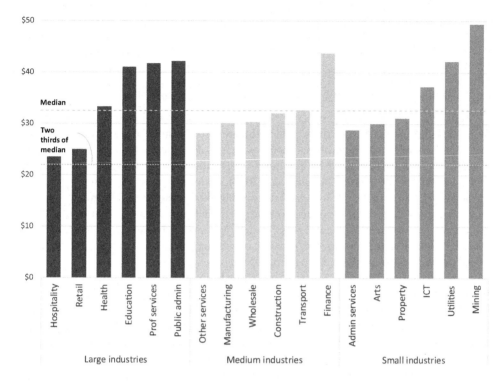

Figure 13.4 Median hourly earnings by industry and industry size category in Australia, 2019.
Note: Size categories obtained by ranking industries in descending order by total employment.
Source: ABS (2019b).

an industry has proportionately more low-paid workers. However, as we seek to understand the drivers of aggregate low pay prevalence, an industry's median wage is not the only influential factor; its employment size also matters. An industry may be lowly paid, but small, in which case its net contribution to low pay prevalence is marginal. Figure 13.4 adjusts for this fact, by grouping the 18 major Australian industries by their total employment size: large, medium, and small. (We exclude Agriculture, as it is not covered by the ABS Survey of Employee Earnings and Hours.)

Two industries stand out clearly in an Australian analysis of low pay: Hospitality and Retail. Both have median earnings that are well below average for the whole Australian workforce, and both are also large by total employment size; together, these two industries employ almost two million Australians. A related feature of these industries is a strong reliance on awards as pay-setting instruments, which gives the Commission a significant direct role in influencing their prevailing wages. Hospitality and Retail both have median earnings below the four other largest industries (Health, Education, Professional Services, and Public Administration). Indeed, the median in both – but especially in Hospitality – is only just above the OECD low-pay threshold. Both these sectors clearly have many low-paid workers. Aside from those two, the next largest low-paid industry is Other Services, which encompasses repair and maintenance activities and personal care services provided to private households. Despite the multiple layers of protection provided through the

NMW and awards, three industries – Hospitality, Retail, and Other Services – remain sites of concentrated low pay and labour market disadvantage in Australia. The ACTU's recent push for a living wage was aimed squarely at the 800,000 workers in these three industries who rely on either the NMW or other award rates to set their pay (ABS 2019a).

Wage theft as an emerging threat to the system's integrity

Having discussed the Australian system's current strengths and weaknesses, we now turn to the insidious problem of 'wage theft', which threatens to accelerate the prevalence of low-paid employment below the proposed living wage – indeed, below the existing minimum wage. In recent years, there have been mounting revelations about employers underpaying their workers (Healy 2016; Thornthwaite 2017). Employer non-compliance has been repeatedly found in the largest low-paid sectors, Hospitality and Retail (Figure 13.4) – in convenience stores, fast-food outlets, post offices, and petrol stations – but also extends beyond these, to airlines, banks, and other large corporations. In Australia, the problem of wage theft finally 'went mainstream' in 2019, becoming a focus of sustained public, managerial, and judicial concern (Clibborn 2020).

There are strongly opposing views of why some businesses fail to meet their obligations to workers. On the employer side, explanations often centre on information deficiencies and regulatory complexity. By these accounts, employers are either unaware of their obligations or inadvertently 'caught out' by arcane laws. Awards are portrayed as too complex, despite recent simplification efforts, which means, according to this view, that even well-meaning employers struggle to 'do the right thing' (Patty 2019). Such interpretations tend to overlook or downplay both the possibility and the revealed extent of wilful employer misconduct.

Going against the more lenient view, unions and other workers' advocates often regard underpayment as at least employer opportunism, if not deliberate malfeasance. The notion of 'wage theft' captures this interpretation. In many cases, malpractice has undoubtedly occurred. Investigative reporter Adele Ferguson has uncovered egregious examples of employers that knowingly violate minimum standards by, for instance, recording only half the hours that employees actually work, or forcing workers to repay part of their wage; for migrant workers, there is often an accompanying threat of deportation if they report these practices to enforcement authorities (Ferguson et al. 2015). Academic observers have suggested that, for certain types of organizations, wage underpayment is indivisible from the business model – some franchises, for instance, would not be viable if they were compliant with minimum wage standards and denied the 'strategy' of underpaying workers (Stewart et al. 2018). Recently, some Australian jurisdictions have legislated to criminalize wage theft, thereby moving to impose more forceful punishments and deterrents for these practices (Schofield-Georgeson and Rawling 2020). The laudable intention is to discourage otherwise viable businesses from treating contravention of minimum labour standards as if it is a legitimate source of competitive advantage.

While the reasons for non-compliance do vary, there is no doubt about its prevalence. The extent of the problem was starkly revealed in a recent report by the consulting firm PwC, which used information from Australia's industrial inspectorate, the Fair Work Ombudsman, to estimate the annual value of underpaid wages. It found that Australian workers lose 'in the order of $1.35 billion in underpayments per year', with those in certain sectors being most 'at risk': Construction, Healthcare, Hospitality, and Retail (PwC

2020). The latter two sectors are low paid, as shown in Figure 13.4, so the preponderance of wage theft within them is perhaps not surprising. Construction and Healthcare are *not* low-paid sectors overall, but both do contain sizeable 'pockets' of employment disadvantage. Healthcare includes aged and disability care, where wages are lower than in other settings, and where many workers are temporary migrants (Charlesworth and Isherwood 2020). In Construction, widespread use of 'labour hire' and other non-standard employment arrangements creates opaque chains of responsibility for compliance that serve to incentivize underpayment of wages (Toner and Coates 2006).

It is extraordinary that workers are deprived of $1.35 billion in earnings annually, but the scale of that loss is difficult to comprehend without a meaningful comparator. We can gain perspective by calculating the expected benefits from the ACTU's recent living wage claims. In 2018, the ACTU made the largest of its claims, asking the Commission to raise the NMW and other award rates by 7.2 per cent (ACTU 2018: 9). At that time, there were some 2.23 million award-reliant, non-managerial employees, earning an average of $788 per week (ABS 2019a). The ACTU claim would have thus added $57 to the average award-reliant employee's weekly pay. Annualizing this and multiplying it out over the 2.23 million workers, we estimate that the ACTU's 2018 claim was worth an additional $6.6 billion in compensation to workers.

Returning to PwC's $1.35 billion wage theft estimate, these calculations mean that *more than one-fifth* of the expected gains from the ACTU living wage claim would have been forfeited through underpayment. It must also be recalled here that, ultimately, the Commission only granted a 3.5 per cent wage increase: less than half of what the ACTU had asked for (FWC 2018). So, proportionately, NMW recipients were denied an even larger portion (42 per cent) of the eventual wage rise, because of employer minimum wage non-compliance. In short, it can no longer be assumed that the full benefit of annual wage reviews reaches workers, as may have once been the case. Instead, there is substantial 'leakage'. Raising minimum wage rates in this context is analogous to pouring yet more water into an already leaking bucket. Or, to borrow another metaphor from Australia's industrial relations lexicon, there would be merit in first mending the 'safety net' before attempting to raise it further.

We are not arguing that, because wage theft undermines workers' gains in practice, the ACTU should abandon any pursuit of a living wage. Australia has developed a wage-setting process and the ACTU is a crucial contributor to that process. It will no doubt continue to avail itself of that forum, pushing the Commission for wage increases on whatever basis it sees as most advantageous. But, within the current framework for minimum wage determination, use of the living wage concept has not given the ACTU much leverage. None of the Commission's recent decisions raise the possibility of an Australian living wage – nor did it adopt this terminology in earlier decisions (Buchanan et al. 2004). The living wage concept is mentioned, but only in passing references to the UK's National Living Wage (e.g. see FWC 2018: 64).

Without 'changing the rules' – which the ACTU has previously campaigned for (Gahan et al. 2018) – there are significant practical limitations to the Commission proclaiming a living wage in Australia. Again, this does not mean that living wage arguments and evidence per se are without merit. They may serve a rhetorical purpose for unions, signalling a commitment to a substantially higher minimum wage and helping 'frame' campaigns around ideals of equity and social justice (Behrens and Pekarek 2020; Gahan and Pekarek 2013). The next triennial ACTU Congress, to be held in 2021, will reveal whether Australian unions continue to support efforts to institute a new living wage, as they did in 2018.

Conclusion

Australia is renowned for its distinctive and long-standing approach to wage determination. From its earliest days, the Federal arbitration system recognized workers' normal 'needs' as an important factor aiding in the prevention and settlement of industrial disputes. Over the course of the twentieth century, that initial acceptance of needs as a wage-setting criterion was retained as a core guiding principle, even as the system's workforce coverage and economic significance expanded greatly. The latter meant that a second main consideration, 'capacity to pay', was quickly incorporated into the mechanisms of wage setting, alongside, and often in opposition to, needs-based claims. Nonetheless, by the close of the twentieth century, Australia retained a basic minimum wage that was high, compared with other advanced countries, and that was bolstered by an interlinked structure of higher (skills-based) award minimum rates of pay.

The past 20 years have seen a raft of new challenges and pressures arise in the system. The original dispute-resolution function of national wage fixation has long been jettisoned, in favour of a process driven by evidence, expert judgement, and pre-specified legislated criteria. Consideration is still given to 'relative living standards and the needs of the low paid', but this is only one among a larger set of considerations that emphasize macroeconomic and labour market goals, such as employment levels, cost factors, and business competitiveness. In an increasingly fragmented and individualized labour market, the award system directly sets pay for nearly one in four non-managerial Australian employees, while trade union density is lower still.

Australia's recent track record on minimum wage determination has been respectable, but not outstanding. Australia's minimum wage has risen in real terms, and it remains among the highest in the world. At the same time, other major countries have outperformed Australia, by gradually 'ratcheting up' their minimum wages in the earnings distribution. Australia's NMW has slipped relative to median earnings, and relative to the performance of comparable economies. The prevalence of low pay has also increased slightly, as the NMW has lagged further behind median earnings. We argued that this slide in the Australian minimum wage's position was not due to economic (in-)capacity constraints. Instead, recent decades have seen robust per capita GDP growth (prior to the Covid-19 crisis), suggesting that there was scope for Australia to have taken a different, more progressive path in adjusting its NMW and other award pay rates.

Against this backdrop, the ACTU recently sought to reintroduce the notion of a 'living wage' to the Commission's annual wage review proceedings. Notably, and in contrast to overseas living wage movements, this tactic was not born of community campaigning, but was essentially a vehicle for persuading the Commission to give greater priority to needs when determining the NMW and award rates of pay. The high watermark of this push came in 2018, when the ACTU asked for and sought to convince the Commission to raise minimum wages by 7.2 per cent. This high-level advocacy for a living wage may seem unusual to overseas observers, but it makes sense in light of Australia's particular institutional arrangements. The Commission, historically, was 'the main game' for adjusting wages and, although its aggregate influence is now much diminished, the safety net remains immensely important for lower-paid workers and industries. The ACTU's effort to reinject historical living wage norms into the contemporary wage-setting proceedings failed, however. The Commission granted much lower increases than the ACTU sought and, tellingly, gave no credence to the notion of an Australian living wage. We have argued that this will remain the case, without a broader reworking of the Commission's operating parameters.

Outside the Commission's annual proceedings, problems of wage evasion have taken hold. Employer underpayment of workers' entitlements has become a mainstream phenomenon – worst in, but not confined to, the largest low-paid industries of Hospitality and Retail. This issue, which unions and Labor governments have denounced as 'wage theft', threatens to derail what remains of Australia's wage-fixing system. It saps the Commission's credibility and casts doubt on the merits of pursuing a living wage through that forum. We suggested that, because underpayments deny workers a part of what they otherwise stand to gain from minimum-wage adjustments, unions must make difficult strategic choices about whether other avenues (outside the Commission) are more conducive to realizing their living wage objectives. With wage theft undercutting employees' earnings, and more workers contending with low and volatile pay in the 'gig economy' (Healy and Pekarek 2020), there is likely to be a need, and an opportunity, for broader, community-led calls for the restoration of a decent and inviolable living wage.

References

ABS (Australian Bureau of Statistics) (2019a). *Employee Earnings and Hours, Australia, May 2018*, cat. no. 6306.0, Australian Bureau of Statistics, Canberra.

ABS (Australian Bureau of Statistics) (2019b). *Characteristics of Employment, Australia, August 2019*, Table 3 'Distribution of earnings for employees by industry', cat. no. 6333.0, Australian Bureau of Statistics, Canberra.

ACTU (Australian Council of Trade Unions) (2004). *Minimum Wages Case: Written Submission*, Australian Council of Trade Unions, Melbourne.

ACTU (Australian Council of Trade Unions) (2017). *Living up to the promise of Harvester: Time for a living wage.* Australian Council of Trade Unions, Melbourne.

ACTU (Australian Council of Trade Unions) (2018). *ACTU Submission to the Annual Wage Review 2018*, Australian Council of Trade Unions, Melbourne.

Behrens, M., and Pekarek, A. (2020). 'Divided we stand? Coalition dynamics in the German union movement'. *British Journal of Industrial Relations*, Online ahead of print, doi: https://doi.org/10.1111/bjir.12565

Behrens, M., Colvin, A., Dorigatti, L., and Pekarek, A. (2020). 'Systems for conflict resolution in comparative perspective', *ILR Review*, 73(2): 312–344.

Bray, J.R. (2013). *Reflections on the Evolution of the Minimum Wage in Australia: Options for the Future.* Crawford School SPI Working Paper No. 01/2013, Australian National University, Canberra. https://dx.doi.org/10.2139/ssrn.2342026

Buchanan, J., Watson, I., and Meagher, G. (2004). 'The living wage in Australia: History, recent developments, and current challenges'. In D. Figart (ed.), *Living Wage Movements: Global Perspectives.* Routledge, London, pp. 122–137.

Charlesworth, S., and Isherwood, L. (2020). 'Migrant aged-care workers in Australia: Do they have poorer-quality jobs than their locally born counterparts?' *Ageing and Society*, Article in press, doi: https://doi.org/10.1017/S0144686X20000525

Clibborn, S. (2020). 'Australian industrial relations in 2019: The year wage theft went mainstream'. *Journal of Industrial Relations*, 62(3): 331–340.

Fair Work Act 2009 (Cwth) s70.

Ferguson, A., Danckert, S., and Toft, K. (2015). '7-Eleven: A sweatshop on every corner'. *Sydney Morning Herald*, August 29. Available at: www.smh.com.au/business/workplace/7eleven-a-sweatshop-on-every-corner-20150827-gj8vzn.html (Accessed November 30, 2020).

Freeman, R. (1998). 'War of the models: Which labour market institutions for the 21st century?' *Labour Economics*, 5(1): 1–24.

FWA (Fair Work Australia) (2011). *Waltzing Matilda and the Sunshine Harvester Factory: The Early History of the Arbitration Court, the Australian Minimum Wage, Working Hours and Paid Leave*. Fair Work Australia, Melbourne.

FWC (Fair Work Commission) (2018). *Decision: Annual Wage Review 2017–18*, Fair Work Commission, Melbourne. [2018] FWCFB 3500

Gahan, P., and Pekarek, A. (2012). 'The rise and rise of enterprise bargaining in Australia, 1991–2011'. *Labour & Industry: a journal of the social and economic relations of work*, 22(3): 195–222.

Gahan, P., and Pekarek, A. (2013). 'Social movement theory, collective action frames and union theory: A critique and extension'. *British Journal of Industrial Relations*, 51(4): 754–776.

Gahan, P., Pekarek, A., and Nicholson, D. (2018). 'Unions and collective bargaining in Australia in 2017'. *Journal of Industrial Relations*, 60(3): 337–357.

Hamilton, R. (2018). *The History of the Australian Minimum Wage*. Fair Work Commission, Melbourne. Available at: www.fwc.gov.au/documents/documents/archives/exhibitions/minwage/exhibitionpaper-100yrsminwage.pdf (Accessed 9 October 2020).

Hancock, K. (1998). 'The needs of the low paid'. *Journal of Industrial Relations*, 40(1): 42–62.

Harcourt, T. (1997). 'The economics of the living wage'. *Australian Economic Review*, 30(2): 194–203.

Healy, J. (2011a). 'What role do safety net wage adjustments play in alleviating household need?' *Journal of Industrial Relations*, 53(2): 169–192.

Healy, J. (2011b). 'The quest for fairness in Australian minimum wages'. *Journal of Industrial Relations*, 53(5): 662–680.

Healy, J. (2015). 'The Australian labour market in 2014: Still ill?' *Journal of Industrial Relations*, 57(3): 348–365.

Healy, J. (2016). 'The Australian labour market in 2015'. *Journal of Industrial Relations*, 58(3): 308–323.

Healy, J., and Pekarek, A. (2020). 'Work and wages in the gig economy: Can there be a High Road?' In A. Wilkinson and M. Barry (eds.), *The Future of Work and Employment*. Edward Elgar, Cheltenham, UK, pp. 156–173.

Leigh, A. (2007). 'Does raising the minimum wage help the poor?' *Economic Record*, 83(263): 432–445.

McGuinness, S., and Freebairn, J. (2007). 'Who are the low paid?' *Australian Journal of Labour Economics*, 10(1): 17–37.

McKenzie, M. (2018). 'The erosion of minimum wage policy in Australia and labour's shrinking share of total income'. *Journal of Australian Political Economy*, 81: 52–77.

OECD (Organization for Economic Cooperation and Development) (2020a). 'LFS – Real minimum wages'. OECD. Stat, https://stats.oecd.org/Index.aspx?DataSetCode=RMW (Accessed October 4, 2020).

OECD (Organization for Economic Cooperation and Development) (2020b). 'LFS – Minimum relative to median wages of full-time workers'. OECD. Stat, https://stats.oecd.org/Index.aspx?DataSetCode=MIN2AVE (Accessed October 4, 2020).

OECD (Organization for Economic Cooperation and Development) (2020c). 'Level of GDP per capita and productivity'. OECD. Stat, https://stats.oecd.org/Index.aspx?DataSetCode=PDB_LV (Accessed October 4, 2020).

OECD (Organization for Economic Cooperation and Development) (2020d). 'LFS - Decile ratios of gross earnings' Organisation for Economic Cooperation and Development, OECD. Stat, https://stats.oecd.org/Index.aspx?DataSetCode=DEC_I (Accessed October 4, 2020).

Pasquier, V., Daudigeos, T., and Barros, M. (2020). 'Towards a new flash-mob unionism: The case of the Fight for 15 movement'. *British Journal of Industrial Relations*, 58(2): 336–363.

Patty, A. (2019). '"Beyond hopeless": Complaints about award system "excuse" for underpayments'. *The Sydney Morning Herald*, October 31.

Plowman, D. (1995). 'Protecting the low income-earner: Minimum wage determination in Australia'. *Economic and Labour Relations Review*, 6(2): 252–287.

Prowse, P., Lopes, A., and Fells, R. (2017). 'Community and union-led living wage campaigns'. *Employee Relations*, 39(6): 825–839.

PwC (PricewaterhouseCoopers) (2020). *Navigating Australia's Industrial Relations*, Melbourne. Available at: www.pwc.com.au/publications/australia-matters/navigating-australias-industrial-relations.html (Accessed October 12, 2020).

Richardson, S., and Harding, A. (1999). 'Poor workers? The link between low wages, low family income and the tax and transfer systems'. In S. Richardson (Ed.), *Reshaping the Labour Market: Regulation, Efficiency and Equality in Australia*, Cambridge University Press, Melbourne, pp. 122–158.

Saunders, P. (2006). 'The historical development of budget standards for Australian working families'. *Journal of Industrial Relations*, 48(2): 155–174.

Saunders, P., and Bedford, M. (2017). *New Minimum Income for Healthy Living Budget Standards for Low-Paid and Unemployed Australians*. SPRC Report 11/17, Social Policy Research Centre, University of New South Wales, Sydney.

Schofield-Georgeson, E., and Rawling, M. (2020). 'Industrial legislation in Australia in 2019'. *Journal of Industrial Relations*, 62(3): 425–445.

Stewart, A., Stanford, J., and Hardy, T. (2018). *The Wages Crisis in Australia: What It Is and What to Do about It.* University of Adelaide Press, Adelaide.

Thornthwaite, L. (2017). 'The living wage crisis in Australian industrial relations'. *Labour & Industry: A Journal of the Social and Economic Relations of Work*, 27(4): 261–269.

Toner, P., and Coates, N. (2006). 'Competition and the growth of non-standard employment: The case of the Australian construction industry'. *Labour & Industry: A Journal of the Social and Economic Relations of Work*, 17(2): 99–118.

14 Employer and employee perspectives on the living wage in New Zealand

*James Arrowsmith, Jane Parker, Amanda Young-Hauser,
Darrin Hodgetts, Jarrod Haar, Stuart Carr, and
Siautu Alefaio-Tugia*

Introduction – New Zealand's living wage context

Aotearoa/New Zealand (NZ) is an important country for the development and application of the 'living wage' (LW) concept. It was one of the first to introduce a national system of minimum-wage laws when the Industrial Conciliation and Arbitrations (IC&A) Act 1894 established a Court of Arbitration to set minimum rates of pay across sectors and occupations. Court deliberations balanced the profitability of industries and firms with the cost of living for workers, elaborating the principle of 'a fair wage, or a ruling wage in the locality in which the decision applies' (Hammond 1917: 417). It soon came to set general minimum rates for all workers in accordance with 'the doctrine of a living wage' following the precedent established by the 1907 Harvester judgement in Australia (Hammond 1917: 421). This idea of a 'living wage' explicitly referenced the need of wage earners to earn enough to provide for a family. It was formalized by a 1936 amendment to the IC&A Act that required award rates to be 'sufficient to enable a man in receipt thereof to maintain a wife and three children in a fair and reasonable standard of comfort' (Riches 1937).

By the 1980s the growth of female labour force participation had undermined the idea of a 'family wage', but wages had been maintained by the mandate provided by the IC&A Act for compulsory union membership and (sector-wide) collective bargaining. This was removed by the Employment Contracts Act 1991, which prompted a dramatic decline in trade unions across the private sector. Low-paid workers increasingly had to rely on the safety net of the statutory minimum wage, which was introduced by the 1983 Minimum Wage (MW) Act as part of the Muldoon government's prices and incomes control policy. The incoming Labour government increased the rate by 70 per cent in 1985, and it remains relatively generous by international standards, at seventh in the world in purchasing power parity terms and second relative to median wages at around 60 per cent (Schulten and Luebker 2019). Annual growth of the adult MW has exceeded general wage growth and inflation for the past 20 years, accelerating after the election of a Labour-led government in 2017 following nearly a decade of centre-right rule. The government announced increases in the MW to reach a goal of $20 by 2021, some 27 per cent on the 2017 rate and closing the gap on the LW rate pursued by campaigners. The new government also endorsed the LW by stating that it would apply it to its own employees.

However, the wider context in NZ is that average wages are relatively low, reflecting poor productivity growth (OECD 2019). The economy is small and geographically

DOI: 10.4324/9781003054078-14

remote, dominated by commodity exports and tourism, and with a preponderance of small firms in low-skill sectors. Also relevant is the sharp decline of collective bargaining following deregulation in 1991 as well as the decline of manufacturing employment due to globalization. A second defining issue is that living costs are high, mainly due to the rapidly increasing cost of housing. House prices rose fivefold from 1980, compared to 60 per cent for the OECD, and higher rents and mortgage payments mean that housing now directly absorbs 45 percent of income for bottom quintile households (Perry 2019). As a result, many households 'can be left with insufficient income to meet other basic needs such as food, clothing, basic household operations, transport, medical care and education', even when in paid employment (Perry 2019: 64).

The Living Wage Movement Aotearoa New Zealand (LWMANZ) was launched in 2012 by a coalition of faith-based, union, and community groups within this context of growing inequality and the 'working poor' (Skilling and Tregidga 2019). It defines a LW as 'the income necessary to provide workers and their families with the basic necessities of life. A living wage will enable workers to live with dignity and to participate as active citizens in society' (LWMANZ 2015). The independent Family Centre Social Policy Research Unit determines the LWMANZ rate using a formula based on a household of two adults earning 1.5 full-time incomes with two dependent children and considering government transfers (King 2016). The LW thus recalls the notion of a 'family wage' and attracts some controversy given the disparity of individual and household circumstances as well as regional living costs (Anker 2011).

The LW is also contentious from an employer perspective as voluntarily paying more to employees might make good or bad business sense depending on circumstances. According to orthodox economics, paying above 'market clearing' wages is uncompetitive and will lead to job losses and/or work intensification (Leonard 2000). However, other theories suggest that low pay reflects unequal bargaining power rather than market forces, resulting in a pay 'range of indeterminacy' (Arrowsmith et al. 2003). Concepts such as 'efficiency wages' and insights from motivational psychology and social exchange theory also suggest that higher pay could deliver offsetting returns, especially in the longer term, through better recruitment and retention, development and training, improved commitment and healthier employment relations, including in small firms (Card and Krueger 1995). Hence, a LW can in theory develop both individual and organizational 'capabilities' (Carr et al. 2017). Case study work also suggests that employer agency, notably commitment to ethics or social responsibility, can also be important (Carr et al. 2018). Hence, in the real world, employers do not necessarily choose to act as simple profit maximizers in setting the wages of their employees (Lester 1946). However, little is known about employer attitudes towards the LW, particularly in low-pay sectors (Werner and Lim 2016). Many firms might be supportive in principle, from a business and/or ethical view, but see it as competitively risky. Others might be in a strong position to pay higher wages but prefer to maintain profit or investment rates, or see a LW as problematic for existing wage structures. The role of employers as agents in the living wage debate is potentially significant, as at pivotal times it has been 'progressive' employers protecting their interests from undercutting by 'nefarious' employers that has furthered the cause of wage regulation, but this is not yet sufficiently understood.

This chapter explores these issues, drawing on a major research project running from 2018 to 2021, involving a national survey of low-paid workers and interviews and case studies of employers. The employee results, which are presented elsewhere (e.g. Carr et al. 2019), indicate that employee well-being (both work and non-work) spikes at around the LW figure, suggesting that it can have a significant positive effect. Here we focus on employer attitudes and practices in the context of a rising MW, drawing primarily on a round of 25 interviews with sector-level employer representatives and other stakeholders. The interviews were conducted in late 2018 with senior representatives of sector associations that have a large proportion of low-paid workers. These included Retail NZ, the Tourism Industry Association, Hospitality NZ, the Food Grocery Council, Federated Farmers, Horticulture NZ, the NZ Aged Care Association, Manufacturing NZ, the Employers and Manufacturers Association and the peak body Business NZ. Senior managers at five Chambers of Commerce (Hawkes Bay, Otago, Auckland, Wellington, and Manawatu) were also interviewed to capture regional perspectives and especially the views of small employers. In addition, a number of other stakeholders were interviewed including two pay consultancies (Strategic Pay, Premium Business Solutions), the LWMANZ, the trade union peak body (CTU), the human resource professionals' association HRINZ, and also senior managers at Auckland and Wellington city councils, where a Living Wage strategy had been formally adopted.

The results suggest employer sympathy for the LW, including in small firms where the financial struggles of employees are often evident. This was informed by the then-prevalent context of low unemployment and skills shortages. However, adoption of the LW is inhibited for many firms by a dual temporal uncertainty – they do not know what future rates will be, nor whether any future productivity or labour market benefits will materialize and outweigh immediate cost implications. In these circumstances, ethical considerations are likely to motivate firms to formally become LW Employers. We thus briefly discuss two of our organizational case studies (Auckland Council and the food manufacturer Chalmers Organics) that demonstrate the importance of ethical and political motivations as well as testifying to unfolding challenges and positive effects. These cases were conducted in 2019–2020 based on a comprehensive set of management and employee interviews and a management survey at Auckland Council.

Employer perspectives

Perhaps surprisingly, employer representatives did not express huge alarm at the accelerating MW rate and shared some sympathy for the notion of a living wage. However, they noted that member firms faced increasing constraints and additional pressures year on year. Businesses had to cope with rising rents and other costs such as rates, utility bills, and other employment expenses such as extended leave entitlements. Other than absorbing or passing on any cost increases, responses noted so far were threefold: reductions in numbers of workers or their hours; upskilling; and automation. Employers also argued that low pay was not simply an employment issue but was a social problem related to the increasing cost of living, especially housing. Policymakers therefore needed to look to a wider set of interventions to address the squeeze on worker incomes.

Coping with the rising minimum wage

Many of the employer representatives were sanguine about the increases to the minimum wage to date, reflecting an ongoing reality of tight labour markets that were putting upwards pressure on pay for some time. The unemployment rate of 3.9 per cent in the second quarter of 2019 marked an 11-year low, down from 5.2 per cent in

2016 and 6.3 per cent in 2012, and many regional rates were even lower. According to the Auckland Chamber of Commerce, 'the minimum wage is not an issue to business at the moment […] there are no big issues', especially as the government's pre-announcement of successive rate increases enabled businesses to plan more effectively. However, Business NZ expected that when the $20 per hour is reached (which occurred in April 2021), 'that's going to get some screams of outrage'. This would impact not just labour-intensive and low-paying sectors such as retail; but also manufacturers such as the EMA and FGC said that experienced staff saw the MW as a benchmark for their own pay and would seek to restore differentials with entry-level workers in an increasingly sellers' market for labour. Problems were therefore seen as likely to accumulate over the coming few years.

At the time of the research, three sets of responses to the rising MW were observed by impacted employers. The first was reduction in employee numbers or the hours that they work:

> Some of our clients have done things like changed the contracts so people are working less hours; some people have gone from 40 to 38, so effectively it's a pay increase, but it doesn't cost the organization any more and they're looking for ways to get the work done. Some are just cutting staff numbers, particularly supervisory staff.
>
> (Strategic Pay)

The second response was automation, which was expected to accelerate in coming years as the cost of labour increased and the price of robots and 'co-bots' continued to fall:

> The predicted [MW] and cost changes are making automation more affordable. With automation you don't have all the other challenges of dealing with human beings. Some of the warehouses within our membership that I visit now, you don't even keep the lights on.
>
> (FGC)

In sectors such as Horticulture, labour retained a competitive advantage due to its dexterity and versatility, though fruit-picking and packaging machines were increasingly deployed. The Covid-19 restrictions on overseas seasonal workers will undoubtedly reinforce this trend. Labour substitution was expected to increase as technology advanced, though not entirely displacing workers:

> Automation will have some impact, but not in the immediate term, not in the next couple of years. It brings a whole suite of new problems in terms of maintenance of your robotics. You will always need entry level workers and always need to bring them on and upskill them.

Manufacturing NZ also noted that automation was more likely to be adopted by successful firms. In such firms a shift away from labour-intensive and/or low-skill production could facilitate higher pay for remaining staff:

> Over the last six years [plastics manufacturer] Sistema have both heavily automated and increased their workforce, and what they've done in a very good way is basically trained people who used to do manual work to become machine operators.

The third response was to reorganize work to upskill staff and increase productivity. However, many firms were constrained in how they could respond to cost increases in this way. Productivity growth could be hindered by access to capital, the limited scope to reorganize work processes in sectors such as personal services, or because most effective changes had already been made.

Respondents also referred to the difficult trading environment for many businesses. In retail, firms were increasingly subject to price scrutiny due to shoppers making online price comparisons and purchasing from across the country and overseas. Manufacturers also mentioned growing international competition limiting price growth, and food manufacturers reported margins constantly squeezed due to dependence on a few key customers; with only two national supermarket chains, food producers faced tight price and delivery expectations. Hence many firms, especially smaller companies, were helpless to address the pressures that their employees were facing, even when it adversely impacted on firm performance:

> A lot of our members don't have a problem with a living wage concept. I recall a story from an Auckland manufacturer with two of his machine operators lured away by a bigger company offering better salary. He said, 'I wish I could have matched that, but I just can't, but I don't berate the guys because their rent has just gone up from $700 to $750 a week and they've got a young family'. The high cost of living in Auckland, which is specifically tied to the high cost of accommodation, it just really drives up not only wage expectations but also objective wage pressures. But the problem is that the money has got to be earned before it's spent.
>
> (Manufacturers Network)

The living wage: rethinking jobs and careers

Employer representatives were largely sympathetic to the notion of the LW in principle and saw opportunities for individual employers to leverage productivity and marketing advantages from it. At the time of the research, competition for workers was increasing, and several associations saw initiatives such as the LW as a way to broaden the appeal of employment in the sector and to rebrand careers more generally. The New Zealand Tourism Industry Association, for example, had a new 'Sustainability Commitment' for its members which included being a 'quality employer' and paying a 'fair wage':

> One of the commitments we're asking businesses to do is to pay a fair wage to staff ... this might be the minimum wage for a new starter with no skills but look different for an experienced employee. One of the default mechanisms for a fair wage is the Living Wage.

Hospitality NZ suggested that the LW could be a way for firms to indicate their commitment to employees and reconfigure work, for example through job enlargement and training so that staff delivered more to the business. Upskilling, alongside higher base pay, could help enhance productivity and retention by building clearer career pathways. Firms needed to break the cycle of low pay, low skills, and poor recruitment:

> The perception is we don't pay very good money, and in some instances we don't, so you don't get a good calibre of people generally, or people who really are keen to

be in it ... and then we're not paying very well because we're not getting the good calibre of people. So, sometimes, it's a bit of a catch-22.

Federated Farmers also indicated that its latest workplace action plan was considering advising members on 'aspiring to the Living Wage ... (for) the ones that can afford it. In order to recruit staff, you really have to make an attractive proposition for them'. Again, the circumstances of individual farmers varied immensely, with most businesses performing as price takers subject to the vagaries of commodity markets. However, the voluntary nature of the LW was a way to encourage those in a better position to rethink market entry-level work as part of a more appealing employment proposition.

The living wage: a social, not simply employment problem

Though largely sympathetic to the LW idea, employer representatives were of course sensitive to the commercial pressures on many individual employers. Margins and profits were tight for many businesses, and opportunities to pass on cost increases were often limited. Small business owners also often worked long hours and took limited incomes in many cases. A wider observation was also made that NZ was not so much a low-wage economy as an expensive place to live, and this had increased in recent years. A small population and geographical remoteness made consumer products expensive, for example, and there was a growing crisis around rising housing costs:

> For unions and the government it's very convenient to frame this as the miserable employers are not paying enough when in fact the social policy and the public policy issue sits really around other things. We've got universal healthcare, more or less free education, highly subsidized public transport. But none of those are enough when you can't afford to find a house to live in.
>
> (EMA)

> Does [the LW] essentially mask an underlying problem? So, for Auckland, for example, it's house affordability. And in some ways potentially it just feeds on itself, it just ratchets up, and if the underlying cause is not dealt with then [the LW] might provide a short-term gain, but ultimately does it provide a long-term shift in what the underlying problem is? For example, my daughter's going to university in Auckland, there was an announcement where they got an increased $50 a week in their living allowance. Lo and behold, rents went up $50 a week. It just followed it, and kind of my feeling is that if it's simply just around the wage side of it, minimum or living, doesn't matter.
>
> (Retail NZ)

Housing costs have increased drastically in recent years, with the harshest impact on lower earners, and employers argued that such factors were way beyond their discretion. A second issue raised by some was that higher pay would be of limited net use to many low-paid workers because in-work benefits would be abated as a result:

> You can't look at the living and minimum wage in isolation, because at that level almost everyone is on some form of benefit and of course they get obviated very quickly as you move up.
>
> (EMA)

The abatement of accommodation supplements, family tax credits, sole parent support, and state pensions disincentivizes many low earners from working additional hours or securing higher-paid work (Nolan 2018). These problems are starting to be addressed following a recent government review (Welfare Expert Advisory Group 2019).

Going living wage: mutual gains, distinct challenges

Voluntarily 'going living wage' incurs costs for employers where they have a significant number of staff paid around the MW, putting many at an immediate competitive disadvantage. However, it also promises gains by helping deliver better recruitment, retention, motivation, and development of employees. Employers also noted that increased awareness of social responsibility was generating interest in the LW:

> NZ is a nation of small businesses, they tend to have very personal relationships with staff, and even with the larger ones … certainly within the food industry, because food's quite a personable product, they do want to do the right thing and make sure that there's value in what people are paid. And I think we'll see more of our firms making public statements about supporting the LW … It will be part of that set of ethical statements that firms are expected to make.
>
> (FGC)

Two of our organizational case studies illustrate the importance of a 'non-business' rationale in becoming a LW Employer, as well as the benefits to employers and challenges in sustaining the commitment over the longer-term.

Internal complexities in larger organizations

Implementing the LW was a political decision of a new mayor and elected members at Auckland Council, linked to the notion of Auckland becoming the 'world's most liveable city'. Unlike some other local authorities, notably Wellington, Auckland chose to implement the LW rate, phased between 2016 and 2019, without accreditation from LWMANZ. This was partly because of its size and complexity, being formed by a merger in 2010 of the previous regional council and seven local authorities with their own extensive use of contractors. The policy applied only to directly employed staff, but impacted a quarter of the workforce (ca. 2,500). Central funding of an additional $7.5 million was allocated to cover the increased wage costs of departments such as Leisure and Libraries, where a significant proportion of staff were paid between the MW and LW rates.

Senior managers supported the policy as it had little short-term impact on budgets. They also felt that staff were undervalued in these customer-facing but ostensibly 'lower-skilled' roles. Low pay was seen as having adversely impacted on recruitment and retention in a buoyant local labour market with rapidly increasing housing and other living costs. The phased LW would provide pay increases for the lowest paid staff of around 8 per cent per year for three years over and above their annual increase. However, one anticipated difficulty was managing the potential impact on pay differentials. The LW policy significantly benefited the lowest paid staff, but could leave others disgruntled that they were not receiving similar increases, and that their service or seniority was no longer sufficiently recognized through the pay system. The industrial relations partnership – or 'interest-based, problem-solving approach' as the PSA union official explained it – was invaluable here. According to HR, the union was an important advocate for the LW on the understanding that pay differentials could not be maintained:

> With the unions and the LW, what we've done is we've said, 'Here's what it is. We are going to move these people up, but you need to partner with us to manage that expectation that it's not going to go all the way up [through the scale]' … and, they've been quite receptive.
>
> (Senior HR manager)

The union acknowledged that 'it was hard to get members to understand that, because all they see is, they've [the low paid] got more money'. Overall, the process was managed by transitioning the LW increases over time and building in temporary allowances to address pay 'compression' for those above these rates earning up to around NZ$50,000. Many staff were also assuaged by lump-sum settlements for shift workers working weekends and public holidays that was necessitated by a legal reinterpretation of the Holidays Act 2003. The union also achieved some success in gaining broader changes to the remuneration scheme, including replacing managerially determined merit pay with a market-based band scheme that facilitated staff progression. This was linked to changes in the perform-ance management system, which abandoned appraisal in favour of an 'employee-led' pro-cess with workers responsible for instigating monthly one-on-one conversations.

More broadly, the LW 'has prompted us to consider what we're doing and how we're doing it' (HR manager). The lowest paid staff received wage increases of up to a third over the period of the LW implementation, and senior managers in Libraries and Recreation described strategies to redesign job roles and hiring practices in order to improve their development and contribution. This included multi-skilling and cross-centre deploy-ment for Leisure Services staff such as swimming pool attendants, reconfiguring hiring in Libraries from shelvers to higher-skilled library assistants, and shifting recruitment from casual and temporary workers such as students. The competency framework for lifeguards, for example, was replaced by a more condensed grade system, leading to changes in per-formance management, skills, and deployment arrangements to enable progression based on performance rather than length of service. In libraries, the LW enabled management to drive a restructuring plan based on fewer but more skilled, better paid staff, including implementing a redundancy programme. Hence, the LW triggered extensive changes to performance management and reward; skills and training; job roles and deployment; working time and employment contracts. Wellington Council referred to similar changes. For example, when bringing its parking inspection services in-house, staff moved from the MW to the LW and so were recruited, deployed, and developed differently:

> We changed them much more from being just ticket revenue collectors and compli-ance officers, to having a role in the city that was a bit more ambassadorial. And, so our recruitment processes became a lot more rigorous. We put staff through assessment centres … I think it has helped us attract a better calibre of person.

This case illustrates how maximizing the potential benefits of moving to a LW-based pay system, and minimizing the potential problems, can require a lot of thinking around wider HR/ER issues. In relatively large and complex organizations that have a significant proportion of low-paid staff, this can include matters such as role design, training, career pathways, and performance management, as well as grading and pay structures generally.

At Auckland Council the biggest and most enduring difficulty related to pay differentials, as indicated by a survey of managers and team leaders in Libraries and Recreation, the two departments most impacted by the LW, in July 2020. Almost all of the 22 managers surveyed supported the LW policy and reported positive effects including better recruitment, retention, and development of lower-paid workers, especially where this had been aligned to role redesign. However, nearly two-thirds also said that the LW had caused difficulties due to the reduction in pay rates between new starters and the lowest paid, to their more skilled, experienced, and senior colleagues, including team leaders themselves:

> Senior staff with many more responsibilities are still on the wage they were on originally, so are disgruntled that the others are [now] on $1 an hour less than them.

> The value of my income as a team leader has dropped where I haven't received an increase myself. In comparison to the rest of my team I am now paid less for the same responsibilities.

Managers reported difficulties such as teamwork and securing interest in promotion into supervisory or more responsible roles as a result. Some of these issues might help explain why the LW had had little if any overall impact on the Council's employee engagement metrics. There was also concern at the ongoing cost implications of maintaining a commitment to the LW in the difficult Covid-19 environment:

> I support the living wage. The issues arise in the implementation, especially issues around fairness, employee engagement, and budget pressures ... The council is currently under financial pressure, and cuts have been signalled already. I'm concerned whether the living wage would affect the numbers of positions being cut. If so, I'd be concerned at the workload of the staff in the remaining positions. I would love for all my staff to have high wages, but in reality, the trade-off would be reduced staffing numbers.

Sustaining the 'win–win' in small firms

Long-term affordability was also an issue in our small manufacturing case, which had also committed to the LW primarily for ethical rather than business reasons. Chalmers Organics is a family-owned firm producing soybean food products mainly through its Tonzu brand. It has grown in recent years with the expansion of the vegetarian food market and now employs 39 mostly female staff, around three-quarters of whom are of Pacific Island origin. This food market has also become more competitive in recent years as larger companies entered, using automation and economies of scale to provide lower-price products. Investment in Tonzu was constrained by its private ownership structure and aversion to debt.

The company was amongst the first to be LW accredited after one of the directors, in her capacity as a local board (sub-Council) member, attended a presentation by LWMANZ in 2012. At that time, the company was thinking about how to set and benchmark its standard pay rate, and the LW was seen as useful and aligning with company values. Managers emphasized that the main rationale was ethical, 'doing the right thing' by its staff. The firm was embedded in its local community, having been established in the 1970s in an area of west Auckland with a large Pacific population. A positive spin-off was that the LW 'gives you more options for selecting when you're recruiting because you've got a larger pool', though this had not been a problem as the company had a well-established reputation as a good place to work. The LWMANZ convenor who worked with the company observed that adoption was serendipitous with company growth and a concern to reinforce and capitalize on its culture:

> They see it as an important part of who they are as a business … they were one of the companies that said, 'We actually decided to invest more; get an HR Manager, because we wanted to make sure that we made the best use of the resource that we had'.

The introduction of the LW also helped reduce a reliance on long working hours by employing more part-time staff and cutting back on overtime:

> Working with machinery down there, people get so tired and also sick leave goes up as they work longer. … we're talking, 'You're working 55 to 60 hours a week so let's just slowly reduce that.' So, I guess the living wage has helped to be able to do that without them feeling it too much in their pocket.
>
> (HR Manager)

> They don't need to work as much. They actually don't want to work 60 hours, funnily enough. They'd like to spend time with their family … I've noticed them pulling back over the years.
>
> (Co-director/manager)

Wage costs were higher than they could be ('$9k a week or something crazy' at the outset), which had implications such as limited discretionary pay:

> Financially, it's a stretch for the company, there's no doubt, and it's definitely a stretch when it comes to reviewing performance and wanting to give pay reviews based on performance.
>
> (HR Manager)

However, the company did have skills-based pay to reward longer-serving staff, and the flatter hierarchy meant there was little impact in terms of differentials. The company also noted that the accelerating MW had narrowed the gap with what competitors were paying, reducing any competitive cost disadvantage.

For their part, staff referred to the fun, inclusive culture as an important motivator, as well as working time flexibility around family commitments:

> I love working here. I like the family that owns the business. They're really nice, kind people. … We're like a big family working together so we all help out each other. We have all sorts of culture here. We have Samoan, Tongan, Ethiopian, Rarotongans, Fijians. It's really nice to get to know all those different people and what they like. I really enjoy working here.
>
> (Production supervisor 1)

> You can hear everybody laughing … We have music in there. Yeah, so it's really good.
>
> (Production assistant)

Our manager actually works with us. She gets her hands dirty. Right down, even if she has to come into work early … Awesome leader … She treats everybody fairly … This place is like a really good place where everybody gets respected. And … we give the supervisors the respect that they deserve as well in return.

(Production assistant)

At the same time, the LW made a material difference to staff, especially as many had financial commitments to extended family and made remittances overseas:

You're not stressing about thinking about what are you going to do with this bill. When are you going to pay this or, you know, if you don't have enough money for the food for the kids the next day, so all that stress has gone.

(Production supervisor 2)

I see a lot of families struggle with low income … I'm thinking this is so good that they brought that up, the living wage, because they can now help a lot of other families out there … I know how hard it is. But now, it is more expensive than before.

(Production supervisor 1)

It motivates me to come to work knowing that this living wage is enough for me to support my family, to finance stability for my family. Better than what I had before … I want to keep that going.

(Production assistant)

This case suggests that in terms of the LW, ethical concerns are not easily differentiated from the 'business case'. A socially responsible concern to be a good employer led to the introduction of the LW in Tonzu, which also helped reinforce its positive workplace culture, recruitment and retention, and the returns to training. This HR strategy, aligned to a premium product strategy, had so far served the company – and its workforce – well. Unlike larger and public-sector organizations, the difficulties for smaller firms lie less in terms of internal complexities than in sustaining the cost of the LW in the face of external competition. In Tonzu, a consistently growing market and the company's niche position within it had sustained its social commitment to the LW and delivered mutual gains. It remains to be seen what the impact of the Covid-19–induced recession might be on pay, but the positive culture and mutual commitment within this family firm puts it in a good position to navigate difficult times.

Conclusions

Many employers are well aware of the need to address low pay in a NZ context of what was until very recently tight labour markets and rising living costs. Owners and managers in small firms in particular observe the struggles of employees first-hand, and would often like to raise pay to better attract, retain, and motivate labour. In this context the accelerating MW prompted few cries of anguish and some strategic thinking about job and career redesign to improve the quality and productivity of work.

However, uptake of the LW remains limited if growing, especially in the private sector. In part this may be because the MW itself is relatively high. Small businesses in competitive sectors like retail and hospitality often have low margins and are concerned that increasing pay further might incur first-mover disadvantages. A fundamental constraint on adopting the LW is its temporal ambiguities and risk. Committing to a LW involves committing to future wage increases linked to a formula shaped by living costs and government transfers without qualification by sector and region. Though companies can put accreditation on hold if they experience affordability problems, this might incur some psychological contract breach. The second risk is that whereas costs are incurred immediately, the potential LW benefits to employers such as improved recruitment, retention, and motivation might take longer to pay dividends and may also require wider changes such as role redesign, and training and performance management systems. Many LW Employers are therefore already high-paying organizations or are motivated strongly by an ethical as well as economic rationale.

This ethical commitment means that the adoption of the LW may not be driven by a 'business case', but at the same time might enable it given it allows a longer-term time frame to prevail. Employers in such cases concede the possibility of some negative consequence in the shorter term (e.g. reduced profits, and some dissatisfaction due to wage compression), but in persisting with the LW as 'the right thing to do' can realize greater benefits over time. The research suggested that sector associations can play a key role here in helping firms think about how they organize work and upskill staff (Edwards et al. 2002).

Employers also argued that there was a limit to what they could deliver in the face of rapidly rising living costs, a view shared by LW and social policy campaigners. Low pay is a 'public bad' that inhibits human and organizational development because it perpetuates stress inside and outside of work (Johri 2005; Perry 2009). It is linked to a disposable view of human resources that sustains low skills and insecure work (Tomlinson et al. 2016). Low pay helps drive inequality and social disintegration and suppresses macroeconomic growth. Paradoxically, low pay is subsidized through in-work benefits such as income and housing support at the same time as the costs of low pay (such as poor physical and mental health and family dysfunction) are externalized to the very public which help sustain it.

Public policy needs to address the problem of low pay by focusing on living costs as well as incomes. The LW concept draws attention to low pay and in-work poverty as social not just employment problems. Employers, where they can afford it, are likely to see significant returns from investments such as the living wage. However, governments also need to attend to housing affordability and welfare structures if much of any pay increase is not simply to disappear (Bennett 2012). For example, the average rent increased by a quarter between 2012 and 2017 (Johnson et al. 2018); NZ ranks equal fifth-lowest among OECD countries for rent control and tenure security (Kholodilin 2018). Pay is also only part of the picture for employers too; they need to look more widely at providing decent working conditions and a positive workplace culture if they are to maximize benefits such as better recruitment, retention, and employee motivation. In short, the focus of the living wage debate needs to more firmly address *Living* and not just wages if it is to materially improve the lives of low-paid workers and the performance of the organizations in which they work.

References

Anker, R. (2011). *Estimating a Living Wage: A Methodological Review*. Conditions of Work and Employment Series No. 29. Geneva: ILO.

Arrowsmith, J., Gilman, M., Edwards, M. and Ram, M. (2003). 'The Impact of the National Minimum Wage and Employment Relations in Small Firms', *British Journal of Industrial Relations*, 41(3): 435–456.

Bennett, F. (2012). 'The "Living Wage", Low Pay and in Work Poverty: Rethinking the Relationships', *Critical Social Policy*, 34(1): 46–65.

Card, D., and Krueger, A. (1995). *Myth and Measurement: The New Economics of the Minimum Wage.* Princeton, NJ: Princeton University Press.

Carr, S., Haar, J., Hodgetts, D., Arrowsmith, J., Parker, J., Young-Hauser, A., Alefaio-Tuglia, S., and Jones, H. (2019). 'An Employee's Living Wage and Their Quality of Work Life: How Important Are Household Size and Household Income?', *Journal of Sustainability Research*, 1(1): 1–19.

Carr, S., Parker, J., Arrowsmith, J., Haar, J., and Jones, H. (2017). 'Humanistic Management and Living Wages: A Case of Compelling Connections?', *Humanistic Management Journal* 2(1): 215–236.

Carr, S., Parker J., Arrowsmith, J., Yao, C., and Haar, J. (2018). 'The Living Wage in NZ and Its Implications for Human Resource Management and Employment Relations', in J. Parker with M. Baird (eds), *The Big Issues in Employment: HRM and Employment Relations in Australasia.* Auckland: CCH, pp. 95–108.

Edwards, P., Gilman, M., Ram, M., and Arrowsmith, J. (2002). 'Public Policy, the Performance of Firms, and the 'Missing Middle': The Case of the Employment Regulations, and a Role for Local Business Networks', *Policy Studies*, 23(10): 5–20.

Hammond, M.B. (1917). 'The Regulation of Wages in New Zealand', *The Quarterly Journal of Economics*, 31(3): 404–446.

Johnson, A., Howden-Chapman, P., and S. Eaqub, (2018). *A Stocktake of New Zealand's Housing.* Report commissioned by the Minister of Housing and Urban Development.

Johri, R. (2005). *Work Values and the Quality of Employment: A Literature Review.* Wellington: Department of Labour.

Kholodilin, K. (2018). 'Measuring Stick-Style Housing Policies: A Multi-Country Longitudinal Database of Governmental Regulations', *DIW Berlin Discussion Papers 1727*.

King, P. (2016). 'Setting the New Zealand Living Wage: Complexities and Practicalities', *Labour & Industry: A Journal of the Social and Economic Relations of Work*, 26(1): 8–23.

Leonard, T. (2000). 'The Very Idea of Applying Economics: The Modern Minimum-Wage Controversy and Its Antecedents', *History of Political Economy*, 32 (Suppl_1). 117–144.

Lester, R. (1946). 'Wage Diversity and Its Theoretical Implications', *Review of Economics and Statistics*, 28(3): 152–159.

Living Wage Movement of Aotearoa NZ (LWMANZ). (2015). *Accredited Living Wage Employers of NZ.* Auckland: LWMANZ.

Nolan, P. (2018). 'Effective Marginal Tax Rates: The New Zealand Case'. *TTPI Working Paper 7/2018*.

OECD (Organization for Economic Cooperation and Development) (2019). *OECD Economic Surveys: New Zealand 2019.* Paris: OECD.

Perry, B. (2009). *Non-income Measures of Material Wellbeing and Hardship.* Wellington: Ministry of Social Development.

Perry, B. (2019). *Household Incomes in New Zealand: Trends in Indicators of Inequality and Hardship 1982 to 2018.* Wellington: Ministry of Social Development.

Riches, E.J. (1937). 'The Fair Wage Principle in New Zealand', *Economic Record*, 13(1–2): 224–239.

Schulten, T., and Luebker, M. (2019). *Time for Substantial Minimum Wage Rises and a European Minimum Wage Policy,* WSI Minimum Wage Report 2019. www.boeckler.de/pdf/p_wsi_report_46e_2019.pdf

Skilling, P., and Tregidga, H. (2019). 'Accounting for the "Working Poor": Analysing the Living Wage Debate in Aotearoa NZ', *Accounting, Auditing & Accountability Journal,* 32(7): 2031–2061.

Tomlinson, M., Walker, A., and Foster, L. (2016). 'Social Quality and Work: What Impact Does Low Pay Have on Social Quality?', *Journal of Social Policy*, 45(2): 345–371.

Welfare Expert Advisory Group (2019). *Whakamana Tāngata: Restoring Dignity to Social Security in New Zealand.* Wellington: Ministry for Social Development.

Werner, A., and Lim, M. (2016). 'The Ethics of the Living Wage: A Review and Research Agenda'. *Journal of Business Ethics*, 137(3): 433–447.

15 Living wage initiatives in the garment sector

Insights from Southeast Asia

Michele Ford and Michael Gillan[1]

Introduction

Home to well over half a billion people, Southeast Asia is a labour-intensive manufacturing hub that sits at the heart of multiple global production networks (GPNs). Despite this, employment is still characterized by high levels of informality and precarity, as well as by limited social protection. Southeast Asia is also a region in which the capacity of trade unions varies considerably, and the potential of industrial relations institutions is constrained by a range of economic and political conditions (Ford and Gillan 2016). In short, it is vibrant and fast growing in its economic profile while at the same time lagging in some key social indicators and the development of effective labour institutions.

Southeast Asia's pivotal role within various manufacturing GPNs has drawn international attention to its labour standards and employment conditions. In the garment sector, in particular, concern over low wages and weak social protection has been amplified by international consumer, union, and non-governmental organization (NGO) activism that targets high-profile global brands. Unions and NGOs also play a significant role within specific national contexts, lobbying for policy change, representing workers in national labour institutions, and engaging with brands and their suppliers. In many cases, these different actors collaborate across scale in an attempt to advocate for labour rights within these particular national settings, but also throughout the garment manufacturing production networks.

An area where there has been some progress in Southeast Asia has been in mobilizing and campaigning around the processes and outcomes of wage determination institutions, which offer formal sector workers some prospect of regulated wages in contexts where workplace collective bargaining is uniformly weak (Caraway et al. 2019; Ford and Gillan 2017). One aspect of this struggle has been the deployment of the 'living wage' concept. The influence of this concept is evident within government discourse around wage setting in a number of countries in the region. It is also present within international debates around the governance of the business activities and social impact of the multinational enterprises (MNEs) that produce branded consumer goods. Yet, while living wage discourse can be observed sporadically within the mobilizations and campaigns of unions and labour NGOs, especially those that target MNEs and their suppliers, it is not well incorporated into formal wage-setting institutions. Instead, these are shaped primarily by the economic interests and political contestations associated with minimum-wage determination processes, which can be national, sub-national, or sectoral in their scope of application.

DOI: 10.4324/9781003054078-15

Using the region's garment sector as a case study, the chapter examines various global and regional living wage initiatives driven by brands, NGOs, unions, or a combination thereof. In doing so, we distinguish between three different logics of living wage interventions in Southeast Asia. The first of these is the 'technical fix', whereby an actor, or actors, propose(s) a formula that can be used to calculate living wage levels. The second is collaboration, whereby unions or NGOs work with lead firms and other actors to improve compliance and reconfigure network governance, while the third is contestation, whereby workers, their unions, or their other allies engage in public campaigning on the absence of a living wage. As we demonstrate, different wage initiatives each have limitations in scope and effectiveness, which affect their capacity to translate their goals and aspirations into concrete outcomes for workers. While our analysis is developed with reference to the garment sector, the dynamics we discuss are relevant to other sectors such as electronics and food and beverages that are characterized by dominant lead firms.

The regional context

Southeast Asia has been a focus for many living wage initiatives in the garment sector, reflecting the concentration of garment production for export in the region. Its prominence in this respect also reflects the fact that, as the International Trade Union Confederation (ITUC) has noted, (a) wages are 'dismally low compared to the cost of living in most countries' and (b) this situation is exacerbated by the uneven coverage of (and compliance with) minimum-wage systems and the 'compromised' capacity of unions to organize and engage in collective bargaining to fight for 'fair wages' (ITUC 2020a).

Vietnam, Cambodia, and Indonesia are Southeast Asia's three most significant garment-producing countries. While Myanmar is further down the list, it is both an emerging player in the sector and the focus of intense international attention. As Table 15.1 shows, the garment sector in each of these countries generates billions of dollars in export earnings and employs millions of workers. Notably, also, all four countries have an official minimum wage – which, in Cambodia's case, applies only to the garment industry.

These four countries have very different political and industrial relations systems. At one end of the spectrum, Vietnam is a one-party state with a single, state-controlled union. At the other, Indonesia is the region's best-functioning – albeit still troubled – democracy, and home to the region's most vibrant labour movement. Both formally structured as electoral democracies, Cambodia tends towards electoral authoritarianism, while Myanmar continues to struggle with the legacies of military rule. Industrial relations, labour regulation, and state capacity for enforcement are therefore uneven and characterized by significant gaps. At the same time, the garment industries in all four are highly exposed to the global economy, and thus to the demands of lead firms and consumers; but also to the attention of the global unions and international NGOs with an interest in the garment sector. This creates pressures and incentives for different actors or coalitions of global and local organizations to develop industry-specific initiatives to address institutional deficiencies and specific problems, such as the gap between the wages paid to workers and what they actually require for a living wage.

Living wage initiatives

Initiatives to address the problem of a living wage reflect the motivations of the different actors that drive them and the 'institutional logics' that frame and condition actions in

Table 15.1 The garment sector as a source of revenue and employment in Southeast Asia

	Cambodia	Indonesia	Myanmar	Vietnam
Population (million)	16.2	267.7	53.7	95.5
Labour force (million)	9.1	132.7	24.5	56.9
Employment (millions)	9.1	126.8	22.5	54.2
Manufacturing workers (millions)	1.5	18.25	2.4	9.6
Garment workers (millions)	0.9	4.0	0.8	2.3
% Women in the garment industry	79	58	90	80
GDP (USD billion)	24.6	1,042.2	76.1	245.2
GDP per capita (USD)	1,512	3,894	1,418	2,567
Export earnings (USD billion)	12.7	180.2	16.7	243.7
Export earnings garments (USD billion)	7.8	8.6	4.1	28.2
Monthly Minimum Wage (USD)	170	262	91	175
Overall union density (%)	10	2	1	50
Union density in sector (%)	60	15	5	5

Sources: BFC (2018), Comtrade (2020), FLA (2019), FWF (2018), Hieu, Phuc, and Schweisshelm (2017), ILO (2020), ILOSTAT (2020), Jannah (2019), SPD (2019), World Bank (2020).

Note: Figures are for 2018 unless otherwise stated. Employment figures for Cambodia are from 2017. Indonesia uses regional minimum wages; the figures here are for Tangerang, a major garment-producing district. Vietnam has minimum wages for four different regions. The figure cited here is the highest rate available. Myanmar has a daily wage and a standard working week of six days in the private sector. We have calculated the monthly minimum wage by generating an annual minimum wage (assuming no weeks off) and dividing by twelve. January 2018 currency conversions were used. There are no reliable figures available for union density in the garment sector in Myanmar. The figure here is an estimate calculated using membership claims from various unions. The union density figures for Vietnam are for 2017. The garment sector figure is calculated using the stated membership of the Vietnam Textile and Garment Workers Union.

this domain. As Thornton and Ocasio (2008:103) suggest, the key premise of the institutional logics approach 'is that the interests, identities, values, and assumptions of individuals and organizations are embedded within prevailing institutional logics'. In other words, organizations have a form of 'embedded agency', with differing logics shaping their actions in a 'variety of contexts, including markets, industries, and populations of organizational forms' (Thornton and Ocasio 2008:100). If we accept this premise, it is not surprising that wages are framed differently by governments, unions, and other actors within the GPNs that connect investors, buyers, supplier firms, and social and political organizations across multiple geographies (Coe and Hess 2012).

For emerging economy governments, labour costs are linked to the need to secure foreign direct investment, most often through the development of labour-intensive manufacturing industries. At the same time, the level and sufficiency of wages is a consideration in terms of growing domestic markets, which are crucial to national economic development but also to social-political stability and, ultimately, the very legitimacy of the state (Ford and Gillan 2016). These intersections are nowhere clearer than in Cambodia, whose economic viability as a nation depends on garment production for export. Faced with large numbers of militant garment workers, and fearful of the economic *and* political consequences of collective action, the government more than doubled garment workers' minimum wage in the seven years to 2020, while simultaneously working to undermine their unions (Ward and Ford in press). It is perhaps not surprising, then, that the governments of the outward-looking economies of Southeast Asia are particularly sensitive in regard to minimum-wage initiatives.

When considering the interests of business in relation to wages, it is necessary to distinguish between lead and supplier firms. On the one hand, lead firms look to emerging economies as locations for production precisely because of their low labour costs. On the other hand, the visibility and centrality of particular lead firms within governance networks has stimulated debate on their moral and regulatory obligations to ensure that their suppliers pay fair and living wages. Supplier firms are wedged between these two different impetuses. They, too, seek to maximize their profits, but at the same time must meet buyer expectations regarding wages and also a raft of other working conditions. Suppliers typically produce for a number of lead firm brands and orders are contingent on the cost, timeliness, and quality of production in addition to their capacity to conform to the compliance requirements of multiple client firms. As Anner (2018: 76) explains, this 'sourcing squeeze' means that 'lead firms are continuously able to pressure their suppliers to produce for low prices and with accelerating turn-around times', which 'puts pressure on management to keep wages low and working hours long'.

Unions, of course, have a very different perspective on the living wage question. They see this as a problem linked to social inequality, but also symptomatic of inadequate worker voice and representation in wage bargaining or wage determination processes. These concerns are reflected in global union campaigns. For example, the ITUC's communications suggest that the 'world needs a pay rise' to compensate for labour's declining share of income within different countries, noting the absence of an 'adequate wage floor that ensures a decent livelihood for workers and their families' (ITUC 2020b). Not surprisingly, then, an important element of global unions' claims is their emphasis on the role of enabling measures that involve their national affiliates and other unions in wage setting, either through multi-stakeholder arrangements or national and workplace collective bargaining mechanisms.

Finally, international NGOs generally adopt a similar frame on the importance of enabling rights, albeit often with more emphasis on the need for global brands to take responsibility for ensuring fair wage practices and less emphasis on engaging with local unions. For example, the Clean Clothes Campaign (CCC) has linked the responsibility for ensuring a living wage to human rights obligations, suggesting that – as per the UN Guiding Principles on Business and Human Rights (UNGPs) – 'businesses have an obligation to remedy state failures' 'in cases where legal minimum wages fails to meet the minimum subsistence level (living wage) for workers in production countries' (CCC 2020).

Examples of living wage initiatives

The exposure of lead firms to pressure from consumers, sometimes also from home-country governments, creates some leverage for local unions or other governance intermediaries. The garment industry is especially prominent in this regard, with a plethora of initiatives launched that lay claim to working towards enhanced and fairer wages for workers. As we note in Table 15.2, initiatives to address the establishment and governance dynamics of a 'living' wage can be driven by various agents (or combinations of agents) located in both business and civil society domains. For the former, engagement is clearly linked to attempts to establish or defend the legitimacy of business practices and mitigate potential regulatory and reputational risks. For the latter, engagement is driven by a desire to contest the morality and legitimacy of business practices but also to create space in which to establish themselves as credible and effective organizational intermediaries in labour governance.

Table 15.2 Examples of living wage initiatives in the garment sector

	Example	Goals	Targets	Strengths	Weaknesses	Dominant Logic
Brands	H&M's Living Wage commitments	Enhanced compliance and sustainability reporting performance	Target for enhanced wage outcomes for corporate supplier base	Public commitments create potential for monitoring and reputational sanctions	Self-regulation and reporting; uneven and temporary gains	Collaboration (lead firms and suppliers)
MSIs	Fair Wear Foundation	Corporate member adherence to codes and improved living wage practices	Brands	Living wage strategy, monitoring, benchmarking, and implementation tools	Limited coverage and risk of decoupling of practices	Technical fix + collaboration
Unions + Brands	ACT	Industry-wide collective bargaining and minimum wage protection	State, local suppliers and other brands	Potential for more effective and coordinated wage regulation	Complexity of implementation; uncertain capacity to influence governments and local business actors	Collaboration (unions and lead firms)
Unions	IndustriALL's regional strategy on living wages	Lift wage floor via institutional reform	States and industry stakeholders	Highlights need for regional institutional reform	Weak impact on state policy agendas	Contestation
Unions + NGOs	Asia Floor Wage Alliance	Mobilization behind the demand for an Asia Floor Wage (Living Wage)	State, brands, buyers, local suppliers, national unions	International campaign that offers a regional solution to wage-based competition	Weak impact on states and brands; limited union involvement at the country level	Technical fix + contestation
NGOs	Global Living Wage Coalition	Adoption of a common definition and method for determining a living wage	State, brands	Accommodates national and subnational variation	Limited scope and weak participation of unions and civil society	Technical fix

As Table 15.2 suggests, these diametrically opposed imperatives manifest in different ways. In many cases, civil society organizations openly criticize brands and suppliers for failing to take responsibility for the payment of a living wage. In other cases, however, the living wage issue is framed as a shared problem that can be resolved by means of a collaborative search for improved practices over time and/or via the application of a technical solution.

In the Southeast Asian context, many living wage initiatives are specifically targeted at the garment sector because of its contribution to employment and export revenues in several key countries in the region. In a subsequent section, we discuss an exemplar of each main type of initiative targeted at that sector, noting its strengths and limitations in effectively and comprehensively addressing the idea of a living wage.[2] However, it is first necessary to note some of the general features of these actor-configured regulatory interventions.

The institutional logics of different living wage initiatives

As Table 15.2 shows, living wage initiatives can be driven by different logics, whether they be a technical fix, collaboration, or contestation – or a combination of two or all three of these logics. Brands' initiatives address living wages in ways that are responsive to their market-driven interests and imperatives. They frame them within their corporate social responsibility obligations and pursue them by means of system-based oversight of relational and stakeholder interactions, largely focused on suppliers based in emerging economies. The likelihood that a brand will enter into a formal commitment to support a 'living wage' depends on a range of factors, the most important of which is its visibility to consumers. The extent to which such a commitment is enforced through a brand's supply network depends on the rigour of its implementation but, in general, the 'decoupling' of CSR commitments from actual practices and impacts at the point of production has been widely observed (Bartley and Egels-Zandén 2016; Kuruvilla et al. 2020). The definition and modalities of brands' living wage initiatives are typically ambiguous; however, it is clear that their dominant logic is collaboration with suppliers and other organizational intermediaries to measure and enhance performance on social indicators like living wages, which can be quantified and communicated to corporate stakeholders, investors, and consumers.

Here NGOs, often structured to incorporate 'multi-stakeholder' interests, have emerged as important organizational intermediaries, which monitor – and, arguably, afford some degree of legitimacy to – brands in dealing with the wages issue. Multi-stakeholder initiatives (MSIs) are defined as 'an entity that works with multiple stakeholders (usually business and civil society, along with others, including governments, universities, and/or investors) to solve a business and human rights problem that no actor can solve alone' (Baumann-Pauly et al. 2017: 772). There are a number of MSIs that, among other goals and activities, are especially focused on the garment industry and the problem of how to measure, monitor and implement a living wage for workers (Edwards et al. 2019; ETI 2020). Their dominant logics and modalities of working are, self-evidently, premised on the value of collaboration between industry stakeholders – most prominently, and even contentiously, brand corporate partners – as well as the development and application of various technical interventions to address the living wage problem.

By contrast, union-controlled initiatives on living wages are driven by a desire to influence lead firm and supplier practice, but also government policy. At the national level, the living wage discourse has become linked with ongoing national and local worker mobilizations to drive improved wage outcomes in minimum-wage determination processes, such as those described by Caraway and Ford (2017) in the Indonesian context. Internationally, unions' living wage initiatives involved broader and more general appeals to the need for a wage floor in the sector, and in some cases, across the region. The key modality at the regional and international level has been public campaigning and affiliate mobilization. While some of these campaigns have targeted particular lead firms, others have targeted states (and, to a lesser extent, regional authorities such as ASEAN) in an attempt to secure meaningful institutional reform. The primary logic in play in both cases is contestation, calling out lead firms and government on the immorality of paying inadequate wages and on the consequences of poorly functioning institutions.

Union–NGO initiatives are also driven by a shared interest in pressuring lead firms, suppliers, and governments with the aim of improving workers' voice and rights at the workplace and their capacity to influence wage processes and outcomes. Although unions and NGOs work on very different institutional logics (Ford 2009; Egels-Zandén et al. 2015), they are quite often drawn into joint initiatives that leverage their different strengths – for example, NGOs' generally superior campaigning capacity and the mobilization potential of unions' membership base. By contrast, union–brand initiatives, which are a relatively new phenomenon, are based on a collaborative logic which manifests in pacts and other forms of institutionalized collaboration not dissimilar to the much more established MSI tradition. Finally, NGO-only initiatives are much more heterogeneous, although they are more likely than either brands or unions to propose a technical logic that can be used by corporations, civil society organizations, or states to monitor and deliver a living wage.

Selected living wage initiatives in Southeast Asia's garment industry

There are several examples of company-specific living wage initiatives relevant to the region, which are driven by the social responsibility, sustainability and business and human rights reporting, and due diligence requirements of brands. MSIs and NGOs also work to promote their living wage benchmarks and improved business practices in Southeast Asia. In the civil society domain, unions and NGOs have also developed regional campaign-based initiatives designed to pressure governments and businesses. IndustriALL, the global union federation responsible for the manufacturing sector, has also developed a collaborative initiative with a select group of brand buyers to address the wage issue.

Brand-driven initiatives: H&M's living wage commitments

Southeast Asia has been an important site for the development of brand-driven initiatives, many of which take the form of pilot programmes designed to improve costing and purchasing practices and/or to develop 'model factory' programmes with suppliers in producer countries (Miller and Hohenegger 2017). According to an assessment of 13 major brand-based companies in the garment sector produced by a Netherlands-based investor network, such pilot projects may be 'inspiring', but the living wage issue can only be addressed by corporations changing their 'mainstream' business practices (ASN Bank 2019: 9). The report named Adidas as the leading performer for, among other reasons, identifying and reporting gaps between paid and living wages in its supplier base and developing a 'standard minute costing system' with suppliers to facilitate wage improvements. H&M is another often-cited example of a company that has committed to 'improved wage management systems supporting fair living wages at business partners' (H&M 2016). Its stated means of achieving this aim has been through the progressive application of its 'Fair Wage Method' in supplier factories (H&M 2015). The company has also engaged in dialogue with government authorities on minimum wages and established partnerships with the International Labour Organization (ILO) in producer countries to support industrial relations, training and skills development, and wages systems in those factories (H&M 2015).[3]

Multi-stakeholder initiatives: Fair Wear Foundation

The Netherlands-based Fair Wear Foundation (FWF) is a multi-stakeholder initiative involving unions, NGOs, and 137 brands, which requires member companies to commit to paying a living wage (FWF 2019; 2020b). The FWF centres its living wage efforts on a technical fix, promoting the use of its 'labour minute calculators' and 'wage ladder' benchmarking tool to encourage progress towards fairer wages. However, the FWF's approach is also 'process-based'. After calculating the relationship between prices and wages, it identifies where the money will come from, and verifies that additional funds are used for the purpose for which they were intended (FWF 2019: 13). This technical fix is embedded in a broader Code of Labour Practices, which is policed through brand performance checks, factory audits, and a complaints helpline, as well as through factory-based education programmes. As of 2020, the FWF's 11 priority countries included Indonesia, Myanmar, and Vietnam. In Myanmar, the FWF works with 13 brands sourcing from 22 supplier factories and alongside an 'enhanced' monitoring programme as a consequence of ongoing human rights concerns in that country. There, as in Vietnam and Indonesia, it also supports education programmes, country-specific research on the living wage issue, and access to a country-specific calculator (FWF 2020a; 2020b).

Union–brand initiatives: Action, Collaboration, Transformation

Action, Collaboration, Transformation (ACT) is a partnership based on a formal agreement between IndustriALL – the global union federation (GUF) responsible for manufacturing – and leading brands to support living wages by building capacity for industry-wide collective bargaining at national level in the garment industry. Established in 2015, ACT has been interpreted as a positive 'spillover' of IndustriALL's increased leverage with major brands in the wake of the Rana Plaza disaster (Ashwin et al. 2020), with the creation of the Accord on Fire and Building Safety in Bangladesh paving the way for the establishment of a more comprehensive initiative. As of 2020, 21 companies – including major firms Inditex, C&A, H&M and PVH – were members of ACT (ACT 2020a). Having initially targeted Cambodia, ACT later shifted its focus to Myanmar after experiencing difficulties in gaining traction and coordinating unions in that country (IndustriALL 2019b).

ACT's key feature is that it links living wages, freedom of association, and 'national industry-level collective bargaining between unions and employers' with 'the purchasing practices of brands' (Holdcroft 2015:102). The rationale for this approach is that industry-wide bargaining takes labour costs out of competition (IndustriALL 2015b). Its other main purpose from a union perspective has been to encourage brands to reform their purchasing practices (IndustriALL 2019a). To this end, ACT has developed an 'account-ability and monitoring framework' and 'labour costing protocol', and required member companies to complete a 'Purchasing Practices Self-Assessment' to review practices and performance with a view to identifying changes required to 'support the move towards living wages on an industry level' (ACT 2020b). Its third strategic goal is to leverage brand support in targeting state authorities, suppliers, and employer associations in key producer countries, with the aim of convincing them to support the core demand for industry-wide collective bargaining.

Union initiatives: IndustriALL's regional strategy on living wages

In many ways, ACT represents a continuation of work begun by the International Textile Garment and Leather Workers' Federation (ITGLWF), one of the manufacturing GUFs that merged to form IndustriALL in 2012. The ITGLWF had launched a 'Bargaining for a Living Wage' campaign in 2008. In what it claimed was the 'first global trade union mobilisation of its kind', it asked its affiliates to generate their own estimations of the living wage needs of workers and to incorporate this figure into their wage demands (ITGLWF 2008). Asia was the centre of much of the public advocacy and union education work associated with this campaign, which coupled a demand for a living wage with the demand for freedom of association and collective bargaining rights in the garment industry (ITGLWF 2012). The ITGLWF's assessment of the campaign's first four years claimed that it had 'helped to fundamentally alter the discourse on wages by placing the living wage firmly on the agenda both within the union movement and amongst external stakeholders such as employers, government, the ILO and multinational companies' (ITGLWF 2012). However, even this self-assessment acknowledged that the campaign had 'produced positive, yet limited, results.

After its formation in mid-2012, IndustriALL established a regional living wage campaign in Asia. This campaign has focused on communicating with brands, suppliers, and states about wage gaps and the deficiencies of state institutions of wage determination in key producer countries.[4] Much of the work of the campaign focused on capacity development for affiliates and support for their engagement with the living wage issue. For example, in 2014 IndustriALL held a regional living wage workshop in Cambodia to discuss advocating for a living wage and bargaining beyond the enterprise level, rather than just engaging with national minimum wage-setting mechanisms (IndustriALL 2014). In 2015, it convened a similar workshop in Myanmar (IndustriALL 2015a). Such efforts continued with, for example, a joint meeting of unionists from Cambodia and Myanmar in 2018 (IndustriALL 2018). As evident at this workshop, IndustriALL has placed increasing emphasis on sectoral bargaining, as exemplified by ACT. However, the regional campaign also provides a platform for ongoing union advocacy on the living wage issue at a country level (IndustriALL 2020).

Union–NGO initiatives: Asia Floor Wage Alliance

The Asia Floor Wage Alliance (AFWA) is a union–NGO initiative premised on the need to develop a regional living wage to improve the well-being of workers while also ensuring that gains in one country do not lead to the relocation of production to lower-cost locations (Ford and Gillan 2017). Although the AFWA incorporates NGO partners based in major consumer regions (Europe, North America), it consciously positions itself as Asia-led, involving unions and NGOs in Cambodia, India, Indonesia, Pakistan, and Sri Lanka (AFWA 2020). AFWA has sought to communicate with brand buyers, suppliers, and governments in the region to support both its broad campaign goals and also to generate awareness of its regional living wage approach (Merk 2009; Roy 2015).

The AFWA is driven by the logics of public contestation and the 'technical fix' approach to living wages. Based on its technical elements, its proponents claim that its regional floor wage method offers 'a credible and legitimate living wage benchmark across the industry' – contrasting it to ACT and other collaborative efforts, which they have described as 'a bunch of whitewashing strategies' (Godrej 2020). As this insight suggests, while the AFWA is willing to engage in dialogue with industry stakeholders, it frames actions and impact as standing quite apart from such collaborative efforts, focusing instead on campaigning for its living wage benchmark. This approach is exemplified by its 'People's Tribunals', which it has convened in Cambodia and Indonesia, as well as in India, and Sri Lanka, to investigate workplace rights, conditions, and wage gaps in the industry, and pursue its campaign goals (Barria 2014).[5]

NGO initiatives: Global Living Wage Coalition

A number of NGO initiatives also apply technical logics to the issue of living wages in the garment industry. One technical fix that has gained some traction is that proposed by the Global Living Wage Coalition (GLWC), an umbrella group that brings together Fairtrade International, GoodWeave International, the Rainforest Alliance, Social Accountability International, and the ISEAL Alliance in an attempt to 'Provide high quality and consistent knowledge and information about living wage levels, implementation, and impact necessary for stakeholders of all types to collaborate in a non-competitive environment toward wage increases globally' (GLWC 2020). In Southeast Asia, the GLWC has worked to develop living wage assessment reports for Vietnam.

The GLWC seeks to support the realization of living wages by facilitating the use of the Anker living wage method by companies, governments, and civil society organizations. Named after the experts who designed it, this method was developed in response to concerns that a lack of methodological rigour and reliability was limiting progress in changes to institutions and business practices to achieve a living wage. The GLWC produces reports that capture detailed estimates of living wage requirements in the context of the specificity of labour markets and costs in regions and urban areas. Its goal is to extend the number and scope of such assessments across the region and for them to assist unions, governments, and companies in their bargaining and relational interactions by enabling access to clearly defined and accurate estimates of living wage needs. In this sense, the GLWC leans towards *promoting* collaboration, while itself remaining primarily technical in its approach.

Conclusion: strengths and weaknesses of different approaches

The public commitment of brands to living wage policies and implementation strategies is a notable and increasing trend, especially in the garment sector, where a feminized workforce toils for long hours to make enough money to sustain themselves and their families. Because of its labour-intensive nature, the garment sector is characterized by among the greatest power imbalances between workers and employers. Layered onto this is the ability of lead firms in apparel production networks to largely dictate the terms under which suppliers operate, not only with regard to cost but also with regard to wages and working conditions. Brushing aside these power differentials, brand-led living wage initiatives are framed around the purported virtues of collaboration and interest alignment between lead firms and suppliers. At the core, these initiatives seek to identify labour costs and reform purchasing practices to gradually work towards the realization of a living wage for workers. Over several decades now, civil society organizations, and in particular NGOs, have both lent legitimacy to such programmes, by participating in them as monitors, and applied reputational sanctions with regard to their non-implementation.

However, most companies fall short on the required transparency and detail of their reporting on wage systems, making limited progress in moving from 'effort-based reporting to impact-based reporting' that actually tracks and supports change on the ground – and, crucially, reforming purchasing and costing practices to enable them to pass on a living wage increment to workers (ASN Bank 2019: 9–10). Such concerns are echoed in a study of leading corporations in the sector with many continuing to rely on social auditing, a process 'widely known to be ineffective and open to abuse' (Edwards et al. 2019: 28). Brand-driven initiatives also often lack measures to enable freedom of association and trade union rights, which are crucial for the effective monitoring and realization of any wage commitments, in their supplier base (Edwards et al. 2019). In addition, it is important to note that brands' attempts 'to unilaterally drive wage increases' – when most factories produce for multiple buyers – are 'fraught with challenges', including the impermanent nature of any wage gains and the industrial relations implications of potentially raising wages for some but not all workers in a single factory (Miller and Hohenegger 2017: 24–25).

MSIs are similar to brand-led initiatives insofar that they focus on improving brands' living wage practices, often supported by technical interventions in the form of strategic plans for upgrading performance and access to benchmarking and implementation tools. Where they differ is that they tend to be driven primarily by an NGO or other civil society organization (or group of organizations) rather than by the brand itself. MSIs – many of which adopt a corporate membership model – are, however, often limited in their reach. Their emphasis on collaboration with brands has also been a source of contention and critique. The Fair Labor Association, for instance, has both been represented as an effective industry-specific MSI (Baumann-Pauly et al. 2017) and condemned for its client-like relationship with brands, the limited impact of its auditing and compliance systems, and its lack of progress in promoting freedom of association rights, which many see as an essential precondition for better wages (Anner 2012; Sethi and Rovenpor 2016).

Union–brand initiatives share many of the features of MSIs, among them a commitment to a logic of collaboration. However, they tend to be more ambitious in the scale of their endgame ambition. This is certainly true of ACT, which seeks to transform the institutional landscape of the industry in key producer countries towards industry-wide collective bargaining as the most effective means of realizing a living wage. However, doing so requires sustained and effective coordination with local union affiliates, which has proven to be difficult to achieve. Moreover, while the power of brand lead firms is evident in their interactions with suppliers, it cannot be assumed that their participation in a union-driven initiative – or MSI, for that matter – necessarily generates enough horizontal influence with employer associations, states, and labour governance institutions to deliver a living wage.

Further along the spectrum are examples of initiatives involving NGOs and unions, but not brands, the underpinning logics of which tends to be contestation or technical support. As we have discussed, some NGO initiatives are focused on the development of rigorous technical benchmarks for the measurement of a living wage in specific labour markets. While also referencing a technical standard, the AFWA – an NGO–union initiative – seeks to build campaign capacity across geographic scale. Challenges for campaign-based regional initiatives such as the AFWA, but also the regional living wage campaign of IndustriALL, include effectively and consistently coordinating with affiliates, but also translating public advocacy into concrete impact. While both the AFWA and IndustriALL's living wage campaigns have succeeded in diffusing the idea and discourse of the living wage, they have also confronted difficulties in coordinating and sustaining campaigns with national and local unions.

Our analysis shows a plethora of living wage initiatives that arguably contribute to the diffusion of the concept, techniques for its calculation and implementation – and public pressure – on brands, suppliers, and governments to develop better wage solutions for Southeast Asia's garment workers. At the same time, most actors at national level, including unions, remain focused on domestic minimum-wage determination processes and outcomes rather than on these externally driven initiatives. As we have also identified, there remains a gulf between the goals of each initiative and their depth of impact in contributing to the realization of a living wage. As such, the living wage remains an unfulfilled aspiration even in the garment sector, despite all the international attention that sector receives. Although workers do better in some other manufacturing GPNs, the struggle to achieve a living wage for all workers is an important but far more challenging ambition, given the region's political complexion and its economic and industrial relations structures.

Notes

1 This chapter was written as part of Australian Research Project DP180101184, entitled 'Global Production Networks and Worker Representation in Myanmar'. Authors have made an equal contribution to the chapter and are listed in alphabetical order.
2 For a longer list of wage initiatives, see ETI (2020).
3 Such initiatives are not always as straightforward as they seem. The Clean Clothes Campaign (CCC) has raised questions about H&M's commitment to transparency with regard to defining a living wage figure, the design and application of its Fair Wage Method, and backing up its aspirations with enforceable and time-bound implementation measures (CCC 2015).
4 In January 2014, IndustriALL, UNI, and ITUC, together with 30 brands, sent a letter to the Cambodian government urging that the government set up a functioning minimum wage negotiation process and respect freedom of association and trade union rights. IndustriALL affiliates took action in Thailand, Korea, and Australia in support of the Cambodian garment workers' demand for an increase in wages (IndustriALL 2014).
5 The AFWA has faced challenges in sustaining an organizational network and campaign impact at the national level in Cambodia and Indonesia. For details, see Ford and Gillan (2017).

References

ACT. (2020a). 'ACT Members'. https://actonlivingwages.com/members/.
ACT. (2020b). 'Purchasing Practices'. https://actonlivingwages.com/purchasing-practices/.
AFWA (Asia Floor Wage Alliance) (2020). 'Our Partners'. https://asia.floorwage.org/our-partners/#toggle-id-1.
Anner, M. (2012). 'Corporate Social Responsibility and Freedom of Association Rights: The Precarious Quest for Legitimacy and Control in Global Supply Chains'. *Politics & Society* 40 (4):609–644.

Anner, M. (2018). 'CSR Participation Committees, Wildcat Strikes and the Sourcing Squeeze in Global Supply Chains'. *British Journal of Industrial Relations* 56 (1):75–98.

Ashwin, S., Oka, C., Schuessler, E., Alexander, R., and Lohmeyer, N. (2020). 'Spillover Effects across Transnational Industrial Relations Agreements: The Potential and Limits of Collective Action in Global Supply Chains'. *ILR Review* 73 (4):995–1020.

ASN Bank. (2019). *Living Wage in the Garment Sector: Results of the 2019 Reviews*. Amsterdam: ASN Bank.

Barria, S. (2014). *National People's Tribunals on Living Wage for Garment Workers in Asia*. New Delhi: Asia Floor Wage Alliance.

Bartley, T., and Egels-Zandén, N. (2016). 'Beyond Decoupling: Unions and the Leveraging of Corporate Social Responsibility in Indonesia'. *Socio-Economic Review* 14 (2):231–255.

Baumann-Pauly, D., Nolan, J., Van Heerden, A., and Samway, M. (2017). 'Industry-Specific Multi-Stakeholder Initiatives That Govern Corporate Human Rights Standards: Legitimacy Assessments of the Fair Labor Association and the Global Network Initiative'. *Journal of Business Ethics* 143 (4):771–787.

BFC (Better Factories Cambodia) (2018). *Annual Report 2018: An Industry and Compliance Review*. Phnom Penh: International Labour Organization.

Caraway, T., and Ford, M. (2017). 'Institutions and Collective Action in Divided Labour Movements: Evidence from Indonesia'. *Journal of Industrial Relations* 59 (4):444–464.

Caraway, T., Ford, M., and Nguyen, O. (2019). 'Politicizing the Minimum Wage: Wage Councils, Worker Mobilization, and Local Elections in Indonesia'. *Politics & Society* 47 (2):251–276.

CCC (Clean Clothes Campaign) (2015). *H&M's Sustainability Promises Will Not Deliver a Living Wage*. https://cleanclothes.org/news/press-releases/2015/04/09/h-ms-sustainability-promises-will-not-deliver-a-living-wage.

CCC (Clean Clothes Campaign) (2020). *Poverty Wages*. https://cleanclothes.org/poverty-wages.

Coe, N.M., and Hess, M. (2012). 'Global Production Networks, Labour and Development'. *Geoforum* 44:4–9.

Comtrade (2020). *UN Comtrade*. https://comtrade.un.org/data/.

Edwards, R., Hunt, T., and LeBaron, G. (2019). *Corporate Commitments to Living Wages in the Garment Industry*. Sheffield Political Economy Research Institute: SPERI.

Egels-Zandén, N., Lindberg, K., and Hyllman, P. (2015). 'Multiple Institutional Logics in Union-NGO Relations: Private Labor Regulation in the Swedish Clean Clothes Campaign'. *Business Ethics: A European Review* 24 (4):347–360.

ETI (Ethical Trading Initiative) (2020). *Living Wage Initiatives*. www.ethicaltrade.org/issues/living-wage-workers/living-wage-initiatives.

FLA (Fair Labor Association) (2019). *Toward Fair Compensation in Vietnam: Insights on Reaching a Living Wage*. Washington, DC: Fair Labor Association.

Ford, M. (2009). *Workers and Intellectuals: NGOs, Trade Unions and the Indonesian Labour Movement*. Singapore: NUS Press/Hawaii University Press/KITLV.

Ford, M., and Gillan, M. (2016). 'Employment Relations and the State in Southeast Asia'. *Journal of Industrial Relations* 58 (2):167–182.

Ford, M., and Gillan, M. (2017). 'In Search of a Living Wage in Southeast Asia'. *Employee Relations* 39 (6):903–914.

FWF (Fair Wear Foundation). (2018). *Indonesia Country Study 2018*. https://api.fairwear.org/wp-content/uploads/2018/11/Indonesia-Country-Study.pdf.

FWF (Fair Wear Foundation) (2019). *Understanding Fair Wear's Approach to Living Wages*. Amsterdam: Fair Wear Foundation.

FWF (Fair Wear Foundation) (2020a). *Labour Minute and Product Costing Calculators*. www.fairwear.org/resources-and-tools/labour-minute-costing-calculators/.

FWF (Fair Wear Foundation) (2020b). *Meet the 137 Brands that Move with Us*. www.fairwear.org/brands.

GLWC (Global Living Wage Coalition). (2020). *About the Global Living Wage Coalition*. https://www.globallivingwage.org/about/

Godrej, D. (2020). 'For a Few Cents More: Interview with Anannya Bhattacharjee'. *New Internationalist*, March/April, 524: 32–33.

H&M (2015). *H&M Conscious Actions Sustainability Report 2014*. www.wearefuterra.com/wp-content/uploads/2016/03/Conscious-Actions-Sustainability-Report-2014_en.pdf: H&M.

H&M (2016). *H&M Conscious Actions Sustainability Report 2015*. http://sustainability.hm.com/content/dam/hm/about/documents/en/CSR/2015%20Sustainability%20report/HM_SustainabilityReport_2015_final_FullReport_en.pdf: H&M.

Hieu, D., Phuc, P., and Schweisshelm, E. (2017). *Trade Unions in Transformation*. Berlin: Fredrich-Ebert-Stiftung.

Holdcroft, J. (2015). 'Transforming Supply Chain Industrial Relations'. *International Journal of Labour Research* 7 (1):95–104.

ILO (International Labour Organization). (2020). *World Employment and Social Outlook Data Finder*. www.ilo.org/wesodata/.

ILOSTAT. (2020). *Statistics on Union Membership*. https://ilostat.ilo.org/topics/union-membership/.

IndustriALL. (2014). *Cambodian Workers Fight for a Living Wage*. www.industriall-union.org/cambodian-workers-fight-for-a-living-wage: IndustriALL.

IndustriALL. (2015a). *IndustriALL in Myanmar*. www.industriall-union.org/industriall-workshop-on-living-wage-in-myanmar: IndustriALL Global Union.

IndustriALL. (2015b). *Industry Bargaining for Living Wages*. www.industriall-union.org/industry-bargaining-for-living-wages.

IndustriALL. (2018). *Garment Unions in Cambodia and Myanmar Step Closer to a Living Wage*. Accessed 4 October.

IndustriALL. (2019a). *ACT Brands Adopt Accountability on Purchasing Practices*. www.industriall-union.org/act-brands-adopt-accountability-on-purchasing-practices.

IndustriALL. (2019b). *Myanmar Unions Call on Brands to join ACT in Fight for Living Wage*. www.industriall-union.org/myanmar-unions-call-on-brands-to-join-act-in-fight-for-living-wage.

IndustriALL. (2020). *Living Wage*. www.industriall-union.org/issues/social-justice-and-globalization/living-wage.

ITGLWF (International Textile, Garment and Leather Workers' Federation) (2008). *ITGLWF to Kick off 'Living Wage' on World Day for Decent Work*. www.fibre2fashion.com/news/textile-news/newsdetails.aspx?news_id=59920.

ITGLWF (International Textile, Garment and Leather Workers' Federation) (2012). *Background Paper: Global Conference on Bargaining for a Living Wage*, June 17–18 2012, Copenhagen, Denmark. Brussels: ITGLWF.

ITUC (International Trade Union Confederation) (2020a). *ASEAN Fights for +50 – Ensuring Decent Work, Minimum Living Wages and Social Protection are on the ASEAN Agenda*. www.ituc-csi.org/asean-fights-for-50-ensuring.

ITUC (International Trade Union Confederation) (2020b). *Promoting Minimum Living Wages – The World Needs a Pay Rise*. https://www.ituc-csi.org/promoting-minimum-living-wages-the.

Jannah, S. (2019). *Menperin: Industri Manufaktur RI Serap 18,25 Juta Pekerja pada 2018*. Tirto.

Kuruvilla, S., Liu, M., Li, C., and Che, W. (2020). 'Field Opacity and Practice-Outcome Decoupling: Private Regulation of Labor Standards in Global Supply Chains'. ILR Review 73 (4):841–872.

Merk, J. (2009). *Stitching a Decent Wage across Borders: the Asia Floor Wage Proposal 2009*. New Delhi: Asia Floor Wage Alliance.

Miller, D., and Hohenegger, K. (2017). *Redistributing Value Added towards Labour in Apparel Supply Chains: Tackling Low Wages through Purchasing Practices*. Geneva: ILO.

Roy, A. (2015). 'The Asia Floor Wage Alliance'. In *Living Wage Now!*, edited by Tanne de Goei and Carole Crabbé. Clean Clothes Campaign: Living Wage Now. cleanclothes.org.

Sethi, S.P., and Rovenpor. J. (2016). 'The Role of NGOs in Ameliorating Sweatshop-like Conditions in the Global Supply Chain: The Case of Fair Labor Association (FLA), and Social Accountability International (SAI)'. *Business and Society Review* 121 (1):5–36.

SPD. (2019). *Hasil Verifikasi Ngawur, KSPI Protes Menteri Ketenagakerjaan.* https://nyataberjuang. org/afiliasi/hasil-verifikasi-ngawur-kspi-protes-menteri-ketenagakerjaan/.

Thornton, P., and Ocasio, W. (2008). 'Institutional Logics'. In *The Sage Handbook of Organizational Institutionalism*, edited by R. Greenwood, C. Oliver, T. Lawrence, and R. Meyer, 99–128. London: SAGE.

Ward, K., and Ford, M. (in press). 'Labour and Electoral Politics in Cambodia'. *Journal of Contemporary Asia.*

World Bank. (2020). *East Asia & Pacific.* https://data.worldbank.org/region/east-asia-and-pacific.

16 Conclusion

Tony Dobbins and Peter Prowse

The living wage is a central component of (re)distributive justice, serving as a policy lever for addressing low pay. The chapters in this book have provided important new comparative insights from academics and public policy experts and researchers into the operation and outcomes of living wages in a variety of sectors in the UK, Europe, and globally. Part 1 evaluated the living wage in the UK and presented various UK-specific sector studies. Part 2 of the book broadened this out to examine selected international and sectoral living wage developments in the European Union, Nordic countries, the USA, Canada, Australia, New Zealand, and South East Asia.

This concluding chapter identifies a number of important themes that emerge from the book, relating to the living wage and the bigger picture of inequality and imbalances in wage bargaining power. These themes include: why minimum wages are not real living wages; why real living wages have (re)emerged in the contemporary era of neo-liberalism, rising inequality, and declining trade union bargaining power, especially in countries labelled as liberal market economies (LMEs); why the living wage is not a prominent concept in some European countries, including the 'Nordic' countries, which retain stronger trade unions and collectivism; why living wages are insufficient as a stand-alone policy measure to address low pay and inequality, and focus on a broader decent work agenda and a 'new social contract' are required; and, finally, increased interest in a global living wage.

Minimum wages are not living wages

'Real' living wages are distinct from legal national minimum wages, tending to be quite significantly higher than statutory minimum rates. The latter are viewed by many observers as not providing enough for many people to live on, factoring in rising living costs. Moreover, minimum wage legislation only establishes an individual minimum pay floor. But many employers interpret it as a pay ceiling – something they pay, to meet regulation, but will not go above. In contrast, a real living wage is the minimum income deemed necessary for workers to be able to afford their basic needs, notably food, housing, household bills, and other basic essentials like clothing. However, a real living wage is usually voluntarist and non-binding (employers only have to pay it if they choose to do so for business and moral reasons); and is therefore distinct from compulsory legal national minimum wages regulated by the state and its agencies (Prowse et al., 2017).

DOI: 10.4324/9781003054078-16

Living wages in the neoliberal era

Rising contemporary interest in the concept of the living wage from around the world needs to be viewed in a broader political economy context of globalization, economic neo-liberalism, financialization, and austerity politics; which many observers now increasingly acknowledge have contributed to rising income inequalities and associated problems of low pay and in-work poverty (Grady, 2017; Harvey, 2007; Thomas et al., 2020; Thompson, 2013). Harvey (2007: 2) defines neoliberalism as 'a theory of political economic practices that proposes that human well-being can best be advanced by liberating individual entre-preneurial freedoms and skills within an institutional framework characterized by strong private property rights, free markets, and free trade'. Critiques of neoliberalism have not only come from the left of the political spectrum. Even the *Financial Times* has called for 'Radical reforms – reversing the prevailing policy direction of the last four decades' (Financial Times, 2020).

While market forces relating to neoliberalism and globalization are affecting many countries, differences and divergences remain, relating to institutional variations across nations (Bamber et al., 2021). Low pay and in-work poverty are especially pronounced and problematic in those countries often referred to as 'liberal market economies' (LMEs), like the USA and the UK, that have gone furthest in liberalizing their economies and encouraging market forces and competition to reach into all aspects of economy and society (Hall and Soskice, 2001).

This relates to an institutional power vacuum opened up by the demise of trade unions and collective bargaining power, which is most evident in LMEs (Ibsen and Tapia, 2017). The effort-reward bargain (Behrend, 1957) and the balance of power in labour markets have become too skewed in favour of employers under neoliberalism and globalization. Low pay is best addressed by the collective power of organized labour. But for many workers this avenue of collective representation no longer exists (especially in the private sector), and minimum wages are insufficient for addressing increased living costs, hence the emergence of real living wage campaigns in LMEs.

European collectivism and trade unions

Interestingly, the living wage is less prominent in many continental European countries (see Chapter 8 by John Hurley on the living wage in the European Union), especially those that retain strong trade unions and collectivism, notably the Nordic countries (see Chapter 10 by Kristin Alsos and Kristine Nergaard – Are collective bargaining models in the Nordic countries able to secure a living wage?). Often categorized as coordinated-market economies (CMEs), the Nordic countries are an interesting outlier regarding the living wage. While the living wage has emerged in the LMEs discussed in the chapters within this book, it has not been a widely applied concept in the Nordic countries. Living wage campaigns like those seen in English-speaking countries are not evident, and the Nordic countries have also not introduced statutory minimum wages that ensure a minimum wage level for all workers. Wage formation is still the 'volun-tarist' domain of employer organizations and trade unions through coordinated collective bargaining. Therefore, although subject to market liberalization/globalization pressures, 'the Nordics' retain institutional buffers of high trade union density, extensive collective bargaining coverage and wage bargaining coordination, and centralized solidaristic social pacts involving the state, employer associations, and trade union confederations. There is widespread support among the 'social partners' for the egalitarian idea that small wage differences serve the Nordic welfare states well, and that the lowest-paid workers must be guaranteed a decent standard of living. This being said, the 'Nordic model' faces challenges, such as those indicated in Chapter 10.

A new 'social contract' for decent work

Legal minimum wages, and even living wages, are insufficient as stand-alone policy interventions of (re)distributive justice to address wider social problems and causes underpinning low pay and inequality (Dobbins 2019). The overarching issue of the decent work agenda (Carson, 2020) needs to be addressed in the context of increasingly fragmented and under-regulated employment relations systems (Hatton, 2015), most noticeably in liberal market economies. The UK Living Wage Foundation is aware of the bigger picture issue of decent work, hence its launch of subsequent campaigns for living hours and a living pension (see Chapter 2 by Daniel Howard). Moreover, the real living wage is voluntary and an example of 'soft regulation' (Johnson et al., 2019) – it is not compulsory for employers to comply with it, so its coverage is by definition restricted. Also, cost of living increases (like housing and household bills) in many countries discussed in this book need to be addressed as part of a broader 'new social contract' for decent work.

A 'new social contract' for decent work would strengthen collectivism (unions, collective bargaining, codetermination), rebuild and extend public services, and enshrine political commitment to full employment by providing decent work/good jobs of social value in the foundational and green economy in different countries (Dobbins, 2020). This 'new social contract' relates to creating a fairer and more sustainable moral economy underpinning decent work and employment for the many not the few (Sayer, 2019). There is also a further more micro-level 'quality of working-life' element of 'contributive justice' to this new 'social contract', encompassing subjective dimensions of perceived equity, job security, job satisfaction, and overall meaningful work and well-being at work (Sayer, 2009). As our case study of Luton Town Football Club highlights in Chapter 3 (Prowse and Dobbins), the presence of a real living wage also increased morale and commitment at work and a higher level of social skills, staff retention, and positive employment relations, as well as a sense of a wider community both inside and also outside the club. This signifies the importance of exploring the wider development of meaningful work of social value and opportunities for quality of work regarding living wage employment and a broader decent work agenda as a springboard for harnessing human capabilities (Carr et al., 2016; Searle and McWha-Hermann, 2020; Sen, 1999; Yao et al., 2017). Broadening out this decent work agenda is vital for creating more inclusive work environments and societies.

A global living wage

There have also been calls for a global living wage, including through the Living Wage Foundation's (2020) global living wage initiative, which would also encompass workers in the Global South. But this would be difficult to achieve in the current global political economy context. Even if a GLW could be shoehorned into the policy agenda, it would likely be another example of 'soft regulation' with no legal 'bite'. Arguably, the International Labour Organization (ILO) needs to be equipped with greater powers to police and enforce global labour standards (Thomas and Turnbull, 2018; Thomas et al.,

2020). Global labour standards encompass a global living wage and the ILO's four pillars of decent work: full and productive employment, rights at work, social protection, and the promotion of social dialogue (ILO, 2020).

This just leaves us to thank all the chapter contributors to this book. We hope that the book encourages further research and policy debates on the living wage, low pay, decent work, and wider issues relating to inequality and the future of work across the world.

References

Bamber, G., Cooke, F.L., Doellgast, V., and Wright C.F. (2021). *International and Comparative Employment Relations: Global Crises and Institutional Responses,* 7th Edition. Los Angeles: SAGE.

Behrend, H. (1957). 'The effort bargain'. *ILR Review*, 10 (4): 503–515.

Carr, S.C., Parker, J., Arrowsmith, J., Watters, P., and Jones, H. (2016). 'Can a "living wage" springboard human capability? An exploratory study from New Zealand', *Labour & Industry: A Journal of The Social and Economic Relations of Work*, 26 (1): 24–39.

Carson, C. (2020). *In-work poverty and decent working standards in the UK: Why a focus on wage rises is no longer enough.* Centre for Employment Relations, Innovation and Change (CERIC). University of Leeds. https://cericleeds.wordpress.com/2021/02/05/in-work-poverty-and-decent-working-standards-in-the-uk-why-a-focus-on-wage-rises-is-no-longer-enough/

Dobbins, T. (2019). 'National living wage is not enough to fix Britain's low-pay problem – here's why'. *The Conversation*. April 8. https://theconversation.com/national-living-wage-is-not-enough-to-fix-britains-low-pay-problem-heres-why-114867

Dobbins, T. (2020). 'COVID illuminates global inequalities in workers' rights and working conditions'. University of Birmingham Perspectives. June 24. www.birmingham.ac.uk/research/perspective/covid-illuminates-global-inequalities-in-workers-rights.aspx

Financial Times (2020). 'Virus lays bare the frailty of the social contract'. *Editorial*, April 3. www.ft.com/content/7eff769a-74dd-11ea-95fe-fcd274e920ca

Grady, J. (2017). 'The state, employment, and regulation: Making work not pay'. *Employee Relations*, 39 (3): 274–290.

Hall, P.A. and Soskice, D. (2001). *Varieties of Capitalism: The Institutional Foundations of Comparative Advantage*. Oxford: Oxford University Press.

Harvey, D. (2007). *A Brief History of Neoliberalism*. USA: Oxford University Press.

Hatton, E. (2015). 'Work beyond the bounds: A boundary analysis of the fragmentation of work'. *Work, Employment and Society*, 29 (6): 1007–1018.

Ibsen, C.L., and Tapia, M. (2017). 'Trade union revitalisation: Where are we now? Where to next?'. *Journal of Industrial Relations*, 59 (2): 170–191.

ILO (International Labour Organization) (2020). *Decent Work Indicators*. Geneva: ILO. www.ilo.org/integration/themes/mdw/WCMS_189392/lang--en/index.htm

Johnson, M., Koukiadaki, A., and Grimshaw, D. (2019). 'The Living Wage in the UK: Testing the limits of soft regulation?'. *Transfer: European Review of Labour and Research*, 25 (3): 319–333.

Living Wage Foundation (2020). *Global Living Wage Initiative*. London: Living Wage Foundation. www.livingwage.org.uk/global-living-wage-initiative

Prowse, P., Fells, R., Arrowsmith, J., Parker, J., and Lopes, A. (2017). 'Low pay and the living wage: An international perspective'. *Employee Relations*, 39 (6): 778–784.

Sayer, A. (2009). 'Contributive justice and meaningful work'. *Res publica*, 15 (1): 1–16.

Sayer, A. (2019). 'Moral economy, the Foundational Economy and de-carbonisation'. *Renewal: A Journal of Labour Politics*, 27 (2): 40–46.

Searle, R.H., and McWha-Hermann, I. (2020). '"Money's too tight (to mention)": A review and psychological synthesis of living wage research', *European Journal of Work and Organizational Psychology*, (forthcoming) doi: 10.1080/1359432X.2020.1838604

Sen, A. (1999). *Development as Freedom*. New York: Random House.

Thomas, H., and Turnbull, P. (2018). 'From horizontal to vertical labour governance: The International Labour Organization (ILO) and decent work in global supply chains'. *Human Relations*, 71 (4): 536–559.

Thomas, H., Pitts, F. W., and Turnbull, P. (2020). 'The International Labour Organization was founded after the Spanish flu – its past lights the path to a better future of work'. *The Conversation*. June 17. https://theconversation.com/the-international-labour-organization-was-founded-after-the-spanish-flu-its-past-lights-the-path-to-a-better-future-of-work-140461

Thomas P., McArdle L., and Saundry, R. (2020). 'Introduction to the special issue: The enactment of neoliberalism in the workplace: The degradation of the employment relationship'. *Competition & Change*, 24 (2): 105–113.

Thompson P. (2013). 'Financialization and the workplace: Extending and applying the disconnected capitalism thesis'. *Work, Employment and Society*, 27 (3): 472–488.

Yao, C., Parker, J., Arrowsmith, J., and Carr, S. (2017). 'The living wage as an income range for decent work and life'. *Employee Relations*, 39 (6): 875–887.

Index

Printed in the United States
by Baker & Taylor Publisher Services